WITHDRAWN

2 3 APR 2023

Understanding Sexual Homicide Offenders

Understanding Sexual Homicide Offenders

An Integrated Approach

Heng Choon (Oliver) Chan
Assistant Professor of Criminology, City University of Hong Kong, Hong Kong

palgrave
macmillan

First published 2015 by
PALGRAVE MACMILLAN

Palgrave Macmillan in the UK is an imprint of Macmillan Publishers Limited,
registered in England, company number 785998, of Houndmills, Basingstoke,
Hampshire RG21 6XS.

Palgrave Macmillan in the US is a division of St Martin's Press LLC,
175 Fifth Avenue, New York, NY 10010.

Palgrave Macmillan is the global academic imprint of the above companies
and has companies and representatives throughout the world.

Palgrave® and Macmillan® are registered trademarks in the United States,
the United Kingdom, Europe and other countries.

ISBN: 978–1–137–45371–6

This book is printed on paper suitable for recycling and made from fully
managed and sustained forest sources. Logging, pulping and manufacturing
processes are expected to conform to the environmental regulations of the
country of origin.

A catalogue record for this book is available from the British Library.

A catalog record for this book is available from the Library of Congress.

To the Chan Family

with deep appreciation of your unconditional love,
endless support, and encouragement.

In loving memory of my mother

Contents

List of Figures

List of Tables

Foreword

Sexual murders often make headline news. The media coverage is widespread when the victims include those perceived as vulnerable such as children and adolescents, college students, and elderly women. Sexually motivated killings are also frequently publicized if the victims involve middle-class gay males and are particularly gruesome.

Why is it that an event that is statistically so rare warrants such extensive attention? Simply stated, because these events are horrifying. Approximately 30 years ago, Alexander Lowen, world renowned psychiatrist and author of many books, such as *Narcissism The Denial of the True Self*, stated that horrific events both repel and attract audiences at the same time. Consumers of print and electronic media are largely composed of people with a moral compass and feelings for their fellow human beings. Individuals with conventional values and compassion for others are repulsed by thoughts and images of victims who are sexually attacked, possibly humiliated and tortured, and killed by "bad guys" who may afterwards defile, desecrate, and dismember their victims' bodies. At the same time, the members of mainstream society are often fascinated by these killings, drawn to feature stories about the homicidal events. For many media readers, listeners, and viewers, there is an insatiable curiosity about the killers, and perhaps, the nagging question of how different (or similar) are these murderers from you and me?

Against this backdrop comes the publication of Heng Choon (Oliver) Chan's book *Understanding Sexual Homicide Offenders*. Chan moves beyond the sensationalism of media depictions of these crimes and their killers.With the precision of a surgeon doing a complex operation, Chan dissects, synthesizes, and critically evaluates the literature. But Chan does not stop there; he builds on the existing knowledge by using his experience, expertise, and acumen to advance the field.

Understanding Sexual Homicide Offenders is an outstanding resource for researchers. In Chapter 1, for example, Chan reviews the existing definitions of sexual homicide. He points out the flaws in these definitions and then proposes one that addresses these shortcomings. This definition, if adopted, could standardize the identification of sexual homicides, making the detection of killers more certain than it has been.

Chan's synthesis of the literature is an invaluable reference for researchers, clinicians, advanced undergraduate students, and graduate students. In Chapter 1, he discusses the differences between sexual homicide offenders and other violent offenders, including homicide offenders, rapists, and sexually aggressive individuals, and then encapsulates this information in concise and clear tables. In Chapter 2, Chan systematically reviews 13 offender classifications that have been used to categorize sexual homicide offenders. The classification systems include typologies derived from pragmatic methods, clinical studies, theory-led investigations, and statistical models. The tables in this chapter illustrate the main tenets and findings with respect to each of these classifications, and are unparalleled.

Chapters 3 and 4 deal with the theoretical explanations for sexual homicide offending. In Chapter 3, Chan masterfully presents four theoretical models that have been proposed to explain sexuallymotivated murders. Having these models encapsulated in one resource is very helpful. It also provides a natural springboard to a discussion on a model of sexual homicide proposed by Chan, Heide, and Beauregard in Chapter 4 that is based on the integration of two well-known criminological theories: social learning and routine activities.

In Chapter 5, Chan discusses the testing of this integrated criminological model. This chapter serves as a model for the theoretical testing of specific hypotheses related to the sexual homicide offending process. The chapter pays attention to the development of operational constructs for theoretical constructs, to measurement issues, to the selection of a suitable sampling population (Canadian non-serial sexual offenders who victimized females that are incarcerated in a maximum security prison) with experimental subjects (55 homicidal offenders) and control subjects (175 non-homicidal sex offenders), methodological sophistication, and the use of bivariate and multivariate techniques of statistical analyses, including model testing. In the final chapter, Chan discusses the implications and conclusions of his study, which were partially supported, and offers suggestions for future research.

Understanding Sexual Homicide Offenders is a monumental work. It is well-poised to become the launching pad for serious scholars to design further investigations of sexually motivated murder. It is a priceless resource for clinicians tasked with evaluating individuals involved in sexual homicide. In addition, this book is a well-written and organized compendium of information that will hold the interest of lawyers, judges, correctional staff, mental health professionals, and university students who want to know more about the circumstances, backgrounds, and motivations that lead some individuals to engage in sexual homicide.

Kathleen M. Heide, PhD
Professor of Criminology
University of South Florida, Tampa, FL, USA
December 2014

Preface and Acknowledgments

"Oliver, you may wish to get a copy of Jean Proulx and colleagues' latest book on sexual murderers and start reading it." That is what my then major professor and now mentor-for-life Professor Kathleen M. Heide recommended to me when I first conveyed my research interest to her after my admission to the University of South Florida's (USF) doctoral program in the fall of 2007. It has been more than seven years since I began my research on sexual murder and sexual homicide offenders. Who are those who sexually assaulted and subsequently killed their victims? What motivates them to sexually murder their victim? What is their mind set? How do they search for their victim? Are all sexual murderers alike? These are some of the questions I kept asking myself that in part cultivated and subsequently strengthened my interest to learn more about this violent population.

The idea for this book was born when I became aware that only a few academic books on this topic had been published in the past three decades. Despite the high level of public interest and media attention given to sexually motivated homicides, the study of sexual homicide remains an understudied area that involves only a handful of researchers. Given my strong interest in this topic, I envisioned *Understanding Sexual Homicide Offenders: An Integrated Approach* becoming the "one-stop-shop" for readers who were eager to learn more about sexual murder and sexual homicide offenders, and the latest research development in this field. This book is written for a variety of readers, including sexual offending and homicide researchers; forensic professionals; law enforcement practitioners; mental health clinicians; and advanced undergraduate and graduate students in behavioral, social, medical, and forensic sciences. I envisage *Understanding Sexual Homicide Offenders: An Integrated Approach* as distinctive from other similar books in the market because it offers a unique perspective. In the pages that follow, I review various definitions and criteria for sexual homicide with the aim to propose a set of standardized sexual homicide criteria to reduce the confusion among researchers and practitioners. I also try to maintain consistency in the characterization of sexual murder; to synthesize different classifications of sexual homicide offenders and their theoretical explanations; and to introduce a new integrative theoretical approach. I then empirically test that approach to better comprehend sexual homicide offenders.

Understanding Sexual Homicide Offenders: An Integrated Approach could not have been completed without the guidance, assistance, and support of many talented and exceptional individuals. There are so many people who helped, directly and indirectly, to make this book possible. I want to thank, in particular, Professor Kathleen M. Heide for her continuous support and guidance throughout the years. I am greatly indebted to her, especially during my journey of academic quest at USF. Kathleen has generously provided me with academic opportunities, intellectual insights, and encouragement. Her belief in my ability to excel academically and professionally is undoubtedly my primary driving force in my success. I am also indebted to Professor Eric Beauregard of Simon Fraser University for his generosity and enthusiastic support of my research, in particular by sharing his invaluable dataset for the completion of my dissertation research. Both Kathleen and Eric's moral support is sincerely appreciated especially during my down times several years back at USF. Their faith in me has never faltered. I also wish to express my gratitude to Professor Wade C. Myers of Brown University and Rhode Island Hospital, a well-recognized forensic psychiatrist, for his insightful commentary and constructive suggestions throughout my academic quest. Wade's selflessness with his time and intellect has never ceased to inspire and challenge me over the years. Now, Kathleen, Eric, and Wade have become my mentors and role models in my professional pursuits.

I want to thank my other dissertation committee members – Drs Shayne Jones and Wesley G. Jennings – for their critical commentary on my dissertation research. They provided me with constructive suggestions for my quantitative research on sexual murderers. I give special thanks to my previous professors and cohort-mates at USF, particularly Dr Lorie A. Fridell, Dr Autumn M. Frei, Dr Brian Sellers, Erin Mulligan, Rhissa B. Robinson, and Samira Kulsum for their continued support and friendship. Perhaps most importantly, I am deeply indebted to the donors to the USF's Asian Criminology Scholarship for their willingness and generosity to financially support me throughout my doctoral years. I also want to express gratitude to my current colleagues in the Department of Applied Social Sciences at City University in Hong Kong, in particular to our Head of Department – Professor Wing Lo – and my criminology colleagues – Professor Dennis Wong, Professor Eric Chui, Dr Lena Zhong, Dr Lennon Chang, Dr Alfred Choi, and Stanislaus Lai – for creating an environment where I was encouraged and supported to pursue my research.

I am very grateful to the editors at Palgrave Macmillan for their patience and timely assistance throughout the writing of this book.

I truly appreciate Julia Willan for believing in this book project, and Harriet Barker and Dominic Walker for their guidance and support throughout the process. I also want to express my deep appreciation for the academic and professional reviewers, with particular appreciation for Professor Jean Proulx who is a strong believer in my work. Their astute comments helped make the contents of *Understanding Sexual Homicide Offenders: An Integrated Approach* much stronger.

Last but not least, I remain deeply indebted to my family – my loving mother, father, and three elder sisters – for their unwavering and unconditional love and endless support throughout my academic quest. They have taught me so much; especially, to have faith in myself no matter how difficult and challenging the circumstances are in my life. In specific, I deeply appreciate my mother, who recently passed away. She was undoubtedly a loving and devoted mother and an excellent role model for all of us in the family. The older I get, the more I come to realize how privileged I was to have been raised and nurtured in a home in which children were loved, valued, and protected. Certainly, I owe a special debt of gratitude to my beloved wife and soul-mate for life – Courtney – for her love, endless support, and encouragement of me over the years that have fueled me with strength and determination to continue my professional pursuits. I cannot thank her enough for the sacrifices she has made for our family, especially in bringing a new life to our home by the time this book goes to market.

1
Introduction

The cases where sexual assaultive behavior leads to the death of the victim have always concerned the public. However, this distinct type of murderous behavior is not something new to society: It has occurred and has alarmed people throughout the centuries. The earliest recorded rape-murder cases can be traced back as far as the 15th century (e.g., Gilles de Rais). According to Wilson and Seaman (1996), another infamous case involved an 8-year-old girl who was murdered in 1867 in Hampshire in the United Kingdom (UK) by Frederick Baker. This recorded case of sexual killing predated the gruesome career of Jack the Ripper, the most infamous British sexual serial killer whom law enforcement agents believed killed and mutilated five London prostitutes in 1888 (Marriner, 1992). Although the 19th century provides periodic recorded examples of sexual homicide comparable with the evidence documented in current times, it is arguably the 20th century that has attracted the most public attention with the most published individual case studies and empirical research on this topic (Carter & Hollin, 2010).

Fundamentally, sexual homicide, sexual murder, sex-related homicide, sexually motivated murder, and rape homicide are common terms that are used to refer to a homicide that occurs in concurrence with a sexual assault or to signify that a particular homicide was sexually motivated (Chan & Heide, 2009; Henry, 2010; James & Proulx, 2014). The sexual activities that occur before, during, or after a killing can be contact (e.g., oral, vaginal, and/or anal penetration of the victim) and/or noncontact (e.g., masturbation by the offender) in nature. In addition to the overt sexual assault against the victim, sexually symbolic behavior, such as the lack of clothing on the victim and the sexualized positioning of the victim's body, is also frequently observed at the crime scenes of sexual murders (Myers, Burgess, & Nelson, 1998). Despite manifest differences in crime scenes and the offender's behavior, there is a consistent theme that exposes the sexual nature of these offenses.

1.1 Organization of the book

This book consists of six chapters. Chapter 1 presents an overview of the sexual homicide phenomenon. In this chapter, the rarity of the occurrence of sexual homicide is first discussed. One of the possible reasons for the low documented occurrence of this crime is the inconsistency in defining and detecting sexual murder. Within this chapter, the various definitions and criteria of sexual homicide are outlined. Because most of these definitions overlap to a large extent, proposed sexual homicide criteria are offered with the aim of standardizing the definition of sexual murder in order to reduce confusion among scholars and practitioners and to maintain consistency in the characterization of sexual murder. This is an attempt to advance the literature by offering a comprehensive definition in order to better understand sexual murder. Next, a brief overview of the dynamics of offending from the homicidal perspective is presented to lay the groundwork for a comprehensive examination of sexual homicide from the offender's standpoint. The findings of comparative studies between homicidal and non-homicidal sexual offenders are detailed. The differences between these two distinct groups of sexual offenders in terms of demographic characteristics, childhood and adolescence psychological and behavioral development, and crime phases are also described in this chapter.

In order to systematically study sexual homicide offenders (SHOs), clinicians and researchers have attempted to categorize sexual murderers into different types on the basis of their developmental, pre-crime, crime, and post-crime profiles. Therefore, in Chapter 2, 13 offender classifications of sexual homicide are discussed in detail: the widely cited Federal Bureau of Investigation (FBI) motivational model of sexual homicide published in the mid-1980s and 12 other scholarly classifications of SHOs published during the period of 1985 to 2014. Some of these SHO typologies are empirically generated, while others are merely based on the authors' personal clinical or investigative experiences. These offender classifications are categorized into four different types of classification approaches: (a) pragmatic, (b) theory-led, (c) clinical, and (d) statistical. Although numerous SHO typologies have been developed over the years, with some of their offender profiles overlapping to some degree, none of them are above criticism. Thus, in the final section of

Chapter 2, these different offender classifications are critically reviewed to determine their strengths and weaknesses in terms of understanding different types of SHOs.

Many studies on sexual homicide have been published over the years. However, most of these studies are either descriptive in nature because of using different samples of sexual murderers or comparative studies of sexual murderers and other types of offenders. Little is known about the underlying theoretical conceptual accounts of the etiology of sexual homicide. Hence, in Chapter 3, four widely cited theoretical models of sexual homicide (i.e., Burgess et al.'s motivational model, Hickey's trauma-control model, Arrigo and Purcell's paraphilic model, and Mieczkowski and Beauregard's crime event perspective model) are discussed at length. Theorizing different socio-psychological and situational factors, these theoretical frameworks offer distinct explanations of the dynamics of offending in sexual homicide.

To complicate matters further in terms of studying sexual homicide, the theoretical propositions from a criminological standpoint have yet to emerge to advance a more complete understanding of the offending process in sexual homicide. In Chapter 4, two criminological theories that have been commonly used to explain sexual violence and sex-related offenses, namely Akers' (1985) social learning theory and Cohen and Felson's (1979) routine activity theory, are reviewed on the basis of their theoretical propositions and applicability in elucidating sex-related offenses. Next, the incompleteness of applying only a single theory (social learning theory *or* routine activity theory) to the understanding of the complete sexual homicide offending process is highlighted.

As the limitations of using only a single theory to explain the offending phenomenon of sexual homicide are apparent, Chapter 5 subsequently goes on to outline at length the integrated theory of the offending perspective of sexual homicide recently proposed by Chan, Heide, and Beauregard. This theoretical integrative model is discussed in terms of its empirical validity and reliability in understanding the offending process of sexual homicide from a criminological perspective. Due to its unexplained variance, a revised theoretical model is proffered with the inclusion of pre-crime precipitating factors to better explain the offending phenomenon. In order to validate the utility of both Chan et al.'s original model and their revised model, a secondary analysis of an empirical study (via semi-structured interviews) is conducted on a Canadian sample of 230 incarcerated non-serial male sex offenders who targeted female victims (55 homicidal and 175 non-homicidal sex offenders). In order to be considered a homicidal sexual offender, the subject has to meet at least one of the six criteria of the sexual homicide definition set forth by Ressler and colleagues (1988): (a) victim's attire or lack of attire; (b) exposure of the sexual parts of the victim's body; (c) sexual positioning of the victim's body; (d) insertion of foreign objects into the victim's body cavities; (e) evidence of sexual intercourse (oral, anal, or vaginal); and (f) evidence of substitute sexual activity, interest, or sadistic fantasy. Non-homicidal sexual offenders (NHSOs) are those convicted of sexual assaults or sex-related offenses other than sexual homicide. In the latter part of Chapter 5, the research methodology used in this empirical study is discussed at length. Different measures are used to examine the theoretical propositions of (a) a motivated offender, (b) an attractive and suitable target, (c) the absence of a capable guardian, and (d) pre-crime precipitating factors. Bivariate (i.e., chi-square analyses) and multivariate (i.e., logistic regressions) analytic approaches are utilized to test the proposed integrative theoretical models. Following the discussion of the research methodology, the study's findings from both integrative theoretical models are discussed.

Chapter 6 provides an overview and the conclusion of this book. Within this chapter, the implications stemming from the findings, such as crime prevention measures to reduce the potential shaping of a SHO and the occurrence of sexual homicide, are examined on the basis of Chan et al.'s revised theoretical model. This theoretical model contributes to the literature in two key areas: (1) theoretical implications and (2) implications for crime prevention measures and offender profiling. For instance, the presence or absence of a capable guardian or guardianship in the immediate crime scene surroundings (i.e., formal and/or informal social control) is, from the environmental perspective, a critical factor in determining the survival rate of the victim. The extra self-protection measures are also important in reducing the probability of being sexually victimized. From the individual perspective, sexual homicides could potentially be prevented from the outset: Adequate childhood and adolescence psycho-sociological development (i.e., parenting style, skills development programs, and prosocial peer group association) is crucial in shaping an individual with positive and constructive behavioral and attitude patterns toward sex and the avoidance of violence. This chapter concludes with a summary of the study along with its methodological limitations and future research directions.

1.2 Sexual homicide: the definition and classification dilemma

Notwithstanding the great interest in sexual homicide from law enforcement agencies, academic scholars, and the general public, sexual homicide is a relatively rare crime of violence. The reporting rate of sexual murder documented by law enforcement agencies constitutes between 1% and 4% of the overall annual homicide rate in the United States (US), Canada, and the UK (Chan & Heide, 2009). This percentage has remained relatively stable over the years. In the studies with representative data sets for at least three decades, sexual homicide accounts for approximately 0.6% of the total individuals arrested for homicide in the US. (Chan, Frei, & Myers, 2013; Chan, Myers, & Heide, 2010).

The overwhelming majority of sexual homicides are perpetrated by males (Chan, Myers, et al., 2010; Myers & Chan, 2012). Close to 95% of those arrested for sexual homicide are males and the remaining less than 5% are females (Chan, Frei, et al., 2013; Chan & Heide, 2008; Myers, Chan, & Mariano, 2014). Although female SHOs are identified in several studies (Chan & Frei, 2013; Chan, Frei, et al., 2013; Gacono, Meloy, & Bridges, 2000; Harbot & Mokros, 2001; Myers & Chan, 2012), this subpopulation of sexual murderers has been understudied due to its rarity. Relative to male murderers, the lower rate of female murderers are also documented in other nonsexual homicides (e.g., Heide, Roe-Sepowitz, Solomon, & Chan, 2012; Heide, Solomon, Sellers, & Chan, 2011; Mariano, Chan, & Myers, 2014). The sexual homicide studies indicate that 88% of the male SHOs are adults and 12% are juveniles under the age of 18 (Chan & Heide, 2008; Chan, Heide, & Myers, 2013; Chan et al., 2010), with the offenders' mean age at arrest is about 27 years (Chan & Beauregard, 2014; Myers et al., 2014). The research finds that most of the victims are females (Van Patten & Delhauer, 2007) and a large proportion of the victims, from 73 to 80% in the most recent empirical studies (Chan & Heide, 2008; Chan et al., 2010; Greenall & Richardson, 2014; Henry, 2010; Smith, Basile, & Karch, 2011), is at least 18 years old. The mean age of victims is about 33 years (Chan & Beauregard, 2014; Myers et al., 2014).

Although numerous definitions of sexual homicide have emerged over the years, the lack of a standardized definition has hindered the accurate classification of sexual homicides and the accuracy of the reporting systems for national crime statistics (see Chan & Heide, 2009; Kerr, Beech, & Murphy, 2013). Sex-related killing is frequently classified as simply a homicide in official crime statistics in both North America and the UK (Adjorlolo & Chan, 2014; Burgess, Hartman, Ressler, Douglas, & McCormack, 1986; Milsom, Beech, & Webster, 2003). Due to the classification dilemma, the documented statistics on this distinct type of violent crime are often misleading, difficult to estimate, or simply unavailable (Ressler, Burgess, & Douglas, 1988). Specifically, the official US national crime statistics source – the Uniform Crime Reports (UCRs) – indexes sexual homicide under the "unknown motive" category, reflecting the uncertainty regarding the nature of this type of crime within the US criminal justice system.

Notably, Burgess and colleagues (1986) were among the first to attempt to classify sexual homicide and to distinguish a sexual homicide from a homicide resulting from a sexual assault. They maintained that sexual homicides "result from one person killing another in the context of power, control, sexuality, and aggressive brutality" (p. 252). To simplify the classification, Holmes and Holmes (2001) define sexual homicide as the combination of lethal violence with a sexual element. Although succinct, these definitions seem too overly simplistic to accurately characterize the offending dynamics of sexual homicide.

In terms of clearly characterizing sexual homicide, the criteria proposed by Ressler, Burgess, and Douglas (1988) is considered to be one of the most complete and widely used definitions. In order for a homicide to be considered sexually motivated, it has to fulfill at least one of the following criteria: (a) victim's attire or lack of attire; (b) exposure of the sexual parts of the victim's body; (c) sexual positioning of the victim's body; (d) insertion of foreign objects into the victim's body cavities; (e) evidence of sexual intercourse (oral, anal, or vaginal); and (f) evidence of substitute sexual activity, interest, or sadistic fantasy (e.g., mutilation of the victim's genitals). Although this definition for classifying sexual homicide seems comprehensive, with detailed criteria for the physical evidence of sexual assault or of sexual activity, it nevertheless oversimplifies the nature of this crime. Clear evidence of sexual assault or sexual activity, which may not be readily available at the immediate crime scene surroundings, is not sufficient (Clarke & Carter, 2000). The true motive of the offender is also an important aspect that needs to be considered in order to classify a homicide as sexually motivated.

Gacono and Meloy (1994) and Meloy (2000) further revise Ressler and colleagues' (1988) defining criteria for sexual homicide. In order to classify a homicide crime scene as sexually oriented, there needs to be (a) physical evidence of sexual assault or sexual activity (e.g., masturbation) in the immediate area of the victim's body should be present and/or (b) the offender should have made a legally admissible confession of the sexual nature of the homicide. When clear physical evidence of sexual assault or sexual activity is not readily available at the homicide crime scene, it is the offender's confession that becomes the determining factor of whether to categorize the homicide as sexually motivated. However, obtaining an offender's confession of committing a sexually motivated homicide is not easy. The denial of responsibility is often observed among suspects who are accused of committing sexual violence, including a sex-related killing. Some offenders attempt to deny responsibility for their behavior and to suggest that their crime was an accident by reporting drug or alcohol intoxication as an excuse (Folino, 2000).

1.2.1 A proposed standardized definition

On the basis of the previous efforts to define sexually motivated murder, a revised definition of sexual homicide is proposed with the aim of accurately classifying this distinct type of offense and offering a standardized definition. In order to classify a homicide as sexual, one of the following criteria has to be met: (a) physical evidence of pre-, peri-, and/ or post-mortem sexual assault (vaginal, oral, or anal) against the victim; (b) physical evidence of substitute sexual activity against the victim (e.g., genitalia mutilation, exposure of the sexual parts or sexual positioning of the victim's body, insertion of foreign objects into the victim's body cavities) or in the immediate area of the victim's body (e.g., masturbation) reflecting the deviant or sadistic sexual fantasy of the offender; (c) a legally admissible offender confession of the sexual motive of the offense that intentionally or unintentionally results in a homicide; and (d) an indication of the sexual element(s) of the crime from the offender's personal belongings (e.g., home computer and/or journal entries).

1.3 Understanding sexual homicide from a homicide perspective

Homicide is the most lethal form of violence. According to Wolfgang and Ferracuti (1967), homicide typically occurs either as a result of (a) a premeditated or rationalized action or (b) an accident in the heat of passion by an offender with the intent to injure another individual but not to kill; a large majority of homicides can be best characterized as the latter (Silverman & Mukherjee, 1987). Furthermore, Wolfgang and Ferracuti (1967) categorize homicides into premeditated, felonious, intentional, planned, and rational homicides. Homicides can also be simply classified into primary and secondary homicides (Jason, Strauss,

& Tyler, 1983; Jason, Flock, & Tyler, 1983). According to Jason, Strauss, and Tyler (1983), primary homicide is a murder that does not occur during the perpetration of another offense (i.e., the offender's primary aim is to murder the victim), whereas secondary homicide is a murder that occurs during or in conjunction with the perpetration of another offense (e.g., rape or robbery).

Salfati (2000), in contrast, differentiates between the types of homicides on the basis of the crime scene behavior of the offender, a model built upon Feshbach's (1964) two types of aggression (expressive and instrumental). According to Feshbach (1964), expressive (or hostile) aggression typically occurs in response to anger-inducing circumstances (e.g., physical attack, insult) and has the intention of making the victim suffer. Conversely, instrumental aggression often results from the desire to acquire the objects or status (e.g., money, valuable items, territory) possessed by another individual regardless of the cost. Feshbach's (1964) classification of aggression is somewhat similar to Toch's (1969) self-preserving and needs-promoting dichotomy. Toch (1969) posits that violence seems to be an effective functional strategy for some individuals to obtain positive and avoid negative reinforcement in dealing with conflictual interpersonal relationships.

1.3.1   Homicidal versus non-homicidal sexual offenders

Little is known about what makes homicidal sexual offenders (HSOs distinct from sexual offenders who are non-homicidal. Although comparative studies of HSOs and NHSOs have been conducted (e.g., Chan & Beauregard, 2015; Chene & Cusson, 2007; Gratzer & Bradford, 1995; Firestone, Bradford, Greenberg, & Larose, 1998; Firestone, Bradford, Greenberg, & Nunes, 2000; Firestone, Bradford, Greenberg, Larose, & Curry, 1998; Grubin, 1994; Koch, Berner, Hill, & Briken, 2011; Langevin, 2003; Langevin, Ben-Aron, Wright, Marchese, & Handy, 1988; Milsom, Beech, & Webster, 2003; Oliver, Beech, Fisher, & Beckett, 2007; Proulx, Beauregard, & Nicole, 2002; Salfati & Taylor, 2006), the findings generated from these studies vary considerably and at times even contradict one another (see Table 1.1). Over the years, 13 empirical studies (1988–2015) have examined the differences between sexual offenders who kill and those who do not kill. Of these studies, eight sampled Canadian sex offenders, four used British samples, and one used German offenders. The number of SHOs sampled in these studies ranged from 13 to 166, while the number in the comparison group of NHSOs ranged from 13 to 714.

Table 1.1 Findings pertaining to the differences between homicidal (HSOs) and non-homicidal (NHSOs) sexual offenders (1988–2015)

Study (Year)	Country of Study	Number of HSOs	Number of NHSOs	Findings Pertaining to Differences between HSOs and NHSOs
Offenders' Age				
Grubin (1994)[A]	Britain	21	121	HSOs older than NHSOs when they committed their index offense.
Salfati & Taylor (2006)[A]	Britain	37	37	
Koch, Berner, Hill, & Briken (2011)[B]	Germany	166	56	NHSOs older than HSOs.
Offenders' Intelligence				
Oliver, Beech, Fisher, & Beckett (2007)[A]	Britain	58	112	Although the mean IQ of both HSOs and NHSOs was above average, HSOs had a significantly higher estimated IQ than NHSOs.
Koch, Berner, Hill, & Briken (2011)	Germany	166	56	NHSOs more educated than HSOs.
Offenders' Criminal History				
Oliver, Beech, Fisher, & Beckett (2007)	Britain	58	112	Significantly more NHSOs committed violent offenses prior to their index offense than HSOs. Yet, HSOs committed more past sexual offenses than NHSOs.
Firestone, Bradford, Greenberg, Larose, & Curry (1998)[C]	Canada	17	35	HSOs committed more violent and sexual offenses prior to their index crime than NHSOs.

Continued

Table 1.1 Continued

Study (Year)	Country of Study	Number of HSOs	Number of NHSOs	Findings Pertaining to Differences between HSOs and NHSOs
Offenders' Childhood and Adolescence Development				
Grubin (1994)	Britain	21	121	HSOs have more stable family structure than NHSOs. Yet, no significant differences found between HSOs and NHSOs in terms of their sexual and nonsexual victimization.
Langevin, Ben-Aron, Wright, Marchese, & Handy (1988)[D]	Canada	13	13	HSOs have more disturbed relationships with their fathers than NHSOs.
Firestone, Bradford, Greenberg, & Larose (1998)[E]	Canada	48	50	HSOs more likely than NHSOs to have been removed from their family before the age of 16.
Proulx, Beauregard, & Nicole (2002)[A]	Canada	40	101	No significant differences found between HSOs and NHSOs in terms of family background. Yet, more HSOs than NHSOs were victims of incest.
Koch, Berner, Hill, & Briken (2011)	Germany	166	56	Significantly more HSOs than NHSOs physically and sexually abused as a child.
Oliver, Beech, Fisher, & Beckett (2007)	Britain	58	112	Reports of having been physically and sexually abused during childhood similarly high among HSOs and NHSOs.

Continued

Table 1.1 Continued

Study (Year)	Country of Study	Number of HSOs	Number of NHSOs	Findings Pertaining to Differences between HSOs and NHSOs
Offenders' Childhood, Adolescence, and Adulthood Behavioral Problems				
Grubin (1994)	Britain	21	121	No significant differences in childhood conduct disorder found between HSOs and NHSOs. However, HSOs reported a higher level of social isolation in childhood and adulthood (e.g., fewer sexual relationships) than NHSOs.
Proulx, Beauregard, & Nicole (2002)	Canada	40	101	HSOs reported more childhood disciplinary problems than NHSOs.
Langevin (2003)[F]	Canada	33	714	HSOs found to have started their criminal career earlier and were more likely to have been to reform school, been members of criminal gangs, set fires, and been cruel to animals.
Langevin, Ben-Aron, Wright, Marchese, & Handy (1988)	Canada	13	13	HSOs more frequently diagnosed with antisocial personality disorder (APD) and sexual sadism than NHSOs.
Firestone, Bradford, Greenberg, Larose, & Curry (1998)	Canada	17	35	HSOs more frequently diagnosed with APD, sexual sadism, paraphilias, and psychopathic personality traits than NHSOs.

Continued

Table 1.1 Continued

Study (Year)	Country of Study	Number of HSOs	Number of NHSOs	Findings Pertaining to Differences between HSOs and NHSOs
Koch, Berner, Hill, & Briken (2011)	Germany	166	56	HSOs diagnosed with schizoid personality disorder and paraphilias (e.g., sexual sadism and fetishism) more frequently than NHSOs. However, NHSOs diagnosed with pedophilia more often than HSOs. No significant differences found between HSOs and NHSOs in terms of psychopathic personality.
Chan & Beauregard (2015)[B]	Canada	74	96	HSOs found to have diagnosed with more different maladaptive personality traits (i.e., paranoid, schizotypal, borderline, histrionic, narcissistic, obsessive-compulsive, and impulsive) and the overall odd and eccentric traits than NHSOs. Besides, HSOs found to exhibit more paraphilic behaviors (i.e., exhibitionism, fetishism, frotteurism, homosexual pedophilia, sexual masochism, and partialism) than NHSOs.
Milsom, Beech, & Webster (2003)[B]	Britain	19	16	HSOs reported higher levels of grievance toward females in childhood, peer group loneliness in adolescence, and seeing themselves as victims in adulthood than NHSOs.
Offenders' Relationship Status at the Time of the Offense				
Grubin (1994)	Britain	21	121	HSOs more likely than NHSOs to live alone at the time of the offense.
Oliver, Beech, Fisher, & Beckett (2007)	Britain	58	112	HSOs reported to have significantly fewer intimate relationship experiences than NHSOs; specifically reported to have had no relationship at the time of the offense.
Firestone, Bradford, Greenberg, & Larose (1998)	Canada	48	50	HSOs significantly more likely than NHSOs to be married at the time of their offense.
Milsom, Beech, & Webster (2003)	Britain	19	16	HSOs significantly more likely than NHSOs to be married at the time of their offense.

Continued

Table 1.1 Continued

Study (Year)	Country of Study	Number of HSOs	Number of NHSOs	Findings Pertaining to Differences between HSOs and NHSOs
Offenders' Sexual Deviation				
Grubin (1994)	Britain	21	121	HSOs and NHSOs equally likely to have an interest in sexual deviation, aggressive pursuits, and a rich fantasy life.
Proulx, Beauregard, & Nicole (2002)	Canada	40	101	HSOs reported to have more sexually deviant fantasies than NHSOs.
Chan & Beauregard (2015)	Canada	74	96	HSOs reported to indulge in deviant sexual fantasies 48 hours prior to their offense than NHSOs.
Langevin, Ben-Aron, Wright, Marchese, & Handy (1988)	Canada	13	13	HSOs more likely to be aroused by transvestism and sadism than NHSOs.
Firestone, Bradford, Greenberg, & Larose (1998)	Canada	48	50	HSOs reported a greater preference for descriptions of assaultive acts with children (pedophile assault index scores) than NHSOs. Yet, no significant differences found between HSOs and NHSOs in terms of pedophile index scores.
Firestone, Bradford, Greenberg, Larose, & Curry (1998)	Canada	17	35	
Firestone, Bradford, Greenberg, & Nunes (2000)[G]	Canada	27	189	

Continued

Table 1.1 Continued

Study (Year)	Country of Study	Number of HSOs	Number of NHSOs	Findings Pertaining to Differences between HSOs and NHSOs
Offenders' Precrime Characteristics				
Chene & Cusson (2007)[A]	Canada	43	148	HSOs more frequently reported to present a motive of anger or of sex and anger than NHSOs.
Chene & Cusson (2007)[A]	Canada	43	148	HSOs more frequently reported to have used and/or abused drugs and alcohol prior to the offense than NHSOs.
Langevin (2003)	Canada	33	714	
Koch, Berner, Hill, & Briken (2011)	Germany	166	56	HSOs more likely to have consumed alcohol at the time of their offense, while NHSOs more likely to have abused illegal drugs either prior to or during their offense.
Chan & Beauregard (2015)	Canada	74	96	HSOs more likely to select victim of choice that meets their needs. Yet, NHSOs more likely to select victim with distinctive physical and/or personality characteristics.
Offender's Crime Scene Characteristics				
Salfati & Taylor (2006)	Britain	37	37	NHSOs reported to engage in more violent vaginal penetration against their victim than HSOs. Yet, HSOs more likely than NHSOs to penetrate their victim anally and to insert foreign objects in their victim's body cavities. NHSOs more likely than HSOs to bring a weapon to the crime scene and to restrict their victim's actions through binding or blindfolding.
Firestone, Bradford, Greenberg, Larose, & Curry (1998)	Canada	17	35	HSOs reported to engage in more noncontrolled violence and to be more likely to inflict multiple wounds on their victim than NHSOs.
Langevin, Ben-Aron, Wright, Marchese, & Handy (1988)	Canada	13	13	
Salfati & Taylor (2006)	Britain	37	37	
Chan & Beauregard (2015)	Canada	74	96	HSOs reported to engage in victim mutilation during the offense and admitted to the damages caused to the victim upon apprehension than NHSOs.

Continued

Table 1.1 Continued

Study (Year)	Country of Study	Number of HSOs	Number of NHSOs	Findings Pertaining to Differences between HSOs and NHSOs
Victims' Characteristics				
Chene & Cusson (2007)	Canada	43	148	HSOs more likely than NHSOs to target strangers older than themselves.
Firestone, Bradford, Greenberg, Larose, & Curry (1998)	Canada	17	35	
Koch, Berner, Hill, & Briken (2011)	Germany	166	56	
Langevin, Ben-Aron, Wright, Marchese, & Handy (1988)	Canada	13	13	
Oliver, Beech, Fisher, & Beckett (2007)	Britain	58	112	

Note. A (sexual murderers and rapists); B (homicidal and nonhomicidal sexual offenders); C (homicidal and nonhomicidal sexual offenders and child molesters); D (sexual killers and nonhomicidal sexually aggressive males); E (homicidal sexual offenders and incest offenders); F (sexual killers, nonhomicidal sexually aggressive men, nonhomicidal sadists, and nonhomicidal sexual offenders); and G (extrafamilial homicidal and nonhomicidal child molesters).

In terms of the differences in the demographic characteristics between HSOs and NHSOs, Grubin (1994) finds that in his sample of 21 sexual killers and 121 rapists, the sexual killers (M = 30.0, SD = 8.7) are generally older than the rapists (M = 25.9, SD = 6.9) when they committed their index offense. Salfati and Taylor (2006) report similar findings, with the sexual murderers (M = 29.4) being older than the rapists (M = 23.5) in their sample of 37 sexual murderers and 37 rapists. However, a recent study by Koch et al. (2011) reports the opposite: their sample of 56 NHSOs are older (M = 38.9, SD = 10.5) than their sample of 166 HSOs (M = 32.8, SD = 12.2).

In terms of victimology, strangers who are older are more likely to be targeted by sexual murderers than by NHSOs (Chene & Cusson, 2007; Firestone, Bradford, Greenberg, Larose, & Curry, 1998; Koch et al., 2011; Langevin et al., 1988; Oliver, Beech, Fisher, & Beckett, 2007). According to Oliver et al.'s (2007) sample of 58 sexual murderers and 112 rapists, the former have a significantly higher estimated IQ than the latter, although both groups' mean IQ is above the average range. Koch et al. (2011), however, find that their sample of NHSOs are more educated than sexual murderers (82% versus 62% finished school). Oliver et al. (2007) find that in their sample, a significantly greater proportion of the rapists commit violent offenses prior to their index offense compared with the sexual murderers. Although the sexual murderers (49%) commit more previous sexual offenses than the rapists (34%) in Oliver et al.'s (2007) study, this difference is not significant. Conversely, Firestone, Bradford, Greenberg, and Larose's (1998) and Firestone, Bradford, Greenberg, Larose, and Curry's (1998) samples of HSOs and child molesters, respectively, both report to have committed more violent and sexual offenses prior to their index crime than their non-homicidal counterparts.

The findings regarding the childhood and adolescent development differences between homicidal and non-homicidal sexual offenders are mixed. The sexual killers in Grubin's (1994) sample report having a more stable upbringing in terms of family structure compared with the rapists. To illustrate, 66% of the rapists experience a change in their primary caregiver in their formative years compared with 43% of the sexual murderers, and the sexual murderers are more likely to have had a stable father-figure prior to the age of ten than the rapists. However, Langevin et al. (1988) find the opposite to be true. In their sample, the 13 sexual killers report more disturbed relationships with their fathers than the 13 nonsexual killers and the 13 non-homicidal sexually aggressive males. The HSOs in Firestone, Bradford, Greenberg, and Larose's (1998) sample are more likely than their non-homicidal counterparts to have been removed from their family before the age of 16. Nevertheless, Proulx et al. (2002) fail to find any significant differences between sexual murderers ($N = 40$) and rapists ($N = 101$) in terms of their dysfunctional family background (e.g., parental alcoholism or domestic violence).

In Proulx et al.'s (2002) sample, the sexual murderers show more evidence of being victims of incest than the NHSOs. Similarly, the sexual murderers in Koch et al.'s (2011) sample are significantly more likely to have been physically and sexually abused as a child than the NHSOs. In sharp contrast, no significant differences between these two groups of sex offenders in terms of their own sexual and nonsexual victimization is found in Grubin's (1994) study. Oliver et al. (2007) find that their sample of sexual murderers and rapists report a high incidence of having been physically (68% of sexual murderers and 82% of rapists) and sexually (65% of sexual murderers and 52% of rapists) abused during childhood.

In terms of childhood behavioral problems, Grubin (1994) finds no differences in terms of the incidence of childhood conduct disorder in his sample of sexual murderers and rapists. In contrast, in their study of 40 sexual murderers and 101 rapists, Proulx et al. (2002) find that the sexual murderers report more childhood disciplinary problems than the rapists. Likewise, Langevin (2003) finds that compared with the other types of sexual offenders in his sample (33 sexual killers, 80 sexually aggressive males, 23 sadists, and 611 general sexual offenders), the sexual killers start their criminal career earlier and are more likely to have been to reform school, been members of criminal gangs, set fires, and been cruel to animals.

The study by Langevin et al. (1988) indicates that sexual killers are more frequently diagnosed as having an antisocial personality disorder (APD) and being involved in sexual sadism than nonsexual killers and non-homicidal sexually aggressive males. Besides being diagnosed with APD and involved in sexual sadism, the homicidal child molesters in Firestone, Bradford, Greenberg, Larose, and Curry's (1998) sample are also more frequently diagnosed with different types of paraphilias (e.g., fetishism, voyeurism, exhibitionism, frotteurism, and transvestic fetishism) and pedophilia than non-homicidal child molesters. In addition, the homicidal child molesters in their sample are also reported to display more psychopathic personality characteristics than the child molesters who did not commit a homicide.

In a more recent comparative study, Koch et al. (2011) find that sexual murderers are more likely to be diagnosed with a schizoid personality disorder than NHSOs. Relative to NHSOs, sexual murderers are also significantly more likely to be diagnosed with paraphilias, particularly sexual sadism and fetishism (Koch et al., 2011; see also Jones, Chan, Myers, & Heide, 2013). Pedophilia, conversely, is diagnosed more often among NHSOs than among those who killed (Koch et al., 2011). In terms of psychopathy, inconsistent with Firestone et al.'s (1998) finding, Koch and his colleagues find no significant differences in psychopathic personality between HSOs and the NHSOs. Interestingly, HSOs have higher mean scores on Factor 2, which corresponds to social deviance and antisocial personality in Hare's (2003) Psychopathy Checklist-Revised (PCL-R), than their non-homicidal counterparts. Chan and Beauregard's (2015) study of 74 HSOs and 96 NHSOs indicate that HSOs reported to have diagnosed with more different maladaptive personality traits, such as paranoid, schizotypal, borderline, histrionic, narcissistic, obsessive-compulsive, and impulsive traits, and the overall odd and eccentric traits than NHSOs. In addition, Sexual murderers are found to exhibit more paraphilic behaviors (i.e., exhibitionism, fetishism, frotteurism, homosexual pedophilia, sexual masochism, and partialism) than their counterparts who did not kill.

Grubin (1994) finds that the sexual murderers in his sample report a higher level of social isolation, both in childhood and adulthood, compared with the rapists; of particular note, relative to the rapists, the sexual murderers are less sexually experienced and have fewer sexual relationships. Similarly, in their qualitative analysis of 19 sexual killers and 16 nonmurdering sex offenders, Milsom et al. (2003) find that compared with the NHSOs, the sexual killers report higher levels of peer group loneliness in adolescence. In addition, compared with the NHSOs, the sexual killers also report having higher levels of grievances toward females in childhood and higher levels of seeing themselves as victims in adulthood.

In the context of the offense, the sexual killers are more likely than rapists to live alone at the time of the offense (Grubin, 1994). In addition, Oliver et al. (2007) find that the sexual murderers in their sample are involved in significantly fewer intimate relationships than the rapists. Although not specifically profound, 38% of sexual murderers are reported as having had no relationship at the time of their offense compared with 44% of the rapists who were married or had one main partner at the time of their offense. Firestone, Bradford, Greenberg, and Larose's (1998) study also yields similar findings: The homicidal sex offenders in their sample are significantly less likely to have married (30%) than the incest offenders (84%). However, Milsom et al. (2003)

find the opposite to be true: the NHSOs are more likely to have married than their homicidal counterparts.

The findings relating to sexual deviance between HSOs and NHSOs are also contradictory. Grubin's (1994) findings indicate that an interest in sexual deviation, aggressive pursuits, and a rich fantasy life are likely to be found equally in sexual murderers and rapists. Proulx et al. (2002) and Chan & Beauregard (2015), however, find that the sexual murderers report having more sexually deviant fantasies than the NHSOs. Similarly, Langevin et al. (1988) report that compared with sexual offenders who do not kill, sexual murderers show more evidence of being aroused by transvestism and sadism, as measured by phallometric assessments.

In their study of 48 HSOs who killed children and 50 incest offenders, Firestone, Bradford, Greenberg, and Larose (1998) consistently find that the HSOs report a greater preference for descriptions of assaultive acts with children than the incest offenders via a higher pedophile assault index. However, no difference is found between these two groups of sexual offenders in terms of their pedophile index scores. In a follow-up comparative study of 17 extra-familial homicidal and 35 extra-familial non-homicidal child molesters, Firestone, Bradford, Greenberg, Larose, and Curry (1998) again find significant differences in pedophile assault index scores between these two groups of child molesters. The homicidal child molesters are reported to have higher pedophile assault index scores than the non-homicidal child molesters. Similarly, the pedophile index scores of these two groups of child molesters fail to yield any significant differences. These significant findings are confirmed in a third comparative study of 27 homicidal child molesters, 189 non-homicidal child molesters, and 47 non-offenders by Firestone, Bradford, Greenberg, and Nunes (2000).

In Chene and Cusson's (2007) sample of 43 sexual murderers and 148 rapists, the sexual murderers are more frequently reported to present a motive of (a) anger or (b) sex and anger prior to the offense than the rapists. Compared with the NHSOs, the HSOs use and/or abuse drugs and alcohol more frequently prior to the offense (Chene & Cusson, 2007; Langevin, 2003). Interestingly, Koch et al. (2011) report that sexual murderers are more likely to consume alcohol at the time of their crime, while NHSOs are more likely to have abused illegal drugs either prior or during their offense. In terms of victim selection, sexual murderers are more likely to select victim of choice that meets their needs, while NHSOs are more likely to select victim with distinctive physical and/or personality characteristics (Chan & Beauregard, 2015).

In Salfati and Taylor's (2006) sample, the rapists (89%) are found to engage in more violent vaginal penetration against their victim at the crime scene than the sexual murderers (60%). In contrast, the sexual murderers are more likely than the rapists to penetrate their victim anally and to insert foreign objects into their victim's body cavities (Salfati & Taylor, 2006). Compared with the sexual murderers the rapists are more likely to bring a weapon to the crime scene (43% versus 14%) and to restrict their victim's actions through binding (24% versus 8%) or blindfolding (16% versus 5%; Salfati & Taylor, 2006). In contrast, sexual murderers engage in more non-controlled violence (i.e., where the offender engaged in manual violence) and to be more likely to inflict multiple wounds on their victim than rapists (Firestone, Bradford, Greenberg, Larose, & Curry, 1998; Langevin et al., 1988; Salfati & Taylor, 2006). Chan and Beauregard (2015), in their study, indicate that sexual killers are more likely to mutilate their victim during the offense and to admit to the damages caused to their victim upon apprehension than sexual offenders who did not kill.

2
Sexual Homicide Offending: Offender Classifications

In order to systematically study sexual homicide offenders (SHOs), clinicians and researchers have attempted to categorize them into different types based on their developmental, pre-crime, crime, and post-crime profiles. In addition to the widely cited motivational model on sexual homicide by the Federal Bureau of Investigation (FBI), which was published in the mid-1980s, there are 12 other scholarly classifications of SHOs that were published during the period of 1985 to 2014. Some of these SHO typologies are empirically generated, while some are merely based on the authors' personal clinical or investigative experiences.

According to Blackburn (1993), the offender classification systems can be grouped into four different types of approaches: (a) pragmatic (analysis of the offender's demographic characteristics in order to generate useful offender categories), (b) clinical (prototypical features of different types of offenders), (c) theory-led (categorization of the offenders' types based on a particular theory), and (d) statistical (classification of the offenders' different offender profiles psychometrically). While most of the SHO classifications published in the early years are pragmatic in nature, a trend in statistically generated offender typologies has emerged in recent years. The number of offender profiles usually ranges from two simple categories to six elaborate groups of sexual murderers. The sample size ranges from 10 to 350 subjects, with the exception of three classifications which are based solely on clinical and investigative experiences.

Out of the 13 scholarly published sexual murderer classifications, the offender crime scene profile (crime phase) is used in 12 (see 2.1). This approach is not only as an effort to study sexual murderers for the purpose of after-the-fact research but also as a seriously developed measure, namely offender profiling, to aid in police investigations.

Table 2.1 Thirteen scholarly published classifications of sexual homicide offenders (1985–2014)

Author(s)	Type of classification	Number, type, and country of sample	Number of profiles	Type of offense and offender profiles
Ressler et al. (1985, 1986, 1988), Burgess et al. (1986)	Pragmatic	36 male serial/non-serial SHOs who murdered adult women and men, and children; United States	Two	Offender developmental, pre-crime, and crime scene profiles
Geberth (1996)	Pragmatic	None; based on investigative experience	Six	Offense characteristics and offender crime scene profiles
Keppel & Walter (1999)	Theory-led	None; based on investigative experience	Four	Offense characteristics and offender personality and crime scene profiles
Kocsis (1999), Kocsis et al. (2002)	Pragmatic	86 SHOs; Australia	Four	Offender crime scene profiles
Meloy (2000)	Clinical	36 male and 2 female serial/non-serial SHOs who murdered adult women and men; United States	Two	Offense characteristics and offender developmental and pathological profiles
Clarke & Carter (2000)	Clinical	32 male non-serial SHOs who murdered adult women, adult men, and children; England	Four	Offender crime scene profiles

Study	Classification type	Sample	Number of types	Profile types
Beauregard & Proulx (2002)	Statistical	34 non-serial and 2 serial male SHOs who murdered adult women; Canada	Two	Offender pre-crime, crime scene, and post-crime profiles
Schlesinger (2004, 2007)	Clinical	None; based on clinical experience	Four	Offender pre-crime, crime scene, and post-crime profiles
Fisher & Beech (2007)	Statistical	28 male SHOs who murdered adult women and children; United Kingdom	Three	Offender pre-crime, crime-scene, and post-crime profiles
Beauregard & Proulx (2007)	Pragmatic	10 male non-serial SHOs who murdered adult men; Canada	Three	Offender developmental, pre-crime, and crime scene profiles
Gerard, Mormont, & Kocsis (2007)	Pragmatic	33 male non-serial SHOs who murdered adult women, adult men, and children; Belgium	Two	Offender crime scene profiles
Sewall, Krupp, & Lalumière (2013)	Pragmatic	82 male serial SHOs; United States	Three	Offender developmental, pathological, and crime scene profiles
Balemba, Beauregard, & Martineau (2014)	Statistical	350 SHOs (250 solved and 100 unsolved cases); Canada	Three	Offender crime scene profiles

Note: Types of classification system: (a) pragmatic, (b) theory-led, (c) clinical, and (d) statistical classification approaches (Blackburn, 1993).

While most of these empirically generated offender typologies are based on North American samples (the US and Canada), samples from other parts of the world, such as Australia, England, Belgium, and the UK, are not uncommon. These different SHO typologies are discussed in the following sections.

2.1　Pragmatic classification approach

2.1.1　The FBI's motivational model of sexual homicide: organized-disorganized dichotomy

In the early 1970s, the Patterns of Homicide Crime Scene Project was initiated by agents of the FBI's Behavioral Science Unit to analyze offender characteristics by examining crime scene information in order to produce a preliminary crime scene analysis and a criminal profiling framework. A review of the case records (e.g., psychiatric and criminal records, pretrial records, court transcripts, and prison records), direct observations, and the first-hand investigative interviews of convicted and incarcerated murderers in various US correctional institutions was performed between 1979 and 1983 to analyze homicide crime scene patterns. On the basis of the cases of 36 male murderers, mostly serial offenders, a dichotomous motivational model of organized and disorganized sexual murderers was proposed (Burgess, Hartman, Ressler, Douglas, & McCormack, 1986; Ressler, Burgess, & Douglas, 1988; Ressler, Burgess, Depue, Douglas, Hazelwood, Lanning, et al., 1985; Ressler, Burgess, Douglas, Hartman, & D'Agostino, 1986; Ressler, Burgess, Hartman, Douglas, & McCormack, 1986; see Table 2.2).

The profiles of organized and disorganized sexual murderers are derived from the distinctive crime scene behaviors and offender characteristics. Organized SHOs are likely to be individuals of high intelligence who are employed in a skilled occupation. They often plan their offenses to increase their success rates and to avoid apprehension. Activities such as stalking their potential victims and surveying their possible crime scene environments are frequently carried out prior to the commission of the offense. They are likely to experience a precipitating stressor (e.g., financial, marital, female, or job) around that period of time. They are more likely to own a vehicle and to drive to the crime scene. During the time of the offense, they are likely to be intoxicated, angry, and depressed. They may exert tremendous force and restraint against their victim to remain in control throughout the sexual assault. Their crime scene tends to be clean, without many traces left for the police investigation, in order for them to evade apprehension. After committing

Table 2.2 The FBI's organized/disorganized dichotomy of the motivational model of sexual murderers

Organized Sexual Murderers	Disorganized Sexual Murderers
Offender characteristics	
1. They are likely to have high intelligence.	1. They are likely to be a low birth order child.
2. They are likely to be employed in a skilled occupation.	2. They are likely to come from a home where their father's employment was unstable.
3. They are likely to be angry and depressed at the time of the offense.	3. They are likely to have been abused as a child.
4. They are likely to experience a precipitating stress (e.g., financial, marital, female, job).	4. They are likely to be sexually inhibited and ignorant and to have more sexual aversions.
5. They are likely to be intoxicated at the time of the offense.	5. They are likely to have parents with sexual problems.
6. They are likely to own a vehicle in decent condition.	6. They are likely to have been frightened and confused at the time of offense.
7. They are likely to follow the police investigation of their crime through the mass media.	7. They are likely to know their victim prior to the offense.
8. They are likely to change jobs or leave town after the commission of their crime.	8. They are likely to reside alone at the time of the offense.
	9. They are likely to have committed their crime near to their home or workplace.
Crime scene behavior	
1. They are likely to plan their offense.	1. They are likely to leave their weapon at the crime scene.
2. They are likely to use tremendous force and restraints against their victims.	2. They are likely to position and depersonalize (i.e., blindfolding, eradication of features) their victim's dead body.
3. They are likely to perform sexual acts with live victims.	3. They are likely to perform sadistic acts against the victim.
4. They are likely to exhibit control over the victim (i.e., being manipulative or threatening and wanting the victim to show fear).	4. They are likely to perform sexual acts (i.e., necrophilia) and postmortem activity (i.e., mutilation) on their victim's dead body.
5. They are likely to use a vehicle to carry out their offense.	5. They are likely to keep their victim's dead body.
	6. They are less likely to use a vehicle to carry out their offense

Sources: Ressler, Burgess, and Douglas (1988); and Ressler, Burgess, Douglas, Hartman, and D'Agostino (1986).

their offense, they are likely to change jobs or flee town. Through media reports, they are well aware of the police's investigation of their crime.

In sharp contrast, disorganized SHOs are more likely to have experienced an abusive childhood and to have parents with histories of sexual problems. Their fathers tend to have unstable employment. Because of their unhealthy background, they tend to have limited healthy interpersonal relationships. They are also likely to be sexually inhibited and ignorant and to experience more sexual aversions. Their crimes lack planning and are apt to be perpetrated against people they get to know in the course of their employment or people who live near them. They are likely to reside alone at the time of the offense and to walk to the crime scene, which is likely to be within close distance to either their home or workplace. They are probably frightened and confused at the time of the offense. Depersonalization of, and sadistic acts against, the victim and the sexual positioning of the victim's corpse are likely to occur as part of their offense routine. They are also likely to perform necrophilic acts and other post-mortem activities on their victim's corpse. After their ritualistic acts on the corpse, they frequently keep their victim's body parts or belongings as souvenirs or trophies. They often leave the crime scene without any attempt to clean it or to hide traces. Hence, their crime scene tends to reflect haphazard behavior and to provide many critical leads for the police investigation.

2.1.2   Geberth's six-type classification of homosexual homicide

On the basis of his homicide investigation experience, Geberth (1996) proposes a six-type classification of homosexual homicides (see Table 2.3). His attempt is among the first to describe the differential offender and crime scene characteristics of homicides that involve homosexual victims. The offenses in the first three offender profiles are sexually motivated. The sexual murder of men as a result of interpersonal violence-oriented disputes and assaults (first profile) is the most common type of homosexual homicide. The victim-offender relationship is often intimate and personal, usually involving partners, ex-partners, or love triangles. This type of murder usually occurs in a prostitution context where one party does not respect the sexual activity "ground rules" that have been mutually agreed on. Although the second type of homosexual homicide – murder involving forced anal rape and/ or sodomy – is also sexually motivated, the offenders usually do not obtain sexual gratification from their killing. The death of the victim often results from the overuse of force to prevent the victim's resistance and/or identification. Geberth's third type of homosexual homicide,

Table 2.3 Geberth's six-type classification of homosexual homicides

Interpersonal violence-oriented disputes and assaults	Murders involving forced anal rape and/or sodomy	Lust murders
1. Common type of sexual murder of men.	1. The offense is often sexually motivated, but usually there is no sexual gratification associated with the killing.	1. Crime is meticulously premeditated according to the offender's deviant sexual fantasies.
2. Usually triggered by disputes between partners, ex-partners, or love triangles (i.e., "ground rules" are not respected by one of the parties involved in the sexual activity).	2. Death typically occurs as a result of the overuse of force to overcome the victim's resistance or to prevent identification.	2. The offenders are likely to exhibit psychopathic personality characteristics.
3. The offense is often committed in a prostitution context.		3. Crime scene evidence of sadism and mutilation of victim's genitalia.

Homosexual serial murders	Robberies and/or homicides of homosexuals	Homophobic assaults and gay bashing
1. Offenders are motivated by power and control, with sex as a secondary motivation.	1. Offenders target potential victims who engage in high-risk behaviors in locations frequented by homosexuals.	1. Offenders assault homosexual-oriented victims because of their intense hatred of homosexuals.
2. The offenders usually target vulnerable victims who are easy to control.	2. Offenders may act alone or with an accomplice and use homosexual prostitution as a means to assault or rob a gay customer who is willing to pay for sexual services.	
3. The offenses are often homosexual-oriented and involve lust, thrill, child, and robbery homicides.		
4. Evidence of mutilation and dismemberment of victim's body either to shock others, to facilitate transportation of the body, or to avoid the victim being identified.		
5. Three subtypes: murderers who (a) exclusively target other male homosexual victims, (b) target heterosexual and homosexual victims, and (c) target young males and boys.		

Source: Geberth (1996).

lust murder, is associated with elements of sexual sadism and mutilation of the victim's genitalia. The assaults committed by lust murderers who victimize homosexuals are often meticulously premeditated to satiate their deviant sexual fantasies. Offenders of this type usually demonstrate psychopathic personality characteristics such as manipulativeness, superficial charm, and callousness.

Unlike the first three profiles of homosexual homicide offenders, which cover sexually motivated crimes, offenders in the remaining three profiles are primarily motivated by power, financial gain, or hatred. Homosexual serial sexual murderers (fourth profile) are motivated by power and control over their victims: sex is only their secondary motive. They typically target vulnerable victims who are easy to control, such as children and prostitutes. Their assaults are homosexually oriented and can involve lust killings, thrill murders, child killings, and robbery homicides. Sexual murderers of this type often mutilate and dismember their victim's body either to shock those who discover the body, to facilitate the corpse's transportation, or to try to prevent the victim from being identified. Geberth further proposes three subtypes of homosexual serial murders (not mutually exclusive depending on offender opportunity and victim availability): (a) offenders who exclusively target male homosexual victims; (b) offenders who attack both heterosexual and homosexual males; and (c) offenders who target only young males and boys. The offenders in the fifth profile, robbery and/or the homicide of homosexuals, usually target victims who are engaging in high-risk behaviors in locations that are frequented by homosexuals (e.g., gay bars, nightclubs, and saunas). Either acting alone or with an accomplice, this type of offender may use homosexual prostitution as a means to assault or rob a gay customer who is willing to pay for their sexual services. Finally, offenders who commit homophobic assaults and gay bashing (sixth profile) are motivated by their intense hatred for homosexuals.

2.1.3 Kocsis's four behavioral patterns of sexual murderers

With the aim of developing a profiling model of different types of sexual murderers, Kocsis (1999) collects data on 86 cases of sexual homicide that occurred in Australia between 1960 and 1998 from all Australian police jurisdictions (see Kocsis & Irwin, 1998 for their selection criteria). Using a computerized statistical modeling approach, Kocsis produces four distinct offender behavioral patterns: (a) predator, (b) perversion, (c) fury, and (d) rape (see Table 2.4). All of these offender behavioral patterns are comprised of three common behaviors: (a) sexual interaction occurs between the offender and the victim, (b) the weapon is

Table 2.4 Kocsis's four behavioral patterns of sexual murderers

Predator	Perversion	Fury	Rape
Offender behavioral patterns			
1. Offenders' behaviors indicative of a high level of planning.	1. Offenders' behaviors indicative of a high level of organization (simple logical coherence in modus operandi to perpetrate the crime) but with less planning and fantasizing.	1. Offenders' behaviors indicative of a deep hatred of the victim.	1. Offenders' behaviors indicative of an intended sexual assault on the victim.
2. Sadistic acts are performed to satisfy sexually sadistic drives.	2. Crime scene characteristics suggestive of an antisocial perversion theme but with less calculation.	2. The motivation behind the attack is to release a long suppressed rage against what the victim may represent to the offender, but the crime does not necessarily indicate anger toward the specific victim.	2. Murder is often an accident due either to the accidental use of excessive force to subdue the victim or to the offender's sudden fear of apprehension.
3. Crime scene characteristics suggestive of a very violent offending pattern, such as stylized wounds, gagging, and torture of the victim, are often evidenced.	3. Offenders engage in bizarre sexual perversion to gain satisfaction, but not necessarily while the victim is alive.	3. Violent crime scene characteristics, such as brutal, excessive, and unfocused wound patterns on the victim, are evidenced but with much less calculation and deliberation.	3. Offenders are often vaguely acquainted with their victim; the specific victim may have been previously targeted by the offender as a potential victim.
			4. Less violent crime scene characteristics are evidenced; victim brutality is less likely.

Sources: Kocsis (1999); and Kocsis, Cooksey, and Irwin (2002).

brought to the crime scene by the offender, and (c) the offender disrobes the victim. Kocsis (1999) differentiates the levels of sophistication in the modus operandi (MO) employed by SHOs: The predator and perversion patterns are more methodical, while the fury and rape patterns are more haphazard in nature. This profiling model of sexual murderers further refined in Kocsis, Cooksey, and Irwin (2002) by using the multidimensional scaling (MDS) approach to include the characteristics of the offender and the victim and the offender-victim interactions.

Sexual killers identified as following the predator pattern often engage in a high level of premeditated offense. A very violent offending pattern characterized by sadistic features, such as stylized wounds, gagging, and the torturing of the victim, that are designed to gratify the offenders' sexually sadistic drives. In terms of the offender's characteristics, predatory SHOs are apt to be older than their victims, to be bilingual with an accent, to have longer hair length, to have scars or other identifying marks, to be well groomed, to be married or live with others, to own a collection of detective magazines and sexual paraphernalia, to have a history of mental problems, to be on statutory release, to have a history of prior sexual offenses, and to have travelled internationally within the previous ten years. They are less likely to own a vehicle but are likely to use a vehicle (van, jeep, or truck) to commit their series of offenses, possibly with an accomplice. The victims of predatory SHOs are apt to be taller, to have a more criminal lifestyle, and to rely on others for their transportation. The initial contact site between the offenders of this type and their victims is likely to be in an outdoor environment, often in a non-city location. The typical crime scene of this type of offender is in the victim's living quarters, but the recovery site is usually in a non-city location.

The offending behavioral pattern of the perversion type of sexual killers, on the other hand, indicates a high level of organization with a simple logical coherence in their MO. However, compared with the predatory type of SHOs, less planning and fantasizing are disclosed by their offenses. Bizarre sexual perversion often occurs to satisfy their sexually perverted needs but not necessarily while the victim is alive. These SHOs are likely to have homosexual/bisexual habits and a collection of pornography, to be employed, to use drugs and/or alcohol, and to drive an older vehicle in exceptionally good condition. The victims of this type of offender are apt to be non-white, to reside with others, and to be incarcerated at the time of their initial contact with the offender. The location of the initial contact between the offender and the victim is likely to be in the victim's living quarters (e.g., correctional institution), and the offender is likely to have a history of prior activity in this location (i.e., being incarcerated before). Sexual killers of this type are likely to select a public place to commit their offense.

Killings by the fury type of sexual murderer demonstrate an expression of deep hatred toward the victim but with less premeditation and deliberation. These offenders perpetrate their crimes to release a long suppressed rage against what the victim represents to them; the crimes do not necessarily indicate hatred of a specific victim. Because of their intense rage, the SHOs of this type are likely to inflict brutal, excessive, and unfocused wounds on their victims. The victims of this type of SHO are apt to be females with a larger body build, to be older than the offenders, to wear glasses, to have longer hair length, and to have scars or other marks or outstanding features. In terms of their offenses, sexual fury SHOs are likely to select an unfamiliar outdoor location as their crime scene, which is also likely to be their disposal site.

Finally, the primary intention of the rape pattern type of SHO is to sexually assault, but not kill, the victim. The murder is accidental due to an unintentional use of excessive force to subdue the victim or the offender's sudden fear of apprehension. Hence, brutality against the victim is not often seen at the crime scene. These offenders are often vaguely acquainted with their victim. In most cases, they were previously aware of their victim's existence and subsequently targeted this specific victim. In general, the SHOs of the rape pattern type are likely to be non-white, to be taller, to have an unkempt hair style, to rely on others for their transportation needs, and to have a history of mental illness. With regards to their offenses, the initial contact scene, the crime scene, and the disposal site are likely to be at the same location.

2.1.4 Beauregard and Proulx's typology of sexual murderers of men

Apart from Geberth's (1996) classification of homosexual homicides, the only other SHO classification that has been developed for those who sexually victimize male victims is Beauregard and Proulx's (2007) typology. Using a sample of ten sexual murderers who killed male victims aged 14 or older, Beauregard and Proulx (2007) empirically examine the crime phase constructs (e.g., crime scene variables and acts committed while committing the offense), dis-inhibitors (e.g., deviant sexual fantasies, alcohol and drug consumption, and pornography), occupational problems (e.g., compulsive work and loss of job), relationship difficulties (e.g., loneliness, separation, and familial dilemmas), and victim characteristics. On the basis of their examination, Beauregard and Proulx

(2007) propose a classification of sexual offenders who victimize adult male victims with three distinct offender categories: (a) the avenger, (b) the sexual predator, and (c) the nonsexual predator (see Table 2.5).

The avengers are usually involved in prostitution activities and can be either homosexual, heterosexual, or bisexual. A history of childhood psychological, physical, and sexual abuse is common among this type of sexual murderer. The offenders of this type may have a diversified criminal career and may have been convicted of a property or a violent crime prior to the commission of their initial sexual homicide. In terms of their sexual homicide offense, anger is a primary theme, the aim being to unleash their rage. Hence, expressive violence is evidenced on their victim. Alcohol and drug consumption prior to perpetrating the crime is common. Their offense is usually triggered by an event occurring during or after a sexual exchange in a prostitution context that triggers the offender's memory of childhood abuse. The victims of this type of sexual murderer are likely to be older than the offenders. In terms of the method used to kill their victim, strangulation is frequently preferred by avengers; they may also use weapons of opportunity, such as a kitchen knife, a pillow, or a phone cord, to murder their victim.

The sexual predators are usually of a homosexual orientation and have a history of committing sexual offenses, particularly against male children and adolescents, but their victims may not necessarily have a homosexual orientation. The sexual murders committed by sexual predators who target male adolescents and young adults are frequently premeditated, and their key motivation is to satiate their deviant sexual fantasies. Once targeted by a sexual predator, the victim is usually abducted and/or confined. The sexual predator performs sadistic sexual acts with expressive violence on the victim in order to satisfy his deviant sexual fantasies. Therefore, the sexual offense against the victim, who is likely to be a stranger to the offender, usually lasts for more than 30 minutes and can go on for as long as 24 hours.

The nonsexual predators can be either heterosexual or homosexual. Although they are likely to have a diversified criminal career, their offenses are predominantly property related. The sex-related homicides committed by nonsexual predators are usually unplanned, and their key objective is to rob their victim. They may act alone or with an accomplice. Often, offenders of this type hunt for their victims in locations that are reputed to be frequented by homosexuals, such as gay bars and nightclubs. Their victims are targeted on the basis of their vulnerability (e.g., live alone, reluctant to report a robbery to the police, or feel guilty after being manipulated), easy access (e.g., often frequent the gay

Table 2.5 Beauregard and Proulx's typology of sexual murderers who target men

The Avenger	The Sexual Predator	The Nonsexual Predator
Offender Characteristics		
1. Offenders can be individuals of homosexual, heterosexual, or bisexual orientation who are involved in prostitution activities.	1. Offenders are usually homosexual in sexual orientation.	1. Offenders can be of either heterosexual or homosexual orientation.
2. Offenders are likely to have experienced psychological, physical, and sexual abuse in childhood.	2. Offenders are likely to have history of sexual crimes, especially against male children or adolescents.	2. Offenders are likely to have a diversified criminal career but mostly involving property crimes.
3. Offenders are likely to have a history of violent and property crimes.		
Victim characteristics		
1. Victims are likely to be older than the offenders.	1. Targeted victims are usually adolescents or young adults who are strangers but not necessarily of homosexual orientation.	1. Victims are targeted and lured to an isolated area via the use of the victims' visibility and homosexual orientation.

Continued

Table 2.5 Continued

The Avenger	The Sexual Predator	The Nonsexual Predator
Crime characteristics		
1. Offenders are likely to use alcohol and drugs prior to the offense.	1. The offense is premeditated.	1. The offense is unpremeditated.
2. The offense is usually preceded by anger, which is rooted in a triggering event that occurs during or after sexual exchange in a prostitution context that reminds the offender of their memory of childhood abuse.	2. Offenders are usually motivated by deviant sexual fantasies.	2. Offenders may act alone or with an accomplice with aim of robbing the victim.
3. Victims are likely to be killed by strangulation or a weapon of opportunity.	3. Victims are abducted and/or confined.	3. Alcohol and drug use prior to the offense.
4. Expressive violence is evidenced.	4. Sadistic acts with expressive violence are performed during the offense.	4. Violence is used to commit the offense or to overcome the victim's resistance.
	5. The offense usually lasts more than 30 minutes and can go as long as 24 hours.	5. Sexual assault is rare, but sexual contact may occur as a means of manipulation.
		6. The use of a weapon of opportunity or choice.
		7. The duration of the offense is generally short.

Source: Beauregard and Proulx (2007).

district), and visibility (e.g., open about their sexual orientation). Once selected, the nonsexual predator's targeted victim is usually lured to an isolated location, where the crime is perpetrated. Sexual assault is rare, but sexual contact with the victim may occur as a manipulative means to trap the victim. A weapon, either by opportunity or by choice, is usually used to control the victim. Instrumental violence is likely to be used against the victim in order to execute the offense or to overcome the victim's resistance. Often, the offense is short in duration, with the offender leaving the crime scene right after the homicide. It is interesting to note that alcohol and drug use prior to an attack is common.

2.1.5   Gerard, Mormont, and Kocsis's two behavioral templates of sexual murderers

Using the cases of sexual homicide committed within the territory of French-speaking Belgium, Gerard, Mormont, and Kocsis (2007) were the first to empirically examine 33 male non-serial sexual murderers of women ($N = 26$) and men ($N = 2$) aged between 7 and 84 years old. As a result of their MDS analysis, two behavioral templates were proposed for offenders: (a) opportunistic-impulsive and (b) sadistic-calculator (see Table 2.6). Apart from the differential behavioral patterns exhibited by these two types of sexual murderer, several common behavioral patterns are shared by all Belgian SHOs: (a) clothing is missing from the victim, (b) vaginal penetration of the victim, (c) fondling of the victim, (d) defensive injuries found on the victim, and (e) the crime is committed between midnight and 7:00 a.m.

According to Gerard and colleagues (2007), opportunistic-impulsive SHOs are likely to (a) act in an almost spontaneous manner without much planning against victims who are known to them and (b) be drunk during the offense. Clearly, their offenses are opportunistic crimes. In addition, a characteristic of sexual homicides committed by this type of SHO is that the offenders are responding to their urges for immediate gratification in an impulsive manner. Hence, random violence is often evidenced. In addition, vaginal, oral, and anal penetration of the victim are common. Upon the completion of their offense, the victim's corpse is often left outdoors with the face covered. Broadly speaking, opportunistic-impulsive sexual murderers are usually aged between 31 and 47 years old, while their victims are typically aged between one and 17 years old and between 31 and 47 years old.

In sharp contrast, sadistic-calculator SHOs usually engage in more preparation and exercise caution when perpetrating their offense. These offenders usually disguise themselves to prevent identification by their

Table 2.6　Gerard, Mormont, and Kocsis's two behavioral templates of sexual murderers

Opportunistic-impulsive	Sadistic-calculator
Offender behavioral characteristics	
1. Offenders know their victims.	1. Offenders are likely to disguise themselves.
2. Victims are likely to be drunk.	2. Victims are likely to be imprisoned, blindfolded, and gagged.
3. Violence caused by the offender is random.	3. Victims are likely to be drugged, bound, and tortured.
4. Oral and anal penetration against the victim.	4. Insertion of objects into the victim's body cavities is likely.
5. Victim's body is disposed of at an outdoor location.	5. Victim mutilation is likely.
6. Victim's face is covered.	6. Offenders are likely to openly expose and position their victim's corpse.
7. Victims are aged between 1 and 7 years old and between 31 and 47 years old.	7. Victims are aged between 17 and 30 years old.
8. Offenders are aged between 31 and 47 years old.	8. Offenders are aged between 17 and 30 years old.

Source: Gerard, Mormont, and Kocsis (2007).

victim. In order to gratify their sexual sadistic urges, they are likely to imprison, bind, and torture their victims. A blindfold and a gag are also often used by this type of sexual killer. The infliction of pain on the victim is performed to satisfy the killer's sentiment of vengeance and/or retaliation. Such sadistic acts include victim mutilation and the insertion of objects into the victim's body cavities. When their victim is dead, sadistic-calculator SHOs are apt to openly expose and position the corpse. In general, sexual murderers of this type are usually aged between 17 and 30 years old and their victims are likely to be in the same age range.

2.1.6　Sewall, Krupp, and Lalumière's three kinds of Male serial sexual murderers

Sewall, Krupp, and Lalumière (2013) argue that the published sexual homicide typologies tend to be weakly based on either (or both) theoretically or empirically driven research. Hence, they propose a typological model that is derived from the work of Harris et al. (2001) and

Lalumière et al. (2005) to provide a more parsimonious typology than those published in the extant literature. Three kinds of male serial SHOs exist: (a) competitively disadvantaged, (b) psychopathic, and (c) sadistic offenders (see Table 2.7).

According to Sewall et al. (2013), competitively disadvantaged offenders are likely to be life-course persistent offenders who experienced neurodevelopmental defects and poor environmental conditions early in their life. They are less likely to succeed in prosocial activities, which lead them to begin an antisocial career at a young age. They are likely to come from low socioeconomic environments and have poor future prospects. Competitively disadvantaged offenders are likely to perform poorly in school, have low intelligence, begin their delinquent careers as juveniles, and struggle to hold steady employment as adults. As low quality men, they are expected to have limited access to desirable sexual partners. Hence, their sexual relationships are likely to be short-term and involve sexual coercion. They are likely to engage in reactive violence in which the homicide is likely to be spontaneous and explosive as a way to respond to a perceived provocation or rejection. Pertaining to their crime scene behavior, they are likely to leave disorganized crime scenes because they lack the mental capacity to fully plan and execute an organized sexual homicide.

Similarly, psychopathic SHOs are also expected to begin their criminal careers at a young age and persist through adulthood. However, they are likely to appear developmentally healthy with little to no evidence of neurodevelopmental deficits. Instead, they are callous, manipulative, impulsive, lack remorse, and feel little empathy for others. They are also prone to casual and sometimes coercive sexual relationships. Crime scenes left by these psychopathic offenders reflect a mixture of organized and disorganized scenes. On the one hand, these impulsive offenders commit homicides that are spontaneous, much as disorganized offenders do. Nevertheless, their criminal lifestyles equip them with the experience to have some planning over their homicides, which enables them to maintain some degree or order at the scene and to avoid detection. Some signs of sadism and torture at the scene are possible given their psychopathic nature of violence, thrill seeking, and their lack of empathy.

Unlike competitively disadvantaged and psychopathic SHOs, sadistic sexual murderers are not expected to have a criminal history. They are likely to have relatively normal lives, to hold steady employment, and to be involved in marital relationships. However, it is their strong sexual attraction to sadistic behavior that eventually leads them to sexually

Table 2.7 Sewall, Krupp, and Lalumière's three kinds of male serial sexual murderers

Competitively disadvantaged	Psychopathic	Sadistic
Offender characteristics		
1. Offenders are likely to experience early neurodevelopmental problems and poor environmental conditions early in life, which lead them to have a lifelong antisocial behavior.	1. Offenders appear to be developmentally healthy, with little to no evidence of neurodevelopmental defects.	1. Offenders are not likely to have a serious criminal background, but have a strong sexual attraction to sadistic behaviors that eventually lead them to kill.
2. Offenders are likely to come from low socioeconomic status environments and have poor future prospects.	2. Offenders are likely to begin their criminal careers at a young age and to persist through adulthood, and may engage in a variety of violent offenses, including sexual homicide.	2. Offenders are likely to spend a great deal of time in fantasizing excessively over the humiliation and torture of others.
3. Offenders are likely to perform poorly in school, have low intelligence, begin their delinquent career as juveniles, and have problem holding steady employment as adults.	3. Offenders are callous, manipulative, impulsive, lack remorse, and feel little empathy for others.	3. Offenders appear to lead relatively normal lives, with steady employment and marital relationships.
4. Offenders are likely to engage in a short-term mating strategy, which involves sexual coercion employment..	4. Offenders are prone to casual and sometimes coercive sexual relationships.	
Crime scene behavior		
1. Crime scenes of these offenders reflect some disorganization, in which offenders lack the mental capacity to fully plan and execute an organized sexual homicide.	1. Crime scenes of these offenders reflect a mixture of organized and disorganized types, with possible signs of sadism and torture.	1. Crime scenes of these offenders reflect organization, by which they spend hours fantasizing over every detail.
2. Offenders are likely to engage in reactive violence whereby the homicide is spontaneous and explosive, which is likely a response to a perceived provocation or rejection.	2. Although the offender are impulsive, so their homicide is likely to be spontaneous, but their criminal lifestyles equips them with the experience to engage in some planning over their homicide to avoid detection.	2. Evidence of sadistic activities at the crime scene is likely, but little evidence pointing to the offenders.

Source: Sewall, Krupp, and Lalumière (2013).

kill. They typically spend much of their time fantasizing excessively over the humiliation and torture of others. It is the presence of the overwhelming urge for sadistic acts that motivates them to sexually kill. Before they commit the offense, they are likely to spend hours fantasizing over every detail in order to behave methodically and meticulously during their offense. Hence, their crime scenes are likely to reflect an organized type of scene, which shows little evidence pointing to them. Evidence of sadistic activities such as humiliation, torture, and mutilation are common at their crime scenes. Sadistic SHOs are also likely to keep trophies or souvenirs from their offenses.

2.2 Clinical classification approach

2.2.1 Meloy's clinical typology of sexual homicide perpetrators

Meloy (2000) refines the framework of Ressler and colleagues' (1988) organized/disorganized dichotomy model of sexual murderers' characteristics with an emphasis on their psychopathology. Drawing from his clinical Rorschach experience of 38 serial and non-serial sexual murderers of adult women and men[1] incarcerated in various prisons and forensic hospitals in California, Florida, Illinois, Massachusetts, and the District of Columbia during the period between 1986 and 1997 (see Gacono, Meloy, & Bridges, 2000; Huprich, Gacono, Schneider, & Bridges, 2004), Meloy postulates a two-clinical-profile classification of SHOs: compulsive and catathymic (see Table 2.8).

Sexual homicides committed by compulsive sexual murderers are likely to be organized with careful premeditation. Compulsive SHOs, who are often diagnosed with sexual sadism, are apt to engage in sadistic acts on their victim to satiate their deviant sexual fantasies. In order to perfect their fantasies, SHOs who are compulsive, organized, and with above average intelligence are likely to learn from their mistakes and improve their mode of perpetration in their subsequent attacks. In terms of their psychopathological condition, sexual killers who are compulsive are prone to be severely psychopathic in their personality, demonstrating behaviors such as a callous, remorseless disregard of others, and to display chronic antisocial behavior. Hence, full blown diagnoses of antisocial and narcissistic personality disorders are not uncommon among compulsive sexual homicide perpetrators. Looking back into their developmental background, compulsive sexual murderers are apt to be chronically detached from their parents, although early childhood traumatic experiences are less likely to be evidenced. Because of their early pathological attachment, compulsive SHOs' autonomic

Table 2.8   Meloy's clinical typology of sexual homicide perpetrators: compulsive and catathymic murderers

Compulsive profile	Catathymic profile
Nature of sexual homicide	
Organized	Disorganized
Axis I diagnosis	
Sexual sadism	Mood disorder
Axis II diagnosis	
Antisocial personality disorder / narcissistic personality disorder	Various traits and personality disorders
Psychopathy	
Severe (primary)	Mild-moderate
Attachment pathology	
Chronically detached	Attachment hunger
Autonomic nervous system	
Hypo-reactive	Hyper-reactive
Early trauma	
Often absent	Often present

Reproduced from *Aggression and Violent Behavior* 5(1), J. Reid Meloy, The nature and dynamics of sexual homicide: An integrative review, p. 22, 2000, with permission from Elsevier.

hyporeactivity facilitates their social isolation, which in turn leads them to depend heavily on fantasy for narcissistic gratification.

In sharp contrast, catathymic sexual murderers' crimes tend to be disorganized. In terms of their possible clinical diagnosis, catathymic SHOs are likely to be diagnosed with a mood disorder. Although various personality disorder traits are possible, a full blown diagnosis of a particular personality disorder is less likely to be diagnosed among catathymic sexual killers. In addition, a mild to moderate level of psychopathy is expected among this type of offender. Catathymic SHOs' hunger for attachment can be traced back to abusive experiences in their early childhood. Because of the damage inflicted on them by early and extreme physical and sexual trauma, catathymic sexual murderers are likely to be autonomically hyperaroused.

2.2.2   Clarke and Carter's four clinical types of sexual murderers

In order to develop an effective relapse prevention (RP) model appropriate for distinctive types of sexual murderers with different treatment needs, Clarke and Carter (2000) sample 32 SHOs who victimized adult women ($N = 29$; aged 14 and above), adult men ($N = 2$), and a child ($N = 1$). These sexual killers underwent the standard Sex Offender Treatment Program (SOTP), together with a 40-hour cognitive skills program, in an English prison in Brixton in the late 1990s. From an examination of the cases of these 32 treated sexual murderers, four primary profiles were identified: (a) the sexually motivated offender; (b) the sexually triggered/aggressive control offender who commits murder in an aggressive but controlled way; (c) the sexually triggered/aggressive dyscontrol offender who commits murder in an aggressive but uncontrolled way; and (d) the sexually triggered/neuropsychological dysfunction offender (see Table 2.9).

According to Clarke and Carter (2000), the SHOs who fit the first profile are characterized by the primary motivation to commit a sexual murder. Their victims are usually known to them and specifically targeted. The method of killing used by this type of offender is sexually stimulating, often involving sophisticated and detailed masturbatory fantasies to satiate the offender's sexual gratification. Sexual offending is secondary to a sexually motivated murderers; therefore, their victims may or may not be sexually assaulted. If the victims are sexually assaulted, this can occur either before or after they are dead.

Sexual murderers who fit the second profile are primarily motivated to sexually assault their victims, who are either complete strangers to the offenders or only briefly acquainted with them. Sadistic features are commonly evidenced in their perpetration of sexual murder. The murder of the victim is intentional and is likely to be instrumental to the nature of the crime, either to quiet the victim during the offense or to prevent identification by the victim.

Sexual killers whose profile is "sexually triggered/aggressive dyscontrol" typically have no prior intention to murder or to sexually offend. The murders they commit usually occur as a result of something said or done by the victims in a sexual context which triggers the offenders' long held and substantial sense of grievance against an intimate party. To release their rage, these SHOs are likely to inflict extreme violence on or humiliate their victims, suggesting their loss of control and perspective. During their perpetration of the crime, sexual intercourse may or may not occur, but the violence they use against their victims often has sexual characteristics (e.g., genitalia mutilation). Although sexual killers of this type are unlikely to exhibit a similar level of violence in a nonsexual context, they are nevertheless known to be aggressive.

SHOs who fit the fourth profile, sexually triggered/neuropsychological dysfunction, usually do not have a clear motivation to murder or to sexually offend. Sexual murderers of this type either behave sexually in

Table 2.9 Clarke and Carter's four clinical types of sexual murderers

Sexually motivated	Sexually triggered/ aggressive control	Sexually triggered/ aggressive dyscontrol	Sexually triggered-neuropsychological dysfunction
Offender characteristics			
1. Offenders' primary sexual motivation is to kill; sexual offending is secondary.	1. Offenders' primary motivation is to sexually offend and the killing is intentional.	1. Offenders are not intending to kill or sexually offend.	1. Unclear whether offenders' motivation is to kill or sexually offend.
2. Offenders' sophisticated and detailed masturbatory fantasies are involved in the killing.	2. Offenders' sexual offending often includes sadistic features.	2. The murder often results from something said or done by the victim in a sexual context which triggers the offender's sense of grievance that he has held for some time against an intimate party.	2. Offenders often behave either sexually in an aggressive context or aggressively in a sexual context.
3. The victim is usually known to the offender and has been specifically targeted.	3. The murder may be instrumental, either to quiet the victim during the offense or to prevent detection.	3. Behavior of extreme violence or humiliation against the victim suggestive of the offender's loss of control and perspective.	3. Offender's life characterized by a series of events in which sexual encounters lead to feelings of aggression or aggressive encounters lead to sexual arousal.
4. Sexual assault of the victim may or may not occur; if the victim is sexually assaulted, it can occur before or after death.		4. Offenders unlikely to exhibit similar level of violence in a nonsexual context but are known to be aggressive.	4. Penile plethysmography (PPG) profile is likely to indicate that the highest arousal comes from aggression only.
5. The method of killing is sexually stimulating to the offender.		5. Sexual intercourse may or may not occur, but violence against the victim has sexual characteristics (e.g., genitalia mutilation).	5. Offenders have clear neuropsychological deficits.

Source: Clarke and Carter (2000).

an aggressive context or aggressively in a sexual context. Their life is typically characterized by a series of circumstances where sexual encounters trigger feelings of aggression or aggressive encounters have ultimately led to sexual arousal. The penile plethysmography (PPG) profiles of this particular type of offender are likely to suggest that the highest arousal comes from aggressive behavior only. It is of note that these offenders are apt to have clear neuropsychological deficits.

2.2.3 Schlesinger's phenomenological-descriptive model of sexual homicide

In his book, Schlesinger (2004) argues that it is more appropriate to first study sexual homicide using the phenomenological-descriptive approach prior to any empirical examination due to the rarity of this crime. According to the homicide offender motivational spectrum developed by Revitch and Schlesinger (1978, 1981) and Schlesinger (2004), murders can be understood on the hypothetical continuum ranging from being motivated by completely external or sociogenic factors at the one end to being internally or psychologically driven at the extreme opposite end. Consequently, homicides can be divided into the following categories: social-environmental, situational, impulsive, cathathymic, and compulsive. According to Schlesinger (2004), sexual murder falls within the cathathymic and compulsive groups (see Table 2.10). To put it simply, cathathymic homicides are triggered by an infiltration of underlying sexual conflicts, while compulsive murders result from a combination of powerful internally driven sex and aggression.

Cathathymic is a term coined by Hans W. Maier (1912) to offer a psychodynamic explanation for the development of the varying contents of delusions as a result of underlying emotionally charged conflicts, typically a desire, a fear, or an ambivalent predisposition. Wertham (1937) further argues that such cathathymic behavior, especially in respect to severe violence, is not completely delusional but rather quasidelusional. Wertham (1937) defines the catathymic crisis, a clinical disorder that results in homicidal acts, as "the transformation of the stream of thought as the result of certain complexes of ideas that charges with a strong affect – usually a wish, a fear, or an ambivalent striving" (p. 975). Wertham (1941, 1949, 1978) subsequently defines five stages of the catathymic process: (a) early trauma leads to a change in thinking; (b) a violent idea emerges; (c) an extreme emotional tension develops and the violent act is executed; (d) following the violence, a superficial normality occurs and tension is lifted; and (e) subsequent insight and recovery ensue or the process can be repeated.

Table 2.10 Schlesinger's phenomenological-descriptive model of sexual homicide: catathymic and compulsive murders

	Acute catathymic	Chronic catathymic	Planned compulsive	Unplanned compulsive
Compulsion to kill	Not present	Not present	Present; building for years	Present for years
Sadistic fantasy	Not present	Not present; but obsessive thoughts about killing	Present in elaborate form; not in reference to a particular target	Present in simple and undifferentiated form
Motives	Sexual; stemming from feelings of sexual inadequacy	Upsurge of tension; feelings of sexual inadequacy	Fusion of sex and aggression	Sexual; fusing sex and aggression
Victims	Usually strangers; triggered by underlying sexual conflict	Usually current/former intimate partners; targets of obsession	Usually strangers; almost never current/former intimate partners	Victims of opportunity; often known; not triggered by conflicts
Warning signs	Sometimes given but often ignored by others	Offenders inform others about their ego-dystonic ideas; often ignored	Rare; but many ominous behavior signs about the offender's background	Rare; but many ominous behavior signs about the offender's background
Sexual activities	Necrophilia and/or dismemberment	Rare	Common; peri-, ante-, and post-mortem sexual activities	Common; sexual assault and postmortem sexual activities
Post-crime behavior	Attempt to elude authorities, but not for long	No attempt made to elude authorities; suicide attempt may follow	Attempt to elude authorities, often successful due to planning	Attempt to elude authorities, but typically unsuccessful

Sources: Adapted from Schlesinger (2004, 2007).

In an attempt to further develop Wertham's idea of a homicidal catathymic crisis, Revitch (1957, 1965, 1980) and Revitch and Schlesinger (1978, 1981) regard catathymia not as a clinical diagnosis but rather as a psychological or psychodynamic process with an acute and chronic subtype that can occur along with various clinical diagnoses ranging from personality and mood disorders to various psychotic conditions (Schlesinger, 1996a, 1996b). The subtypes of catathymic sexual homicides are proposed to extend Wertham's initial catathymic hypothesis of emotionally charged complexes by including the underlying sexual dynamics of homicide (Schlesinger, 2004). Simply put, a catathymic sexual homicide typically consists of underlying sexual conflicts that stem from the offender's long-standing fixation with, or disturbed attachment to, the victim (Schlesinger, 2007). The perpetration of the crime can either be an unplanned and explosive response or a premeditated attack.

As a subtype of catathymic sexual homicide, acute catathymic sexual homicide is usually triggered by a sudden overwhelming underlying emotionally charged sexual conflict of symbolic significance. Sometimes, there are warning signs, but these are often ignored by those in the offender's surroundings. The sudden explosive outburst of the perpetration, typically affective in nature, is often symbolized as a displaced matricide. Victims of this type of SHO are usually strangers who have symbolic significance to the offenders. A disorganized crime scene as a result of the violent attack and overkill of the victim are evidenced among acute catathymic sexual murderers. Necrophilia and/or dismemberment of the victim are common due to the offender's sexual impotency. Catathymic SHOs of this type are typically puzzled about their homicidal attack after the murder and do not try to elude the authorities.

The chronic catathymic homicidal process, on the other hand, involves three stages: (a) incubation, (b) violent act, and (c) relief. During the incubation stage, the potential murderer may become depressed and obsessively preoccupied by his future victim. This psychological disturbance may later lead to suicidal thoughts and to homicidal ideas regarding the future victim until the killing obsession becomes fixed and dominant. The SHOs of this type, who are usually diagnosed with borderline personality disorder, may inform their family and friends about their obsessive thoughts of killing, but these disclosures are often disregarded or rationalized. The actual killing typically occurs when the SHO's homicidal thoughts have become uncontrollable. The victim in such cases is usually someone who shares a close relationship with the offender (e.g., current or former intimate partner) and may have symbolic significance to the offender. The violent attack that aims to discharge the SHO's catathymic tensions is frequently organized in nature and may involve stalking the victim prior to the actual perpetration of the crime. Ante-, peri-, and post-mortem activities are rare. A feeling of relief often follows the completion of the murder. However, suicide or a suicide attempt regularly follows if the SHO's catathymic tension is not completely discharged during the homicide.

On the other extreme, compulsive sexual murder is the result of a fusion of sexual dynamics and aggression. According to Revitch and Schlesinger (1978, 1981), compulsive offenders are least influenced by external or sociogenic factors. The SHOs of this type possess a powerful internal drive to execute their violent sadistic fantasies, which are eroticized, and have a strong propensity for repetition. In general, compulsive murders are sexually motivated: the violence is sexually arousing and stimulating to the offenders. Schlesinger (2001a, 2001b, 2001c) outlines several ominous signs that indicate that a person is becoming a potentially compulsive SHO: (a) childhood abuse; (b) inappropriate maternal (sexual) contact; (c) pathological lying and manipulation; (d) sadistic fantasy with a compulsion to act; (e) animal cruelty, specifically toward cats; (f) need to dominate and control others; (g) repetitive firesetting; (h) voyeurism, fetishism, and sexual burglary; (i) unprovoked assaults on females, typically associated with generalized misogynous emotions; and (j) evidence of ritualistic behavior.

Compulsive murders, according to Schlesinger (2007), can be viewed as falling somewhere within a continuum between planned attacks and unplanned attacks. The SHOs who commit planned compulsive murders are motivated to act out their elaborated violent sadistic sexual fantasies. Their sexual perpetration of murder is commonly executed according to their detailed killing plan in order to elude the authorities, which they often do successfully. As a result, they tend to have multiple homicide victims, who are usually strangers but are sometimes acquaintances, over an extended period of time. Sadism, fantasy, and a compulsion to kill are frequently the primary themes for this type of offender. Ritualistic behaviors, commonly known as signature elements, are also present.

In sharp contrast, a calculated plan of action is almost never seen in unplanned compulsive sexual murders. Unlike those of their counterparts who commit planned compulsive murders, the violent sadistic fantasies of SHOs who commit unplanned compulsive murders are simpler and undifferentiated in form. These offenders typically select victims of opportunity, often someone they know, once their compulsive killing urge has emerged. The psychological status of SHOs who commit unplanned compulsive murders often reflects disorganized personalities and overt psychopathological traits such as borderline, schizotypal or schizoid personality disorders; schizophrenia; or psychosis. Social immaturity, sexual incompetence, and a poor employment history often lead them to behave in a high-risk manner. Although SHOs of this type attempt to escape detection by law enforcement agencies, they are generally unsuccessful because of the physical evidence left at the crime scene. Hence, early apprehension by the police is not uncommon.

2.3 Theory-led classification approach

2.3.1 Keppel and Walter's rape-murder classification

On the basis of their research, Groth, Burgess, and Holmstrom (1977) developed a rapist classification system to offer a dynamic view of different types of rapists (see also Groth & Birnbaum, 1979). Ten years later, Hazelwood and Burgess (1987) refined this rapist classification system by applying it to the analysis of rape cases to demonstrate its practical utility. Four distinct categories of rapists are proposed: (a) power-assertive (PA), (b) power-reassurance (PR), (c) anger-retaliatory (AR), and (d) anger-excitation (AE; see Table 2.11). Although this classification system was initially developed to describe rapist behavior, Keppel and Walter (1999) further expand these categories for use in homicide investigations, depicting the different types of rape-murder on the basis of distinctive crime scene information, offender profiles, and homicidal patterns.

Sexual assaults committed by PA rape-murderers are planned, and the victims are typically strangers opportunistically acquired through a surprise mode of attack. However, due to the increasing aggression involved to ensure control of the victim, unplanned homicide is likely to occur. The theme behind the offender's overpowering sexual assault is primarily the expression of virility, mastery, and dominance to satiate his need for power and control, which often results in multiple ante-mortem rapes of the victim. The victim is likely to suffer a violent beating and pummeling by the offender, who does this to demonstrate his masculine image. However, mutilation by this type of offender is rare. The PA rape-murderers carefully execute their assault, and the organized crime scene reflects an effort by the offenders to cover up and protect their identity. In general, PA rape-murderers are in their early 20s and rather emotionally primitive. They are sensitive about their masculinity and therefore are persistently preoccupied with projecting a macho image. Perceived by others as antisocial individuals due to their power- and control-oriented attitudes, they are typically school dropouts with a history of property crime, which they commit to demonstrate their potential for power.

Table 2.11 Keppel and Walter's four categories of rape-murder classification

Power-assertive	Power-reassurance	Anger-retaliatory	Anger-excitation
Dynamic characteristics			
1. The rape is premeditated but the murder is not.	1. The rape is premeditated but the murder is not.	1. The rape and murder are premeditated.	1. The rape and murder are premeditated.
2. The sexual assault is characterized by the desire for power through forceful aggression and intimidation.	2. The assault is characterized by the need to act out fantasy and to validate sexual competence via victim's verbal reassurance.	2. The assault is characterized as an anger-venting act for symbolic revenge in a stylized violent burst of sexual attack.	2. The motivation of the assault is to inflict pain and terror on the victim for sexual gratification.
3. The murder is unplanned: caused by increasing aggression to maintain control of the victim.	3. The murder is an unplanned overkill characterized by postmortem mutilation.	3. Overkill may occur.	3. Sadistic acts are performed to act out a sexual fantasy of eroticized anger and power.
Homicidal patterns			
1. The victim selection method and modus operandi are determined by past experience, internal stress, and opportunity.	1. The assault is carried out with no preferred victim type.	1. Victim is typically a substitute for the actual female who belittles, humiliates, and rejects the offender.	1. Symbolic victims are targeted in an organized prolonged, bizarre, and ritualistic attack.
2. The crime scene is organized to evade apprehension.	2. Postmortem mutilation is performed for further fantasy satisfaction and is reflected in a disorganized crime scene.	2. The assault is anger driven for emotional satisfaction.	2. Sexual satisfaction is achieved through sadistic ante- and post-mortem mutilations.
Suspect profile			
1. Usually in early 20s, sensitive to his masculinity characteristics and preoccupied with projecting a macho image.	1. Usually in mid-20s, socially isolated, and uses sexual fantasies to overcome inadequate sexual life.	1. Usually in mid to late 20s, with an explosive personality and aggressive feelings toward women, and links eroticized anger with sexual competence.	1. Usually has committed first murder by age of 35; sociable law-abiding person with a dark side of a sadistic sexual fantasy life

Source: Adapted from Keppel and Walter (1999).

The rape committed by a PR rape-murderer against a victim, who is usually 10 to 15 years older or younger than the offender, is premeditated. The victim can be either preselected or a victim of opportunity. The murder, however, is an unplanned overkill of the victim. The rape-murderers of this type are generally characterized by an idealized seduction and conquest fantasy. Their sexual assaults are motivated by the acting out of a deviant sexual fantasy and the need to seek verbal reassurance of their sexual adequacy from the victim. Threats and intimidation are often used to gain initial control over the victim. The offenders, often referred to as "polite and gentleman rapists," try to act out their preprogrammed fantasy through a planned verbal dialogue in order to seek validation of their sexual competence from the victim. If their sexual assault is uncompleted due to their sexual competency being threatened and ridiculed, they may initiate homicidal attacks to control the victim and to protect their image. Post-mortem ritualistic activities are performed for further fantasy gratification. A haphazard crime scene is evidenced from their post-mortem activities. Small souvenirs and newspaper clippings are regularly collected to enhance their imagined relationship with the victim. Broadly speaking, PR rape-murderers are generally in their mid-20s and are likely to be socially isolated. With their extensive repertoire of rape fantasies, they are likely to reside in their private world without a history of normal sexual activities. Due to the dominating influence of their fantasy activities, they are apt to be underachievers with a criminal history that involves fetish activities, trespassing, and larcenies.

Unlike the power-based rape-murderer, both the rape and the murder committed by an anger-oriented rape-murderer are planned. Because of their poor relationships with women that are often precipitated by criticisms from a woman with authority, AR rape-murderers commit assaults that are characterized as anger-venting acts to express their symbolic revenge on substitute female victims who remind them of the women they hate. Often, the substitute victim, who is likely to be older than the offender, is selected through the offender's daily routine activities. Due to his anger and internal stress, the offender is unlikely to get an erection to complete the rape. Dynamically, the stylized violent burst of rape-murder is committed to retaliate against, get even with, and take revenge on women, and it may result in overkill of the victim. Regardless of whether the victim is alive or dead, the combative assault continues until the offender is emotionally satisfied. The crime scene tends to be disorganized in nature due to the offender's intense expression of anger. Trophies and souvenirs may be taken from the crime scene by the offender to allow him to relive his murder experience later on. Generally speaking, AR rape-murderers are likely to be in their mid to late 20s with a history of violent crime. Because of their explosive personality, their interpersonal relationships are limited and tend to be superficial. Sexually, they are frustrated with their sexual incompetence. Hence, they are likely to link eroticized anger with sexual competence and to favor aggressive behavior toward women.

As for the AE rape-murderers, their use of prolonged, bizarre, and ritualistic torture is intended to cause the victim pain and terror in order to energize their deviant sexual fantasy and to temporarily satiate their lust for domination and control. The offenders may select their victim, often a stranger, on the basis of a certain set of criteria. Equipped with a murder kit and a set of planned ritualistic actions, the offenders exploit, torture, and mutilate their victims with escalated violence to appease their insatiable appetite for the sadistic killing process. The excitement of sadistic sexual murder is heightened by the realization of a rehearsed fantasy of eroticized anger and power. Very frequently, bondage and domination play important roles in their killing process. Ante-, peri-, and post-mortem sexual exploration activities are evidenced, with body parts and souvenirs regularly being taken from the crime scene for later extravaganzas of masturbation. The AE rape-murderers tend to leave an organized crime scene without many forensic traces left behind, and the victim's body may be moved to another location to delay discovery by the police. To avoid detection, these offenders are likely to commit their offense at a location distant from their routine activities and comfort zone.

2.4   Statistical classification approach

2.4.1   Beauregard and Proulx's two nonserial sexual homicide offender profiles

Using a sample of 34 non-serial and two serial sexual murderers of women aged 14 years or older who were incarcerated in the Canadian province of Quebec in 1998, Beauregard and Proulx (2002) empirically examine the pre-crime (e.g., affects before the offense, disinhibitors, relationship dilemma, occupational problems), crime (e.g., crime scene variables, acts committed while committing the offense, affect during the offense), and post-crime (affect after the offense, attitudes toward their offense) phases of their offense(s): from a cluster analysis, two distinct profiles, anger and sadistic, based on the offender's MO emerged (see also Beauregard, Proulx, & St-Yves, 2007; see Table 2.12).

Table 2.12 Beauregard and Proulx's two offender profiles in non-serial sexual homicide

Anger profile	Sadistic profile
Precrime phase characteristics	
1. Offenders are likely to have occupational idleness problems 48 hours before the offense.	1. Offenders are likely to have sexual fantasies and relationship separation problems 48 hours before the offense.
2. Offenders are likely to have loneliness problems and to perceive rejection 48 hours before, and a year prior to, the offense.	2. Offenders are likely to perceive rejection 48 hours before, and a year prior to, the offense.
3. Offenders are likely to be angry and to use alcohol prior to the offense.	3. Offenders are likely to be in positive mood (e.g., joy, sexual arousal, calm, and well-being) and use alcohol prior to the offense.
Crime phase characteristics	
1. Homicides are typically unplanned.	1. Homicides are typically premeditated.
2. Victims are not preselected.	2. Victims are often preselected strangers.
3. Physical restraints are rarely used.	3. Physical restraints are used to control the victims.
4. Victims are not humiliated and mutilated.	4. Victims are humiliated and their bodies are likely to be mutilated and sometimes dismembered.
5. The killing process is likely to last less than 30 minutes, thereby reducing the offender's risk of being apprehended.	5. The killing process is likely to last more than 30 minutes, thereby increasing the offender's risk of being apprehended.
6. The victims' body is often left on its back at the crime scene.	6. The victim's body is likely to be concealed and moved from the crime scene after the murder.
Postcrime phase characteristics	
1. Offenders are likely to give themselves up to the police, admit all the acts committed against their victim, and admit responsibility for their offense.	1. Offenders are less likely to give themselves up to the police, admit all the acts committed against their victim, and admit responsibility for their offense.

Source: Beauregard and Proulx (2002).

Generally speaking, the offenses committed by "angry" sexual murderers are typically unplanned; their victims are usually not preselected. Approximately two days prior to their offense, the SHOs of this type are more likely to be unemployed and to experience loneliness. The use of alcohol prior to the offense is not uncommon. They are also likely to be in a rage immediately prior to perpetrating the crime. During their attack, victims are rarely physically restrained, humiliated, or mutilated. After the completion of their sexual assault, which frequently lasts for less than 30 minutes, their victim's body is often left on its back at the crime scene. Interestingly, angry sexual murderers are likely to surrender themselves to the police, and there is a high likelihood that they will confess to their offense.

In sharp contrast, sadistic SHOs' crimes are likely to be premeditated; they carefully select their victims, who are apt to be strangers. About two days prior to perpetrating their crime, sadistic sexual murderers are likely to have experienced rejection, relationship separation problems, and sexual fantasies. It is interesting to note that sadistic SHOs are likely to be in a positive emotional state immediately prior to committing a sexual assault. The use of alcohol before the offense is also not uncommon. Sadistic SHOs are likely to use physical restraints to control their victims. It is common to find that sexual murderers of this type humiliate and mutilate their victim's body to satiate their sadistic fantasies; sometimes, they may even dismember the body. Before leaving their crime scene, sadistic sexual murderers are likely to conceal and dispose of their victim's body at another location to delay identification and evade apprehension. The whole killing process of sadistic SHOs is likely to last more than 30 minutes. They are less likely to surrender themselves to the police, and even if they are arrested, they are less likely to admit responsibility for their offense.

2.4.2   Fisher and Beech's implicit theories-led classification of sexual murderers

Fisher and Beech's (2007) SHO classification is a refinement model of earlier typologies by Beech, Robertson, and Clarke (2001) and Beech, Oliver, Fisher, and Beckett (2006). Initially, on the basis of Keenan and Ward's (1999) five-ITs (implicit theories) model of sexual offenders, Beech, Robertson, and Clarke (2001) propose a three-profile model of SHOs based on a sample of 50 subjects: (a) grievance motivated, (b) sexually motivated, and (c) motivation to sexually offend (see Table 2.13). Later, Beech, Oliver, Fisher, and Beckett (2006) revise and validate this offender typology, offering more characteristics in each renamed profile,

Table 2.13 Fisher and Beech's offender implicit theories-led classification of sexual murderers

Sadistic	Violently motivated	Sexually motivated
Motivation		
To carry out fantasies	Grievance	Avoid detection
Thoughts/fantasies prior to murder		
Intent to kill, violent and sadistic, or control and domination thoughts and fantasies	Resentment/anger towards women (dominant) or sexual fantasies	Sexual fantasies (dominant) or intent to kill
Targeted victim and age of victim		
Strangers (ranging from 9 to 86 years old)	Known victims (ranging from 14 to 85 years old)	No fixed type (ranging from 18 to 56 years old)
Method of Killing		
Strangulation (dominant), stabbed, stabbed / set on fire, beaten, or beaten/killed by train	Beaten (dominant), drowned, stabbed, or suffocated	Stabbed (dominant), beaten, or strangulation
Sexual mutilation & interference after death		
Highly likely to mutilate, and likely to interfere with, body	Less likely to mutilate, but likely to interfere with, body	Less likely to mutilate, but likely to interfere with, body
History of violence against women		
Highly likely	Less likely	Less likely
Previous sex, violent, and other convictions		
Likely for all types of conviction	Less likely to have convictions for sexual and violent crimes, but highly likely to have other convictions	Likely to have convictions for sexual and violent crimes, and highly likely to have other convictions
Risk of sexual reconviction		
Highly likely	Less likely	Unlikely

Source: Adapted from Fisher and Beech (2007).

on the basis of a sample of 28 post-treatment interviews with convicted sexual murderers: (a) prototypical (or calculated pain infliction), (b) grievance motivated, and (c) rape plus murder.

To further improve Beech et al.'s (2006) SHO classification, Fisher and Beech (2007) conduct semi-structured interviews, using a grounded theory approach, with 28 sexual murderers who are serving life sentences for murder. Most ($N = 24$) of the SHOs commit their offenses against adult women; the remaining SHOs murder young girls ($N = 3$) and a boy ($N = 1$). Through their analysis of the interview transcripts for the presence of the five ITs, Fisher and Beech are able to empirically categorize sexual murderers into three distinctive profiles closely resembling those offered by Beech, Robertson, et al. (2001) and Beech, Oliver, et al. (2006) that fit into the three dominant ITs: (a) sadistic ($N = 14$), (b) violently motivated ($N = 8$), and (c) sexually motivated ($N = 6$).

The first profile, sadistic SHOs, is characterized by the ITs as a "dangerous world," "male sex drive is uncontrollable," and, in half of the group, "entitlement." The intention of sadistic sexual murderers is to carry out their violent and sadistic thoughts and fantasies or to control and dominate. Their victims are likely to be targeted strangers aged between 9 and 86 years old. The possibility of this type of offender committing sexualized violence, sexual mutilation, and sexual interference against their victims after death is high. The ritualistic behavior of sexual mutilation may include acts like exposure of, and bites to, the breast, partial severance of the breast, and vaginal mutilation. The most common method sadistic SHOs use to murder their victims is strangulation because this method demonstrates the offender's complete control over the victim's life at all times until death. The sadistic sexual killers are likely to have a history of previous convictions which includes a history of sexual violence against women. They also pose a very high risk of sexual recidivism.

Violently motivated sexual murderers (second profile) are mainly driven by a grievance towards women. The underlying IT for this group of SHOs is "dangerous world," with thoughts about the punishment and control of women as their primary motivation. Violently motivated SHOs are likely to target known victims aged between 14 and 85 years old. A high level of expressive violence is a key theme in this type of sexual killing, with multiple attacks on the victim using different types of weapons (e.g., knives, blunt instruments, and hands). Overkill of the victim (e.g., gouging the victim's eyes out, attempted scalping, numerous stabbings, and repeated blows such that body parts of the victim are partially severed) is common. Sexual mutilation and interference after death are less likely to be seen in the crimes of this type of offender. In terms of criminal background, previous sexual and violent convictions are less common in this group of violently motivated sexual killers; hence, their risk of sexual reconviction is also low.

Those in the third group of sexual murderers proposed by Fisher and Beech (2007) are sexually motivated to either to satiate their sexual fantasies or to carry out their prior intention to kill. They commit murder either to silence the victim during the offense or to avoid identification by their victim. The method they commonly use to murder their victims is stabbing. The primary IT found in this group of sex killers is "male sex drive is uncontrollable." They generally have no fixed type of victim, but their victims are likely to be aged between 18 and 56 years old. Sexually motivated SHOs are less likely to sexually mutilate and interfere with their victim's body after death. Basically, they are determined to have sex with their victims regardless of what the cost may be. These sexually motivated to offend are apt to have a history of previous sexual and violent convictions, including a history of violence against women. Nevertheless, they are unlikely to sexually reoffend.

2.4.3 Balemba, Beauregard, and Martineau's three classes of sexual homicide

Using the largest sample to empirically generate a typology of SHOs, Balemba, Beauregard, and Martineau (2014) examine 10 crime scene variables of 350 (i.e., 250 solved and 100 unsolved) Canadian sexual homicide cases from a national database operated by the Royal Canadian Mounted Police. Three classes of sexual homicide with different offense patterns emerge by using the cluster latent class analytic approach: (a) the sloppy/reckless, (b) the violent/sadistic, and (c) the forensically aware (see Table 2.14). All three classes result with approximately equal frequency and with differences mainly due to varying offense behaviors or *modus operandi*.

The first type of SHOs is grouped under the sloppy/reckless category, with nearly 84% of such cases being solved. The priority of these SHOs is the sexual component of the rape. Therefore, they are likely to engage in vaginal and/or anal intercourse with their victim. The offenders' semen is likely to be found at the scene, suggesting they either do not use a condom or do not dispose of it correctly. These sloppy/reckless offenders are less likely to use excessive force against their victim. The mutilation of the victim and the insertion of foreign objects are also uncommon. The primary cause of the victim's death for this type of SHOs is likely to be strangulation. Upon the killing of their victims, these sloppy/reckless

Table 2.14 Balemba, Beauregard, and Martineau's three classes of sexual homicide

Sloppy/reckless	Violent/sadistic	Forensically aware
Crime scene behavior		
1. The offense's priority is the sexual component of the rape.	1. The offense's priority is dominated by a need to inflict pain on the victim.	1. The offense's priority in killing the victim is to avoid detection.
2. Offenders are likely to have vaginal and/or anal intercourse with their victim; and often leave semen at the scene.	2. Offenders are likely to mutilate their victim and to insert foreign objects into their victim.	2. Offenders are less likely to have vaginal or anal intercourse with their victim, which thus leave no semen to be discovered at the crime scene.
3. Offenders are less likely to use excessive force against their victim and to employ mutilation techniques or insert foreign objects into the victim.	3. Offenders are likely to engage in physical beating and strangulation against their victim, with the prevalence of overkilling is very high.	3. Offenders are less likely to engage in physical beating or strangulation against their victim.
4. Strangulation is likely to be their victim cause of death.	4. Offenders are likely to take items from the scene either to remove evidence or as an act of greed.	4. For offenders who mutilate their victim, the reason for such is likely to be a detection avoidance technique in an attempt to destroy evidence or a strategy to delay victim identification.
5. Offenders may take items with them when they leave the scene, for reason of either to remove evidence or for an act of greed.	5. Offenders of this type are likely to be apprehended by the police, possibly due to leaving more traces and biological evidence on or near their victim through their acts of torturing.	5. Offenders are less likely to remove items from the scene.
6. Offenders of this type are likely to be apprehended by the police due to either a lack of sufficient planning or a lack of concern for detection avoidance.		6. Offenders of this type are less likely to be apprehended by the police due to the minimal amount of evidence discovered at the scene.

Source: Balemba, Beauregard, and Martineau (2014).

offenders may take items with them when they leave the crime scene either to remove evidence or as an act of greed. The offenders of this type are likely to be apprehended by the police due to either a lack of sufficient planning or a lack of use of detection avoidance strategies.

Violent/sadistic SHOs are the second cluster of offenders to emerge in the latent class analysis. Similar to the sloppy/reckless category, a large majority (81%) of the cases in this category are solved. The SHOs of this type are mainly motivated to inflict pain on the victim for their sexual gratification. Hence, mutilation and the insertion of foreign objects into their victim are possible. Dominated by a need to torture and to create suffering, violent/sadistic SHOs are likely to engage in a physical beating and strangulation of their victim, with a high probability of overkilling. Upon leaving the crime scene, these offenders are also likely to take items from the scene either as a half-hearted attempt to eliminate evidence or as an opportunistic theft. Interestingly, violent/sadistic SHOs are likely to be apprehended by the police, possibly due to leaving more traces or biological evidence on or near their victim through their torturing.

Finally, the forensically aware offenders are the third type of SHOs. Not surprisingly, only half of the cases in this category are solved. The priority of these SHOs when killing their victim is to avoid detection by the authorities. These offenders are forensically aware and are less likely to engage in vaginal or anal intercourse with their victim, thus leaving no semen to be discovered at the crime scene. Unlike violent/sadistic SHOs, a physical beating and strangulation of the victim are less common in offenders who are forensically aware. However, mutilation of the victim is possible in some of these offenders. For those who mutilate their victim, their reason for such act is likely to be an avoidance detection technique in an attempt to destroy evidence or a strategy to delay the victim's identification. Unlike the other two types of SHOs, the forensically aware offenders are less likely to remove any items from the crime scene. Given the minimal amount of evidence to be discovered at the scene, offenders of this type are less likely to be arrested by the police.

Balemba et al. (2014) further analyze the 100 unsolved cases with a two-cluster model: (a) the forensically aware (unsolved) group and (b) the not forensically aware (lucky) group. Not unexpectedly, almost two-thirds of the unsolved cases are from the forensically aware (unsolved) group. Similar to the forensically aware group found using the full sample (i.e., solved and unsolved cases), the SHOs in the forensically aware (unsolved) group are less likely to engage in vaginal or anal intercourse with their victim and to avoid as much contact with their victim as possible (i.e., no mutilation and insertion of a foreign object, and less violence is used), thus leaving minimal evidence at the crime scene. They are also less likely to take items away from the crime scene. A degree of offense planning and sophistication is evidenced in these offenders through their meticulous method of body disposal either to elude detection or to delay the victim's identification.

The not forensically aware SHOs in the unsolved cases are merely "lucky" in not being apprehended by the police. The offenders of this type are likely to engage in vaginal and/or anal intercourse with their victim that may leave their semen at the scene, to be involved in mutilation and the insertion of foreign objects into their victim, to treat their victim violently, and to remove items from the scene. This type of SHOs shows no attempt to hide their victims' bodies. With these sloppy, unplanned, and unsophisticated offense patterns, these offenders simply have luck on their side. Rossmo (2009) reasons that "not all crimes are solvable...in some circumstances, even solvable crimes are not cleared because of incompetence, misfeasance, nonfeasance, resources problems, or simple bad luck" (p. 3).

2.5   Critical review of the current sexual homicide offender classifications

Although numerous SHO typologies have been developed over the years, with some of their offender profiles overlapping to some degree, none of them are above criticism. Among the typologies, the FBI's motivational model of sexual homicide has received the most criticism. Although this typology is one of the most complete and pragmatic classifications of sexual homicide currently available, it is not without its faults. Ressler and colleagues' (1985, 1986) organized-disorganized behavioral dichotomy of sexual murderers is developed from a weak research methodology that thus reduces the validity of their findings (Salfati & Taylor, 2006). Their subjects are not a random sample of sexual murderers (Goodwin, 2000), and no comparison group is used to single out factors specific to sexual murderers only (Meloy, 2000; Proulx, Cusson, & Beauregard, 2007). Even within their group of subjects, no effort is made to differentiate between SHOs who kill women, men, and children despite the fact that these different types of sexual killers may be very distinctive in terms of their offense profiles (Proulx et al., 2007).

Furthermore, the majority of their subjects (25 out of 36 subjects) are serial SHOs. Non-serial sexual killers who murder one or two victims could differ markedly, in terms of their offending patterns, from serial sexual killers who kill multiple victims (Chan & Heide, 2009). For instance, serial SHOs engage in more rape fantasies than non-serial SHOs (Campos & Cusson, 2007; Chan, Beauregard, & Myers, 2014; Prentky et al., 1989). Clearly, this distinction between non-serial and serial SHOs should not be overlooked.

Another critical shortcoming of this behavioral dichotomy is its overemphasis on the crime phase and the scene behavior; the pre-crime (Beauregard & Proulx, 2002; Meloy, 2000) and the offender developmental (Chan & Heide, 2009) phrases are minimally discussed. Rather than differentiating between organized and disorganized sexual murderers, this classification describes the different levels of aggression in sexual homicide (Goodwin, 1998).

Most importantly, the scientific basis of this organized-disorganized maxim has also been questioned. According to Kocsis (1999), the application of this organized-disorganized maxim is highly subjective in the selection of appropriate crime scene behaviors for each profile (see also Canter, Alison, Alison, & Wentink, 2004). In reality, the variations in real events are often continuous rather than dichotomous (Meloy, 2000), from which this contention is empirically supported by Canter et al. (2004) to be more effective as a continuum of organization. Therefore, this method cannot be scientifically replicated. Nevertheless, this pragmatic SHO classification has its inherent strengths as an attempt to offer a simplified understanding of the sexual homicide phenomenon; and most importantly, this organized-disorganized behavioral dichotomy has become a guiding model for many subsequent offender typologies.

It is noteworthy that Geberth (1996) is the first to offer an offender classification of murderers who kill male victims. Although his six-type classification of homosexual offenders is informative, the lack of empirical verification of these profiles is the key drawback of his offender classification. No sample is described in his study (Beauregard & Proulx, 2007); rather, his offender typology is based solely on his investigative experience in homosexual homicides. Besides the reliability of his proposed offender profiles, the validity of his classification framework has also been questioned (Chan & Heide, 2009). The offender profiles offered by Geberth are limited to the crime scene correlates. The variables related to the pre-crime phase and the offender personality characteristics of each profile are not discussed (Beauregard & Proulx, 2007). Hence, Geberth's typology suffers from more limitations than strengths in terms of offering a better understanding of homosexual homicides.

As for Keppel and Walter's (1999) four rape-murder offender profiles, reliability and validity issues emerge regarding their classification. Even though their discussion on the characteristics of different rape-murderers is comprehensive, the correlations among the variables within each offender profile are not examined (Salfati & Taylor, 2006). In addition, no information is provided as to how the prevalence of each offender profile is determined (Salfati & Taylor, 2006). Most importantly, their classification is not empirically validated until 14 years after its publication by Bennell, Bloomfield, Emeno, and Musolino (2013). Unfortunately, using 53 male serial sexual murderers, Bennell et al. (2013) fail to find evidence to indicate the validity of Keppel and Walter's (1999) classification. No evidence of highly concurrent characteristics from the proposed categories is found. Nonetheless, more empirical tests are needed to validate this classification before any conclusive statements about its validity could be offered; or perhaps, a refinement of this classification is necessary.

Kocsis's (1999) offender classification of sexual murderers is the first such typology to use an Australian sample. According to Kocsis (1999), using offender typologies constructed from foreign demographics for profiling purposes is often unreliable; that is to say, behavioral patterns indicative of a foreign population that is virtually nonexistent in another country is highly questionable to the point of irrelevance. Hence, Kocsis (1999) argues that his typology is most appropriately applied to the unique features of Australian demographic elements. Although this classification is constructed empirically by using an MDS approach, it is not without certain faults. First, the descriptions of each profile's characteristics are oversimplified in his initial attempt (Kocsis, 1999). Not all of the dimensional characteristics of the offense, the offender, and the victim are clearly outlined to facilitate easier applicability for profiling purposes. However, Kocsis does make a revision to the initial effort in his subsequent empirical study; more distinctive features of each profile are offered to clearly distinguish the different types of SHOs (Kocsis, Cooksey, & Irwin, 2002). Nonetheless, the lack of continuous empirical testing of this typology reduces its utility value. More rigorous scientific analyses are needed to empirically validate this offender classification as a reliable profiling tool for sexual homicide cases in Australia.

In order to address the flaws of the organized-disorganized behavioral dichotomy, Meloy (2000) refines the FBI's motivational model of SHOs by incorporating psychopathological elements acquired from his clinical practice in order to provide a more complete version of the classification. Although Meloy attempts with his colleagues to statistically examine his refined typological model (Gacono, Meloy, & Bridges, 2000; Meloy, Gacono, & Kenney, 1994), not all of the elements illustrated in the FBI's motivational model are examined in their studies. Instead, these studies primarily test the attachment pathology and other psychopathological issues by using forensic Rorschach protocols. It is noteworthy that a large majority of the subjects tested in the studies are diagnosed as psychopaths. Thus, their sample of SHOs lacks generalizability to the entire SHO population. Furthermore, the offender's crime scene behavior, the key dimension accentuated in the original FBI motivational model, is not addressed in Meloy's refined classification, let alone in their empirical analyses. Clearly, more scientific research is required to validate the complete version of Meloy's typology, which is intended to refine Ressler et al.'s initial sexual homicide motivational model.

Clarke and Carter's (2000) SHO typology is among the first to offer distinctive treatment implications for each type in its proposed profiles. This approach is clearly a strength. Unlike other previous classifications that focus on their utility for investigative purposes, Clarke and Carter (2000) attempt to outline the differing treatment needs of different types of sexual murderers. However, this approach is only briefly mentioned in their published work, especially in regards to the sexual components of a sexual homicide. For instance, little is mentioned about how to deal with the sadistic impulses and the anger and grievance aspects of the two proposed profiles. Although all of the sexual murderers examined by Clarke and Carter are non-serial murderers, the diversity of their victims (adult women, adult men, and children) makes this typology applicable for use in treatment. To illustrate, it might be the case that the SHOs who murder adult women have different treatment needs than the SHOs who sexually kill adult men and children, and vice versa.

Unlike most typologies that are constructed using mixed types of sexual murderers, the offender typology developed by Beauregard and Proulx (2002) is a rare classification in that it examines a specific type of sexual murderer. Although the two proposed types of SHOs (sadistic and angry) are argued to be reliable classifications, the small number of subjects in their study ($N = 36$) limits the statistical power of their typology in quantitative analyses. Despite this drawback, they assert that their sample of SHOs who murder adult women is fairly representative of the sexual murderer population in Quebec, Canada, at the time of their data gathering process. Unlike earlier offender typologies, Beauregard and Proulx's (2002) classification is very comprehensive because they use a quantitative method to measure a wide variety of variables concerning the offense, the offender, and the victim.

Schlesinger's (2004, 2007) discussion is illuminating with its detailed explanations and case studies of the two extreme types of sexual homicide (catathymic and compulsive). However, a major drawback of this offender classification is the lack of empirical verification of this typology, which is constructed on the basis of his clinical judgment. The validity and reliability of this dichotomy model has yet to be examined (Chan & Heide, 2009). Hence, more research evaluating large numbers of SHOs of each specific type proposed by Schlesinger is required.

Fisher and Beech's (2007) work on the profiles of IT-oriented sexual murderers is a more robust and comprehensive version of an earlier work conducted by Beech, Robertson, et al. (2001) and Beech, Oliver, et al. (2006). Unlike most existing SHO typologies, Fisher and Beech's work offers their perspective on the implications for treatment of each type of sexual murderer. Although their SHO categorization is empirically generated, a replication of their classification is needed because their sample of 28 sexual murderers is very small.

Notwithstanding the fact that Beauregard and Proulx's (2007) classification of sexual murderers who victimize men is empirically constructed, its small sample of just ten subjects has severely hampered the generalizability of their results. In addition, only the descriptive findings are generated, and thus advanced statistical analyses are not possible due to their small sample size. Hence, their findings should be studied prudently. Moreover, potential biases related to the use of only imprisoned SHOs are likely to occur (Beauregard & Proulx, 2007). Notwithstanding the inherent shortcomings of their offender classification, Beauregard and Proulx's typology is the first to take into account the entire criminal event (i.e., the offender, the victim, and the context of the crime) of sexual homicides that involve male victims.

Similar to Kocsis's (1999) Australian-based SHO typology, Gerard, Mormont, and Kocsis's (2007) sexual murderer classification is based on a Belgian sample. This uniqueness has proved its strength in terms of its suitability for use as a profiling tool for sexual homicides that occur in Belgium. Nevertheless, this typological model is still in its early stage, with only one validation study. Further empirical examination, evaluation, and refinement of this model are needed. Future attempts using only sexual murderers who victimize a specific type of victim might be able to test the reliability of this typology in terms of applying it to all of the different kinds of SHOs.

Sewall, Krupp, and Lalumière (2013) set out to empirically test the FBI organized/disorganized model of sexual homicide. They propose a typological model of three kinds of sexual murderers with a sample of 82 male serial male SHOs. Neither of these two models are well supported in their study. Instead, a four-cluster model (i.e., sadistic offenders, competitively disadvantaged offenders, slashers, and a heterogeneous group of offenders) is found, with limited evidence for their proposed psychopathic profile. Therefore, Sewall et al.'s proposed typology is not empirically supported. Perhaps, their study is hampered by the use of mainstream media sources as their data of analysis. The quality of the case information is a key study limitation, with the data comprehensiveness varying from case to case. The authenticity of the sources is subject to question. Moreover, the offender clusters in their study could only be applied to serial SHOs. Sexual murderers who only kill once are likely to possess different profiles. Nonetheless, the future studies are needed that use a different set of serial offenders with a more reliable and complete source of data (i.e., official data) in order to examine, evaluate, and refine this proposed typological model.

The sample size ($N = 350$) used in Balemba, Beauregard, and Martineau's (2014) offender classification is, by far, the largest among all of the published offender classifications. This is clearly a strength as it increases the statistical power of their offender typology. Despite its large sample and the use of a quantitative approach in generating the offender profiles, this offender classification is not without any criticism. First, Balemba et al.'s offender profiles focus only on the crime scene behavior of sexual murderers. The offenders' developmental issues and other personal characteristics along with the pre-crime selection of the victim and hunting are not examined. Hence, the "completeness" of their offender classification is in question. Further their offender classification emphasizes the crime scene perspective of the sexual homicide but only ten crime scene variables are tested. It may be difficult for a "complete" picture of the offenders' crime scene behaviors to emerge from just ten crime scene variables. Among these variables, the weapon, the offender's emotional state, and the offense's duration are key crime scene behaviors that could be distinguished between different offender profiles. In the future, a refinement of this empirically supported classification of SHO crime scene profiles could be performed by adding more crime scene factors. Despite these noted limitations, this offender classification is empirically validated by a large sample size, which may prove its utility in aiding police investigation.

3
Sexual Homicide Offending: Theoretical Explanations

Many studies on sexual homicide have been published over the years (mid-1980s to 2008). Most of these studies, however, are either descriptive in nature and use different samples of sexual murderers or comparative studies of sexual murderers and other types of offenders (Chan & Heide, 2009). Hence, little is known about the underlying theoretical conceptual accounts of the etiology of sexual homicide. To date, only four widely cited theoretical models of sexual homicide have been proposed: (a) the motivational model (Burgess, Hartman, Ressler, Douglas, & McCormack, 1986; Ressler, Burgess, & Douglas, 1988), (b) the trauma-control model[1] (Hickey, 1997, 2002), (c) the paraphilic model (Arrigo & Purcell, 2001), and (d) the criminal event perspective model (Mieczkowski & Beauregard, 2010). These distinct theoretical models are discussed in the following sections.

3.1 The FBI's motivational model

In order to comprehend the various socio-psychological factors that influence sexual murderers to kill, a group of FBI investigators and scholars proposed a motivational model for understanding sexually motivated murder and sadistic violence. Using interview data collected from 36 incarcerated sexual murderers, Burgess, Hartman, Ressler, Douglas, and McCormack (1986) propose a five-phase motivation model to explain why an offender commits sexual murder(s): (a) ineffective social environment, (b) formative events, (c) critical personal traits and a cognitive mapping process, (d) action toward others and self, and (e) a feedback filter. They propose that these five components are interrelated (see Figure 3.1).

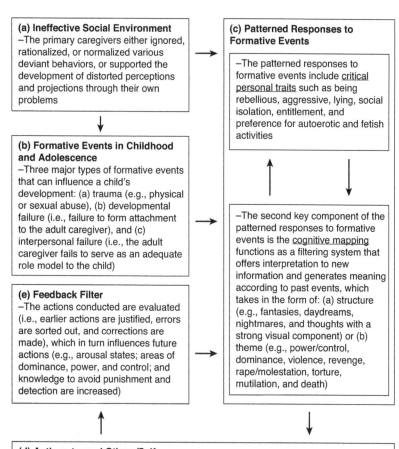

(a) Ineffective Social Environment
–The primary caregivers either ignored, rationalized, or normalized various deviant behaviors, or supported the development of distorted perceptions and projections through their own problems

(b) Formative Events in Childhood and Adolescence
–Three major types of formative events that can influence a child's development: (a) trauma (e.g., physical or sexual abuse), (b) developmental failure (i.e., failure to form attachment to the adult caregiver), and (c) interpersonal failure (i.e., the adult caregiver fails to serve as an adequate role model to the child)

(e) Feedback Filter
–The actions conducted are evaluated (i.e., earlier actions are justified, errors are sorted out, and corrections are made), which in turn influences future actions (e.g., arousal states; areas of dominance, power, and control; and knowledge to avoid punishment and detection are increased)

(c) Patterned Responses to Formative Events
–The patterned responses to formative events include critical personal traits such as being rebellious, aggressive, lying, social isolation, entitlement, and preference for autoerotic and fetish activities

–The second key component of the patterned responses to formative events is the cognitive mapping functions as a filtering system that offers interpretation to new information and generates meaning according to past events, which takes in the form of: (a) structure (e.g., fantasies, daydreams, nightmares, and thoughts with a strong visual component) or (b) theme (e.g., power/control, dominance, violence, revenge, rape/molestation, torture, mutilation, and death)

(d) Actions toward Others/Self
–The thoughts of dominance over others are expressed through a wide range of actions toward others both in childhood (e.g., negative play patterns, disregard for others, abuse of other children, cruelty toward animals, stealing, fire setting, and destroying property), and adolescence and adulthood where the actions become more violent (e.g., assaultive behaviors, arson, burglary, abduction, rape, and nonsexual and sexual murder).

Figure 3.1   Burgess et al.'s (1986) motivation model of sexual homicide

3.1.1   Ineffective social environment

The structure and quality of family and social interactions are pertinent to the general development of a child, especially the manner in which the child perceives his/her family members and their interactions with him/her and with each other. Burgess et al. (1986) asserts that the quality of the children's attachments (also known as "bonding") to their parents as their primary caregivers and to other members of their family is the most important factor in determining how children will relate to and value others in society later in life. Simply put, the early life attachments of the children to their parents are critical in influencing how they will perceive situations outside of their family. In Burgess et al.'s (1986) study, all of the interviewed sexual murderers had either failed to bond with their primary caregivers as children or had developed selective or limited methods of bonding with others. These primary caregivers had either ignored, rationalized, or normalized various deviant behaviors during the process of developing their children or had supported their children to develop distorted perceptions and projections through their own problems (e.g., criminal behavior, substance abuse; Burgess et al., 1986). Thus, these ineffective social bonds contributed to the children's negative perceptions of reality and, most importantly, to their cognitive distortions in relation to sexuality.

3.1.2   Formative events in childhood and adolescence

According to Burgess et al. (1986), there are three major types of formative events that can influence or affect a child's development: (a) trauma (e.g., physical or sexual abuse), (b) developmental failure (i.e., failure to form attachment to his/her adult caregiver), and (c) interpersonal failure (i.e., adult caregiver of the child fails to serve as an adequate role model to the child). In terms of the traumatic events experienced by children, these can either be normative events (e.g., illness, death) that occur as a function of routine life or non-normative events that are not consistent with routine life. The non-normative traumas experienced by the murderers in Burgess et al.'s (1986) sample include direct trauma such as physical and/or sexual abuse and indirect trauma such as witnessing family violence. In an ineffective social environment, children may feel unprotected and confused about the non-normative events they experience. The assumption, as posited by Burgess et al. (1986) with regard to early traumatic events, is that the children's memories of frightening and/or upsetting life experiences are likely to shape their developing thought patterns. These thought patterns can then emerge in the form of daydreams and fantasies, which in turn influence their tendency to become socially withdrawn into their fantasy world in order to find comfort. If these children are unsuccessful at resolving their traumatic events, their feelings of hopelessness and helplessness can be reinforced. Daydreaming and fantasy are ways for adolescents to escape the reality in which they lack control. In addition, daydreaming and fantasizing enable adolescents to have complete control over any situation they create or encounter.

Developmental failure also contributes to the formative events of childhood and/or early adolescence. For various reasons, a strained or a lack of adequate social attachment to parents or other primary caregivers is likely to lead to children or adolescents feeling neglected and emotionally deprived. The third contributing factor in this model component is interpersonal failure, which refers to the failure of parents or primary caregivers to serve as appropriate role models for developing children (Burgess et al., 1986). Examples of negative parental role models for children include parents with problems of substance abuse and parents who offer a violent home environment to their children. If children experience violence at home, "the aggressive acts may become associated with the inappropriate sexual behavior of the adult caretaker" (Burgess et al., 1986, p. 264).

3.1.3 Patterned responses to formative events

The patterned responses or adaptations to formative events include critical personal traits and cognitive mapping and processing that interact with each other to generate fantasies. Personality traits can be both positive and negative. Positive personality traits such as warmth, trust, and security that help to establish positive relationships with others are consequences of children's normal growth and development. As Burgess et al. (1986) contend, "in combination with an effective social environment, the child is allowed to develop competency and autonomy" (p. 264). Negative personality traits, in contrast, are formed as a result of an ineffective social environment which in turns interferes with a child's formation of prosocial emotional relationships with others. As a result, an inability to approach others in a confident manner is likely, thereby increasing the likelihood of social isolation. Increased social isolation encourages a reliance on fantasy as an alternative to prosocial human interaction. Hence, individual personality development may become dependent on fantasy life and its dominant themes rather than on prosocial human interaction (Burgess et al., 1986). In Burgess et al.'s (1986) study, murderers are found to have a sense of social isolation; cynical views of others and society; preferences for autoerotic activities and fetishes; a sense of entitlement; and to be rebelliousness, aggressive, and chronic liars. Their sense of social isolation, coupled with deep-seated anger, may limit their normal sexual development based on caring, pleasure, and companionship. As a result, these individuals can only relate to others through their fantasy life, whereby their "fantasy becomes the primary source of emotional arousal and that emotion is a confused mixture of sex and aggression" (Burgess et al., 1986, p. 265).

Cognitive mapping is the second key component that informs the patterned responses of children that usually stem from their formative events. In simple terms, cognitive mapping functions as a filtering system that provides for interpretation of new information and generates meaning according to past events (Burgess et al., 1986). This process can take the forms of daydreams, fantasies, nightmares, and thoughts with strong visual elements. Common fantasy themes, as reported by the murderers in Burgess et al.'s (1986) sample, include dominance, revenge, violence, rape, molestation, power, control, torture, mutilation, pain infliction on self/others, and death. The fantasy world of murderers is likely to influence and support their self-image. The fantasy that offers these murderers stimulation becomes a preferred substitute for their lack of control over their internal and external involvement in reality. Consequently, their preoccupation with aggressive or sexually deviant fantasy themes, their detailed cognitive activity, and their increased kinesthetic arousal state may ultimately lead these individuals to take action (Burgess et al., 1986).

3.1.4   Actions toward others

Regardless of age, behavioral patterns reflect the private internal world of each individual. Burgess et al. (1986) find this to be true with their sample of sexual murderers. In fact, Burgess et al. (1986) find that the behavioral patterns of their sample of murderers indicates that their "internal worlds were preoccupied with troublesome, joyless thoughts of dominance over others" (p. 266). These thoughts are expressed through a wide range of actions toward others in childhood (e.g., cruelty toward animals, abuse of other children, negative play patterns, disregard for others, fire setting, stealing, and destroying property). In adolescence and adulthood, their actions become more violent (e.g., assaultive behaviors, burglary, arson, abduction, rape, nonsexual homicide), finally leading to sexual homicide involving rape, torture, mutilation, and necrophilia (Burgess et al., 1986).

According to Burgess et al. (1986), a failure to intervene and eradicate early childhood expressions of violence is likely to serve as a catalyst for future abusive behavior. They contend that the early acts of violence are likely to be reinforced if the child or adolescent is not held accountable for his/her antisocial behavior. Burgess et al. (1986) also assert that impulsive and erratic behavior tends to discourage friendship. The failure to make friends leads to social isolation and interferes with the child's or the adolescent's ability to develop positive empathy, conflict resolution, and impulse control skills.

3.1.5 Feedback filter

Burgess et al. (1986) coin the term "feedback filter" to refer to the manner in which an individual reacts to and evaluates his/her action toward him/herself and others, which in turns influences his/her future actions. Through feedback filters, Burgess et al.'s (1986) sample of murderers justify their earlier actions, sort out errors, and make corrections "to preserve and protect their internal fantasy world and to avoid restrictions from the external environment" (p. 267). Also, their arousal states of dominance, power, and control via fantasy variations of their violent actions increase; in addition, an increased knowledge of how to avoid punishment and detection is also evidenced. All of this feeds back into their patterned responses and subsequently enhances the details of their fantasy life.

3.2 Hickey's trauma-control model

Hickey (1997) proposes a trauma-control model to offer a theoretical explanation for serial murder. In addition to addressing several aspects identified by Burgess et al. (1986) in their motivational model of sexual homicide, Hickey (1997, 2002) theorizes a number of predispositional factors and facilitators that can influence the specific behavioral factors that can lead to a serial killing. Hickey's (1997) model includes eight key features: (a) predispositional factors, (b) traumatic events, (c) low self-esteem and fantasies, (d) dissociation, (e) trauma reinforcers, (f) facilitators, (g) increasingly violent fantasies, and (h) homicidal behavior (see Figure 3.2).

3.2.1 Predispositional factors

According to Hickey (1997), a majority of serial murderers are known to have certain predispositional factors, which are biological, psychological, and/or sociological in nature, that can affect or shape their conduct. An example of a biological factor is the extra Y chromosome in males, which could possibly contribute to violent behavior. Mental disorders such as personality disorders are examples of psychological factors that could produce aggressive and dangerous (i.e., risky) behavior. An illustration of a sociological factor is a dysfunctional home environment that could influence the prospects of adolescents acquiring negative or antisocial behavior during their formative years of life.

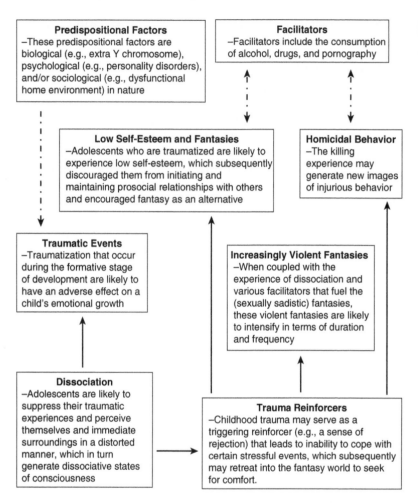

Figure 3.2   Hickey's (1997) trauma-control model of serial homicide

3.2.2   Traumatic events

In their motivational model of sexual homicide, Burgess et al. (1986) assert that traumatic events that occur during the formative stage of development are likely to have an adverse effect on a child's emotional growth. Hickey (1997, 2002), nonetheless, indicates that such childhood traumatic experiences are more likely to be aggravated by social and environmental issues. The models theorized by Burgess et al. (1986) and Hickey (1997) both acknowledge the debilitating outcomes of adolescent abuse caused by parents or primary caregivers. Hickey (1997) states that "the child or teen feels a deep sense of anxiety, mistrust, and confusion when psychologically or physically [harmed] by an adult" (p. 87). Being rejected by parents or primary caregivers is the most common manifestation of childhood trauma. According to Hickey (1997), "an unstable, abusive home ... [is] one of the major forms of rejection" (p. 87).

3.2.3 Low self-esteem and fantasies

The patterned responses to formative events addressed in Burgess et al.'s (1986) model are also discussed in Hickey's (1997) model. According to Hickey (1997), adolescents who experience traumatic events in the early stage of their development are likely to experience inadequacies, self-doubt, low self-esteem, and worthlessness. Because of their poor self-image and depleted confidence, these adolescents are discouraged from initiating and maintaining prosocial relationships with others. Hence, daydreaming and fantasy become alternatives for these socially isolated adolescents.

3.2.4 Dissociation

According to Hickey (1997), children and adolescents who experience physical or psychological trauma in their early development years are less likely to effectively confront and cope with these traumatic experiences. Hence, they may perceive themselves and their immediate surroundings in a distorted manner. As they mature, these distorted perceptions can generate dissociative states of consciousness (Vetter, 1990). Hickey (1997) defines the dissociation process as an "effort to regain the psychological equilibrium taken from [an individual] by people in authority [in which the offender] appear[s] to construct masks, facades, or a veneer of self-confidence and self-control" (p. 88). Generally, serial murderers portray themselves to others as having perfect control over themselves when, in reality, they are morally and socially incompetent. Therefore, under these circumstances, illusion and image become the only reality that sustains them.

Hickey (1997) notes that it is also common for individuals to suppress their traumatic events to the point where they are unable to recall or remember these events. This phenomenon is known as "splitting off" or blocking out the experience. Tanay (1976) describes this phenomenon, from a serial killing standpoint, as an ego-dystonic episode. Offenders execute a homicide in an altered state of consciousness, whereby they are unaware of their own actions. Danto (1982), conversely, believes that when an individual's mind is "overwhelmed and flooded with anxiety"

(p. 6), a state of agitation and/or apprehension is likely to develop as a dissociative reaction.

3.2.5   Trauma reinforcers

According to Hickey (1997), "childhood trauma for serial murderers may serve as a triggering mechanism or reinforcer, resulting in an individual's inability to cope with the stress of certain events, whether they are physical, psychological, or a combination of traumatizations" (p. 87). An example of a triggering factor is a sense of rejection. This sense of rejection is likely to stem from the unrequited displays of affection showered on an intimate partner or the intense and ferocious work-related criticisms of an employer. When these early traumatized individuals experience rejection again in later life, they may internalize the feeling and become immobilized and unable to constructively cope with this adverse experience. In order to find comfort, they may retreat psychologically into their fantasy world, which often consists of cynical and negative sentiments.

3.2.6   Facilitators

In the course of the trauma-control process, it is common for offenders to immerse themselves in facilitators (e.g., alcohol, drugs, and pornography). Hickey (1997) posits that "alcohol appears to decrease inhibitions and inhibit moral conscience and propriety, whereas pornography fuels growing fantasies of violence" (p. 89). From a serial killing perspective, addiction is the first of several stages offenders go through with facilitators. To illustrate, in the case of pornography, offenders are likely to be aroused physiologically and psychologically by pornography consumption, which subsequently generates an appetite for such satisfying effects in their daily activities. As a result, they enter the next stage, known as escalation, whereby their "appetite for more deviant, bizarre, and explicit sexual material is fostered" (Hickey, 1997, p. 89). Ultimately, they become desensitized to pornographic materials that are graphically sadistic and degrading. In the end, offenders are likely to act according to these sadistic imageries in which they immerse themselves.

3.2.7   Increasingly violent fantasies

As aforementioned, traumatizing experiences in early life can adversely affect an individual's social perception of the world and his/her developing sense of self. Serial killers, for instance, are likely to daydream and to indulge in their fantasy world as a way to escape from their socially isolated reality. When coupled with the experience of dissociation, which originates from their trauma reinforcers, and the various facilitators that fuel their (sexually sadistic) fantasies, a synergistic and possible lethal effect is likely to materialize. In the presence of increasingly violent fantasies, this synergistic effect is likely to grow in duration, frequency, and intensity (Hickey, 1997).

3.2.8 Homicidal behavior

According to Hickey (1997, 2002), the killing experience may generate new images of injurious behavior. Each violent act is an attempt to gratify the offender's fantasy fully. If their homicidal act does not resemble the expected outcomes of their fantasy, they are likely to murder again.

3.3 Arrigo and Purcell's paraphilic model

Paraphilias (i.e., sexually aberrant or deviant behaviors), as a behavioral system, commonly function as the motivation for sexual murder, particularly lust murder (i.e., sadistic sexual murder, also known as "erotophonophilia"). Arrigo and Purcell (2001) propose an integrated theoretical paraphilic schema that uses both Burgess et al.'s (1986) motivational model and Hickey's (1997, 2002) trauma-control model coupled with MacCulloch et al.'s (1983) work on sadistic behavior. In their integrated paraphilic framework, they propose seven key dimensions: (a) formative development, (b) low self-esteem, (c) early fantasy and paraphilic development, (d) paraphilic process, (e) stressors, (f) behavioral manifestations, and (g) increasingly violent fantasies (see Figure 3.3).

3.3.1 Formative development

Arrigo and Purcell's (2001) initial dimension of the integrative model explains how childhood and early adolescent experiences contribute to the development of paraphilic behaviors. This dimension is a direct integration of both the "ineffective social environment" and "formative events" phases of Burgess et al.'s (1986) motivational model and the "predispositional factors" and "trauma events" features of Hickey's (1997) trauma-control model. Consistent with Burgess et al.'s (1986) and Hickey's (1997, 2002) assertion, Arrigo and Purcell (2001) state that the formative development of an individual has a significant effect on his/her psychosocial adjustment throughout their lives. In their formative development dimension of paraphilic behaviors, two interdependent concepts are introduced: (i) predispositional factors and (ii) traumatic events.

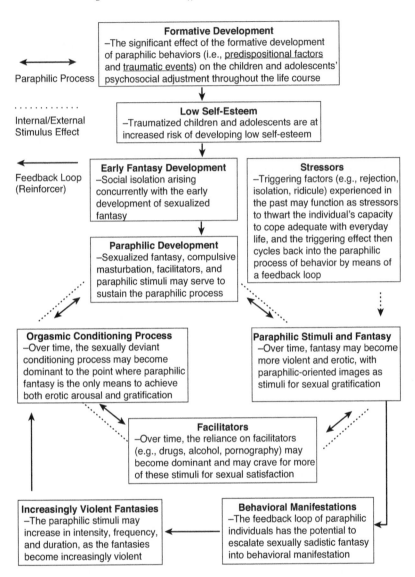

Figure 3.3   Arrigo and Purcell's (2001) paraphilic model of lust murder

3.3.1.1   *Predispositional factors*

Burgess et al.'s (1986) motivational model and Hickey's (1997, 2002) trauma-control model both recognize that certain predispositional factors are capable of affecting an individual's offending behavior. Specifically, Burgess et al. (1986) note that the psycho-sociological influence of dysfunctional family surroundings in childhood can adversely affect the quality of the parent-child attachment, which could result in developmental and interpersonal failures in later life. Hickey (1997) also asserts that mental disorders are inherently psychological and predispositional factors that could produce antisocial behavior.

In addition, Hickey (1997) posits that biological factors (e.g., the extra Y chromosome syndrome) can also influence offender conduct. Interestingly, research indicates that certain biological factors can influence the development of paraphilic behavior. For instance, Money (1990) argues that all paraphilias, especially sexual sadism, develop "due to a disease in the brain which affects the centers and the pathways that are responsible for sexual arousal, mating behavior, and reproduction of the species" (p. 27). With regard to sexual sadism in particular, Money (1990) contends that "the brain becomes pathologically activated to transmit messages of attack simultaneously with messages of sexual arousal and mating behavior" (p. 28). Simply put, all paraphilias stem from certain predispositional factors (e.g., biological, psychological, and sociological) that can, in some circumstances, generate erotically sadistic, aggressive, and even homicidal behavior (Arrigo & Purcell, 2001).

3.3.1.2 Traumatic events

In addition to the influence of predispositional factors on an individual's propensity to engage in erotically deviant behaviors, both the motivational and the trauma-control models also acknowledge the severe effects of traumatic experiences (e.g., physical, sexual, and psychological) on childhood and early adolescent development. Studies on the paraphilia of lust murderers also show that the early years of psychological adjustment "are crucial to the personality structure and development of these offenders" (Hazelwood & Douglas, 1980, p. 21). Simon (1996) argues that it is uncommon for lust murderers to grow up in a nurturing family environment that is free from abuse, alcoholism, and drugs (see also Money & Werlas, 1982). Simply put, paraphilic behaviors are likely to originate from largely unresolved or inappropriately addressed childhood or early adolescent traumatic events (Arrigo & Purcell, 2001).

3.3.2 Low self-esteem

The motivational (Burgess et al., 1986) and trauma-control (Hickey, 1997) models both acknowledge the inherently negative consequences of traumatic events for a child's or adolescent's development of a positive self-image and their learning of prosocial behavior. Traumatized children and adolescents are at increased risk of developing a deep-seated sense of personal failure and a genuine lack of regard for others that eventually interferes with their ability to develop positive interpersonal relationships with others. Consequently, daydreaming and fantasy become a substitute for their socially isolated life. Individuals with paraphilias are likely to come from a dysfunctional background (Abel, Becker, Cunningham-Rather, Muttleman, & Rouleau, 1988; Holmes, 1991). Burgess et al. (1986) also note that negative personality traits are likely to act as catalysts for generating fantasies, which in turn become patterned responses. The anger or rage these individuals experience as a result of previous trauma and rejection is likely to be expressed in the content of their image making in their fantasy (Arrigo & Purcell, 2001). Thus, in addition to having a socially isolated life, these angry individuals are likely to form violent fantasies in their minds (Hickey, 1997).

3.3.3   Early fantasy and paraphilic development

Arrigo and Purcell (2001) posit that several factors are likely to occur simultaneously to produce a synergistic effect in the development of the paraphilia. To illustrate, social isolation arising concomitantly with the early development of sexualized fantasy may subsequently lead to an individual developing paraphilic behaviors. This process (i.e., paraphilic-oriented sexualized fantasy) may eventually become fixated. According to Arrigo and Purcell (2001), fantasy, compulsive masturbation, facilitators, and paraphilic stimuli (e.g., fetishes, unusual objects, sadistic and erotic rituals) may serve to sustain the paraphilic process.

Burgess et al. (1986) specifically identify personality characteristics, such as social isolation, a preference for autoerotic activities, and fetishes, that are indicative of the paraphilic process described by Arrigo and Purcell (2001). Indeed, Ressler et al. (1988) state that "the internal behaviors most consistently reported over the murderers' three developmental periods were daydreaming, compulsive masturbation, and isolation" (p. 30). Furthermore, Burgess et al. (1986) find that in their study of 36 sexual murderers, 83% of those who were victims of childhood sexual abuse engaged in fetishistic behaviors compared with only 43% of those who were not abused. This finding strongly suggests that fetishistic behaviors, as paraphilic stimuli, are initiated at some point in the context of social isolation, fantasy, and prior sexual abuse. Other researchers (e.g., Hickey, 1997, 2002; Holmes, 1991; Simon, 1996) have also acknowledged the importance of fetishistic behaviors as symbolic links in a sexual murderer's life.

3.3.4   Paraphilic process

The paraphilic process, as posited by Arrigo and Purcell (2001), is cyclical and consists of three mutually interactive elements: (i) paraphilic stimuli and fantasy, (ii) orgasmic conditioning process, and (iii) facilitators (e.g., alcohol, drugs, pornography).

3.3.4.1   *Paraphilic stimuli and fantasy*

According to Arrigo and Purcell (2001), fantasy is very influential in facilitating the paraphilic process. Both the motivational (Burgess et al., 1986) and the trauma-control (Hickey, 1997) models claim that feelings of inadequacy as a result of a lack of social-sexual bonding with others may drive individuals into a world of fantasy and social isolation. Over time, the images of their fantasy may become more violent and erotic, incorporating assorted fetishes, rituals, and/or unusual and sexually charged objects as stimuli for sexual gratification. This contention is further supported by MacCulloch et al.'s (1983) study of the sadistic fantasies of sexual offenders. MacCulloch et al. (1983) find that most of the sexual offenders in their study who engage in sadistic fantasies experience difficulty in both social and sexual relationships at a young age. The feeling of sexual arousal and the sadistic fantasies are likely to reinforce each other via classical conditioning, and this increases the likelihood of escalation and habituation (Arrigo & Purcell, 2001). Studies find that lust murderers usually associate sex with aggression in their fantasy systems (e.g., Hazelwood & Douglas, 1980; Liebert, 1985). The common themes are power, domination, exploitation, revenge, molestation, humiliation, and degradation (Simon, 1996).

3.3.4.2   *Orgasmic conditioning process*

Compulsive masturbation through fantasizing and rehearsing paraphilic behavior enables an individual to achieve sexual orgasm. Over time, this sexually deviant conditioning process may become dominant to the point where paraphilic fantasy is the only means of achieving both erotic arousal and satisfaction (Arrigo & Purcell, 2001). The nature and content of the fantasy may become increasingly violent and sadistic, and the paraphilic behaviors may increase in intensity and frequency.

3.3.4.3   *Facilitators*

In his trauma-control model, Hickey (1997) states that the use of drugs, alcohol, and pornography are important components in serial murdering. Similarly, Ressler et al. (1988) find that in their sample of sexual killers, over half of the subjects report having an interest in pornography and approximately 81% indicate "interests in fetishism, voyeurism, and masturbation" (p. 25). Other studies also demonstrate the influential role of facilitators in sustaining and contributing to manifestations of sadistic sexual homicide (e.g., Hazelwood & Warren, 2000; Holmes, 1991; Prentky et al., 1989; Simon, 1996).

Likewise, Arrigo and Purcell (2001) posit that the use of facilitators is also essential to the paraphilic process; these facilitators manifest themselves as addictions for sexually deviant individuals. Paraphilic individuals become firmly embedded in a cycle of addiction, experiencing dependency and craving more of these stimuli for sexual satisfaction. The reliance on drugs, alcohol, and/or pornography may escalate until these paraphilic individuals become desensitized to the facilitators. Ultimately, they may have to act out their depraved and erotically charged deviant sexual fantasies through sexual homicide or lust murder.

3.3.5 Stressors

According to Arrigo and Purcell (2001), the triggering factors (e.g., rejection, isolation, and ridicule) that are experienced in childhood and adolescence may function as stressors to constrain or thwart an individual's capacity to cope adequately with everyday life. These stressors are similar to Hickey's (1997) trauma reinforcers. The stressor activates childhood trauma and regenerates the adverse and vile feelings that are associated with it within the individual (Ressler et al., 1988). Depending on the nature and the seriousness of these triggering factors, the individual may experience a temporary loss of control. This triggering effect subsequently cycles back into the paraphilic process of behavior by means of a feedback loop and is sustained by masturbation, facilitators, and fantasy (Arrigo & Purcell, 2001). In extreme circumstances, the response to the stress may manifest itself in sadistic and erotic conduct, including lust murder.

3.3.6 Behavioral manifestations

If paraphilic individuals are compelled to execute their sexually sadistic fantasy, their feedback loop has the potential to escalate into behavioral manifestations. Through the enactment of paraphilic fantasy and stimuli, these individuals attempt to gratify, complete, and reify their illusions. Each time this behavior is inaugurated, an exhilarating rush of carnal satisfaction and an increased need for stimulation are likely to be experienced by these paraphilic individuals. This behavior is likely to function as a reinforcer and to cycle back into the fantasy system. Both the motivational (Burgess et al., 1986) and the trauma-control (Hickey, 1997) models depict this similar process from the perspective of sexual and serial homicides.

3.3.7 Increasingly violent fantasies

As the fantasies become increasingly violent in nature, the paraphilic stimuli also increase in intensity, frequency, and duration. The need for constant violent arousal is part of the paraphilic feedback loop and sequences into the process accordingly (Arrigo & Purcell, 2001). Similarly, in their motivational model, Burgess et al. (1986) introduce two components that account for the increasingly violent imagery: actions toward others and the feedback filter. Burgess et al. (1986) indicate that when the actions-toward-others factor happens "in adolescence and adulthood, the murderers' [conduct] becomes more violent: assaultive behaviors, burglary, arson, abduction, rape, nonsexual murder, and finally sexual murder involving rape, torture, mutilation, and necrophilia" (p. 266). Subsequently, feelings of dominance, power, control, and an increased arousal state all sequence back into the offenders' "patterned responses and enhance the details of the fantasy life" through the feedback filter component (Burgess et al., 1986; p. 267). Likewise, Hickey (1997) argue that an increasingly violent fantasy component also plays an important part in the serial murders.

3.4 Mieczkowski and Beauregard's criminal event perspective model

Criminal events are distinct from criminal acts (Sacco & Kennedy, 1996). Acts are examples of behavior, while events entail the context of the behavior (Mieczkowski & Beauregard, 2010). To illustrate, sexual penetrations (e.g., vaginal, oral, and anal) are acts, while sexual assault is an event that may consist of different types of sexual penetration. Using a criminal event perspective (CEP), Mieczkowski and Beauregard (2010) propose a model to explain what characteristics are associated with the homicidal outcome of a sexual assault. The CEP simply refers to a technique used to organize ideas and data (Meier, Kennedy, & Sacco, 2001) in order to design explanatory models of crime that emphasize the significance of interactions (Anderson & Meier, 2004). There are three key domains of criminal events in Mieczkowki and Beauregard's (2010) model: (a) victim characteristics, (b) situational characteristics, and (c) crime characteristics.

3.4.1   Victim characteristics

In examining victim characteristics, Mieczkowski and Beauregard (2010) find that the victims with the highest probability of being murdered during a sexual assault are those who are aged 14 or below, come from a non-criminogenic environment, and are strangers to offenders. Interestingly, Mieczkowski and Beauregard (2010) find that the three highest ratio combinations include victims who come from non-criminogenic environments. They reason that coming from a criminogenic environment may serve as a factor that protects a victim from being killed during a sexual assault. Socialization experiences in a criminogenic environment may have "better equipped [them] to detect early cues regarding the malevolent intentions of the offender or escape the circumstances at an earlier moment" that might otherwise have resulted in a homicidal outcome (Mieczkowski & Beauregard, 2010, p. 354). Alternatively, they may be better trained to handle the circumstances once a sexual assault has begun, and thus they may act in a strategic manner to save their lives. Comparatively, victims who are raised in a criminogenic environment are better prepared and more competent to manage the circumstances than victims who are less socialized in such an environment.

Another noteworthy finding of Mieczkowski and Beauregard's (2010) study is that victims who are children under 14 years of age and who are raised in a criminogenic environment are least likely to be murdered during a sexual assault. Mieczkowski and Beauregard (2010) reason that young children are likely to offer no resistance and their compliance to the sexual assault may increase their survivability. However, child victims who come from a non-criminogenic environment and experience an encounter with a stranger are likely to panic and resist, which may lead to a lethal outcome as a result of the offender's escalation of violence as a means to control the circumstances (Mieczkowski & Beauregard, 2010).

3.4.2   Situational characteristics

Looking at the perspective of situational characteristics, Mieczkowski and Beauregard (2010) find that a daytime attack is likely to result in a lethal outcome. This is consistent with the findings in Weaver et al.'s (2004) study, where a higher proportion of homicidal outcomes is found in crimes committed between the hours of 6:00 a.m. and 8:00 a.m. Mieczkowski and Beauregard (2010) reason that daylight assault may increase the tendency of the victim to potentially identify the offender, which in turn may cause the offender to murder the victim to evade apprehension. This is also consistent with Beauregard et al.'s (2007) findings on the hunting process of serial sex offenders; they find that the strategies used by the offenders are likely to be influenced by different environmental and situational factors.

3.4.3 Crime characteristics

In terms of crime characteristics, the presence of a weapon is found to be a dominant factor in determining whether a sexual assault will probably end up in the killing of the victim (Mieczkowski & Beauregard, 2010). This finding is consistent with previous reports indicating that the presence of a weapon makes the killing of the victim easier (Chene & Cusson, 2007; Felson & Messner, 1996). In addition, sexual assaults that involve no intrusive or forced sex with the victim and take more than 30 minutes are found to be more likely to end with a homicide than sexual assaults that do not have these characteristics (Mieczkowski & Beauregard, 2010). Consistent with Beauregard and Proulx (2002), Mieczkowski and Beauregard (2010) reason that the killing of the victim may be due to the offender's frustration and anger over his failure to obtain sufficient sexual release or to accomplish a sexual goal. In sum, the combination of the use of a weapon, an extended period of time with the victim, and a failure to engage in intrusive sex with the victim or a failure to coerce the victim to perform sexual acts on the offender increases the likelihood that a homicide will result from the sexual assault.

3.5 Conclusion: theoretical limitations

This chapter discusses the four widely cited theoretical models of sexual homicide: (a) the motivational model (Burgess et al., 1986; Ressler et al., 1988), (b) the trauma-control model (Hickey, 1997, 2002), (c) the paraphilic model (Arrigo & Purcell, 2001), and (d) the criminal event perspective model (Mieczkowski & Beauregard, 2010). Despite their distinctive efforts to theorize the phenomenon of sexual homicide from different theoretical perspectives, the creators of these models neglect to link the different components in their models to the existing criminological and/or psychological theories. In particular, these models fail to explain from either a criminological or a psychological theoretical standpoint the processes by which potential offenders become motivated to sexually murder or decide to sexually murder and then act on that desire, intention, and opportunity.

Recently, a comprehensive model of sexual killing from the offending perspective has been proposed in the criminological literature (Chan, Heide, & Beauregard, 2011). This theoretical model uses an integrated theory combining social learning theory and routine activity theory to explain the conceptual framework for sexual homicide offending. In order to understand this newly proposed model of sexual homicide from the offending perspective, the following chapter will comprehensively discuss this theoretical framework.

4
Sexual Homicide Offending: In Search of a Criminological Explanation

Two criminological theories, the social learning theory and the routine activity theory, are reviewed in this chapter. In addition, their applicability to explaining sexual violence and sex-related offenses is discussed. The limitations of using the social learning theory or the routine activity theory independently to explain the offending perspective of sexual homicide are outlined. Each theoretical model may complement the other via cross-level explanation of the sexual homicide phenomenon. However, in order to fully explain the complete offending perspective of this distinctive, yet serious violent crime, an integrated theoretical framework is desirable. Consequently, the recently proposed integrated theory of the offending perspective of sexual homicide by Chan, Heide, and Beauregard (2011) is presented below.

4.1 Social Learning Theory

For the last four decades, Akers' social learning theory has been one of the dominant criminological theories (Akers & Jensen, 2003, 2006). The social learning theory, initially proposed by Burgess and Akers (1966), is an explicit effort to extend Edwin Sutherland's theory of differential association (Akers & Sellers, 2009). As stated by Akers (2001), "social learning theory retains all of the differential association processes in Sutherland's theory" (p. 194), but with additional considerations. With an emphasis on the behavioral specification of the learning process, this theoretical perspective focuses on violations of social and legal norms using the new principles of the modern learning theory (Akers, 1985).

The published empirical research on social learning theory is extensive (for a review, see Akers, 1998; Akers & Sellers, 2009; Pratt et al., 2010). The core themes of Akers' social learning theory, as it is currently conceptualized, are *differential association, definitions, differential reinforcement or punishment,* and *imitation.* The differential association concept refers to the direct or indirect interaction and/or exposure to different attitudes and behaviors in different social contexts. Family and peers, which are examples of primary groups, tend to be the most vital social groups within which differential associations have a strong influence on the individual's behavioral learning process. As asserted by Akers (1998), the impact of such exposure nevertheless varies greatly according to the frequency, duration, intensity, and priority of each type of association. Notwithstanding the tremendous influence primary social groups have on the behavioral learning process, the secondary and the other reference groups (e.g., school system, colleagues and work groups, mass media, Internet, computer games) can also contribute greatly to the normative definitions in the learning process (Akers, 1997; Hwang & Akers, 2003; Warr, 2002).

Definitions are simply defined as the attitudes, beliefs, values, and norms with regard to certain behavior that are learned directly or indirectly from particular social groups, typically within intimate primary groups (Akers, 1997; Akers & Jensen, 2006; Batton & Ogle, 2003; Bellair, Roscigno, & Velez, 2003; Sellers, Cochran, & Branch, 2005). Definitions can be revealed in different forms. These attitudes or beliefs can be general (i.e., broadly approving or disapproving of criminal conduct) or specific (i.e., an explicit view of a particular criminal conduct) to a particular act or situation (Akers, 2001). Definitions may also be positive (i.e., favorable view of criminal behavior), negative (i.e., oppositional to criminal conduct), or even neutral (i.e., perceiving criminal conduct as permissible; Pratt et al., 2010).

Differential reinforcement or punishment is another facet of the social learning theory. This element refers to the net balance of anticipated social and/or nonsocial rewards and costs associated with different types of behavior (Akers, 1997; Krohn, Skinner, Massey, & Akers, 1985; Sellers et al., 2005). Although reinforcement can be physical (e.g., physiological changes from drug-taking behavior), Akers (2001) argues that the imperative reinforcers are social in nature (e.g., consequences result from the social interaction with one's intimate social group). Social reinforcement involves "not just the direct reactions of others present while an act is performed, but also the whole range of tangible and intangible rewards valued in society and its subgroups" (Akers, 1997, p. 55) such as financial rewards, positive facial expression, and verbal approval from significant others. Nonsocial reinforcements are "unconditioned positive and negative effects of physiological and psychological stimuli" (Akers, 1998, p. 71) such as the psychophysiological effects of a stimulant. The acts that are reinforced, either positively or negatively, are likely to be repeated, whereas acts that draw punishment are less likely to be repeated.

In addition, criminal behavior can be influenced by the imitation of certain behaviors through the observations of role models (Akers, 1997; Bandura, 1977; Donnerstein & Linz, 1995; Krohn et al., 1985; Sellers et al., 2005), especially when the behavior is first initiated (Akers, 2001). The important sources of imitation usually come from members of primary social groups, such as family and peers, who the individual admires and has personal or intimate relationships with (Donnerstein & Linz, 1995; Sellers et al., 2005). Other sources, such as the mass media, may also be capable of shaping the individual's behavioral orientation, either prosocially or criminally (Akers, 1997). Therefore, under the theoretical principles of the social learning theory, the presence of criminal behavior is more likely when an individual is embedded in a social atmosphere in which differential associations with pro-offending definitions and behavioral patterns are readily available and, most importantly, when his/her misconduct is repeatedly reinforced. Of note, in a recent meta-analysis by Pratt et al. (2010), the differential association and definition measures specified by the social learning theory are consistently found to yield the strongest mean effect sizes; the differential reinforcement and imitation predictors, however, are found to be generally weak across the sample of 133 studies.

4.1.1 Sexual Violence and Sex-Related Offenses: A Social Learning Theory Perspective

From a theoretical standpoint of social learning, deviant behavior is rooted in familial social interaction, especially the parent-child interaction (Fagan & Wexlers, 1987; McCord, 1991a, 1991b, Patterson, 1975). In addition to witnessing parental aggressive attitudes and/or behaviors, personal experience with family violence (i.e., physical and sexual abuse) may enhance an individual's tolerance for violence and his/her propensity to use violence as a coping mechanism (Burgess, Hartman, & McCormack, 1987; Flowers, 2006; Mihalic & Elliott, 1997; Straus, 1990). To illustrate, recent studies find that childhood maltreatment (e.g., physical violence, psychological abuse) and witnessing violence among parents are significant risk factors for future intimate partner violence (e.g., dating violence). These studies lend support to the inter-generational transmission of violence from the social learning perspective (Gover, Park, Tomsich, & Jennings, 2011; Jennings, Park, Tomsich, Gover, & Akers, 2011). Sexual violence, specifically, is argued to be a socially learned behavior related to interpersonal aggression and sexuality as a result of social and cultural traditions (Bandura, 1978; Ellis, 1989). Ellis (1989) contends that sex role scripts, sexual attitudes, and other prosexually deviant cognitions that are associated with physical aggression and sexuality are often mediated by cultural and experiential factors.

For decades, rape and other sexually aggressive behaviors have been widely studied from the social learning perspective (Chan, Heide, & Beauregard, 2011). Social learning theorists assert that sexually aggressive behaviors are typically learned through differential associations with significant others, such as family and close peers. To illustrate, individuals learn sexually aggressive behavior through association with sexually aggressive peers and family members who have a positive perception of sexually aggressive behaviors. These individuals are likely to conform to a supportive behavioral model of sexual hostility whereby sexually aggressive behavior is regarded as appropriate and is differentially reinforced over other nonsexually aggressive behaviors (Boeringer, Shehan, & Akers, 1991; Ellis, 1989; Flowers, 2006).

In addition to differential association, there is some evidence that sexual deviance can be learned through the conditioning effects of differential reinforcement for sexual responses to any stimulus that promotes positive feelings (Benda & DiBlasio, 1994; Ellis, 1989; Harris, Mazerolle, & Knight, 2009; Wilson & Nakajo, 1965). Kinsey, Pomeroy, Martin, and Gebhard (1953) refer to this conditioning process as the "psychologic factors in sexual response." In their study on dating and acquaintance relationships among college male students, Boeringer et al. (1991) find support for their social learning model of sexual aggression and rape. The sexual deviations are learned responses to possibly accidental experiences with sexually deviant behaviors which in turn promote positive feelings that can lead to potential escalation and habituation (Laws & Marshall, 2003; Ward, Polaschek, & Beech, 2006).

Furthermore, other reference social groups, such as the mass media, have also been commonly blamed for being an influential imitation medium of social violence. The long-term exposure to sexually explicit materials and/or violent pornographic materials may increase the tolerance for sexually aggressive behavior (Donnerstein, Linz, & Penrod, 1987; Dworkin, 1979; Gray 1982). Violent erotic materials are likely to desensitize an individual's reaction to violence (Bandura, 1978) and thus might promote a propensity to sexually assault through imitation (Ellis, 1989; Flowers, 2006). Scholars have posited that violent pornographic materials often portray females as sexual objects, which in turn fosters male dominance in society. These materials offer behavioral and ideational support for actual sexual violence (Bandura, 1978; Baron & Straus, 1989; MacKinnon, 1984). Unfortunately, with the advancement of technology, pornographic materials can now be easily obtained by anyone with Internet access.

Limited, conflicting arguments have been made regarding the effects of pornography. The report from the Commission on Obscenity and Pornography (1970) concludes that the consumption of pornographic materials does not necessarily produce any measurable negative effects on sexual behavior and does not lead to the learning of sexually deviant behavior. McCormack (1978) finds similar conclusions; nevertheless, he avers that viewing violent hardcore pornographic materials does promote aggressive behavior against another individual when anger or hostility toward that specific individual is already felt prior to the consumption of the violent pornography.

In his attempt to emphasize the significance of cognitions in influencing an individual's behavioral pattern, Ellis (1989) offers four hypotheses of rape from the social learning perspective: (1) rapists hold more positive attitudes toward rape and violence in general relative to other males; (2) in contrast to the general male population, rapists exhibit more sexual arousal to depictions of rape and violence against women; (3) exposure to violent pornography enhances male tendencies to commit rape and violent conduct against females; and (4) the consumption of sadistic pornography that degrades females further enhances male propensities to subscribe to attitudes that are conducive to the commission of rape.

4.2   Routine Activity Theory

Most of the criminological theories and empirical research developed and conducted in the 1970s primarily focused on the etiological perspective of crime and on the offender's characteristics. In contrast, Cohen and Felson's (1979) routine activity theory proffers an explanation for social change and crime rate trends. As noted by Cohen and Felson (1979), "unlike many criminological inquiries, we do not examine why individuals or groups are inclined criminally, but rather we take criminal inclination as given and examine the manner in which the spatio-temporal organization of social activities helps people to translate their criminal inclinations into action" (p. 589). Their theoretical model is preceded by Hindelang, Gottfredson, and Garofalo's (1978) lifestyle/exposure theory and the work by Hawley (1950).

Cohen and Felson (1979) argue that the possibility of crime occurring in a given community or society is influenced by the convergence in space and time of three key elements in the daily routines of individuals: (a) *motivated and potential offenders*, (b) *attractive and suitable targets*, and (c) *the absence of capable guardians to protect against a violation*. The lack of any one of these elements diminishes the probability of a crime being committed (Felson & Cohen, 1980). This theoretical perspective addresses the differential risks of victimization among individuals based on their daily lifestyles. Two central hypotheses have emerged from the routine activity approach to crime: (a) a criminal-opportunity structure is created from patterns of routine activities and lifestyles through contact between a motivated offender and a suitable target and (b) the selection of a specific victim is determined by the offender's subjective value of this particular victim and his/her level of guardianship (Wittebrood & Nieuwbeerta, 2000). Petersilia (2001) further asserts that from a routine activity perspective, an individual's risk of victimization "is a function of lifestyle and/or patterns of routine activities" (p. 673). Essentially, according to Spano and Freilich (2009), the routine activity theoretical perspective has evolved into four key tenets: (a) increased guardianship reduces the likelihood of victimization and criminal behavior, (b) more attractive targets are more likely to be victimized, (c) participation in deviant lifestyles increases the likelihood of victimization and criminal behavior (which is embedded in the "attractive target" concept), and (d) greater exposure to potential offenders increases the probability of victimization and criminal offending.

A body of literature on the early years of the routine activity theory has focused primarily on the structural level (macrolevel) of analysis. This literature tends to categorize the structural opportunity into three theoretical elements: motivated offenders, suitable targets, and guardianship (Stein, 2010). Since its theoretical development, Cohen and Felson's (1979) original macro-based (structural-level) theoretical framework has evolved over the years to explain criminal events at the macro-level and has also been tested using a micro-level approach (e.g., Arnold, Keane, & Baron, 2005; Bernburg & Thorlindsson, 2001; Birkbeck & LaFree, 1993; Casten & Payne, 2008; Felson, 1986; Gaetz, 2004; Holt & Bossler, 2009; Kennedy & Forde, 1990; Lynch, 1987; Marcum, Ricketts, & Higgins, 2010; Miethe & Meier, 1990; Mustaine & Tewksbury, 1999; Sacco,

Johnson, & Arnold, 1993; Sampson, 1987; Sampson & Wooldredge, 1987; Sasse, 2005; Schreck & Fisher, 2004; Spano & Nagy, 2005; Tewksbury & Mustaine, 2000) or a multilevel approach (e.g., Stein, 2010; Tseloni & Farrell, 2002; van Wilsem, de Graff, & Wittebrood, 2003). The studies that focus on the individual level of analysis are likely to incorporate measures of activities (e.g., going out for leisure) and demographic characteristics that capture lifestyles (Stein, 2010). For instance, the actual routines of individuals indicate that individuals who go to bars, work, or school are at an increased risk of victimization (Arnold et al., 2005; Kennedy & Forde, 1990). In addition, the individuals whose activities take place outside of their home are likely to increase their chances of being exposed to potential offenders, to present themselves as suitable targets, and to often be perceived as lacking capable guardianship (Gaetz, 2004; Messner & Blau, 1987; Spano & Nagy, 2005; Tewksbury & Mustaine, 2000). A cautious interpretation is advised because not all of the findings on these measures of activities from an individual level are consistent across all of the empirical studies. Regardless of this inconsistency, on the basis of the relevant literature, the routine activity theory has support on both the macro- and micro-levels (Marcum et al., 2010; Reynald, 2010; Spano & Freilich, 2009).

Undeniably, crime is not a random occurrence in society (Lunde, 1976). The victim selection process involves a rational decision (Hough, 1987). Offenders typically target victims who meet a set of criteria that holds special significance for them (Bourdreaux, Lord, & Jarvis, 2001; Canter, 1989) and who lack adequate protection at that given moment (Hough, 1987). To a great extent, the vulnerability of becoming a victim is associated with the individual's specific daily activities, lifestyle, and status (Mustaine & Tewksbury, 2002; Tewksbury & Mustaine, 2001). The offender's behavior is assumed to be both repetitive and predictable (Cohen & Felson, 1979; Kennedy & Forde, 1990).

Guardianship, from the routine activity perspective, is simply defined as a formal or informal social control mechanism that restricts the availability and accessibility of an attractive target (Cohen & Felson, 1979; Cohen, Kluegel, & Land, 1981). In Felson's (1995) words, a guardian is anyone or anything that "serves by simple presence to prevent crime and by absence to make crime more likely" (p. 53). Not all guardians are aware of their influence on the occurrence of a criminal event. Guardians may engage in guardianship activities unknowingly or unintentionally (Hollis-Peel, Reynald, van Bavel, Elffers, & Welsh, 2011; Spano & Nagy, 2005). Often, it is the mere presence of an individual that serves to deter the likely offender from committing a crime against a potential target.

Research has further broken down guardianship into three subtypes, which are often referred to as "controllers": handlers, managers, and guardians (Felson, 1995; Felson & Boba, 2010; Sampson, Eck, & Dunham, 2010; Tillyer & Eck, 2011). Handlers are the supervisors of potential offenders who generally have an emotional attachment to the would-be offenders (e.g., parents, schoolteachers, employers), whereas managers are the supervisors of potential settings or places for criminal events (e.g., the owners of places, the owners' representatives at these places; Sampson et al., 2010). Guardians are described as individuals who keep an eye on the potential target of a crime, whether that target is a person or an object (Felson, 2006). Sampson et al. (2010) indicate that "guardians are highly varied" (p. 39). According to Felson and Boba (2010), these three subtypes are interconnected in terms of their influence on whether the crime can be completed: "the offender moves away from handlers toward a place without a manager and a target without a guardian" (p. 30).

Taken together, these findings indicate that victimization is most likely to occur when individuals (a) are positioned in high-risk situations, (b) are in close proximity to motivated offenders, (c) appear to be attractive targets, and (d) lack a capable guardian (Cohen & Felson, 1979; Felson, 2008). Likewise, individuals who are involved in criminal conduct are at an increased risk of victimization as they increase both their proximity to other motivated offenders and the propensity to retaliate; they also reduce social guardianship by associating with other crime-prone individuals (Bossler, Holt, & May, 2012; Jensen & Brownfield, 1986; Lauritsen, Laub, & Sampson, 1992; Zhang, Welte, & Wiecxorek, 2001). Therefore, the routine activity approach to crime can account for both victimization and crime because victims frequently report higher levels of criminal behavior than nonvictims and usually share similar demographic characteristics with the offenders (Jensen & Brownfield, 1986).

4.2.1   Sex-Related Offenses: A Routine Activity Theory Perspective

Constructs relevant to the routine activity approach have long been heavily examined in relation to a wide variety of violent and property offenses. Among others, sex-related offenses have received tremendous attention, particularly within the last decade (Belknap, 1987; Cass, 2007; De Coste, Estes, & Mueller, 1999; Deslauriers-Varin & Beauregard, 2010; Fox & Sobol, 2000; Mustaine & Tewksbury, 2002; Schwartz & Pitts, 1995; Schwartz, DeKeseredy, Tait, & Alvi, 2001; Sherley, 2005; Tewksbury & Mustaine, 2001; Tewksbury, Mustaine, & Stengel, 2008).

Most of these studies utilize a micro-level approach to analyze the role of individual lifestyle behaviors and routine activities on the determination of victimization risk. The victimization risk or target suitability is regarded as the most tested tenet of the routine activity theory in studies of sex-related offenses, especially in the college population. According to Presley (1997), annual victimization research indicates that one in every 20 college students has reported at least one incident of forced sexual touching, while one in every 25 college students has reported at least one incident of forced sexual intercourse.

From a routine activity perspective, lifestyle behaviors and statuses (i.e., healthy or unhealthy ways of life) are pertinent to determining the risk of sexual victimization. Of particular note, college students who are on campus are likely to suffer a higher victimization risk due to their frequent and close proximity to potential offenders and the absence of capable guardianship (Cass, 2007; Mustaine & Tewksbury, 2002; Sampson & Lauritsen, 1990; Schwartz & DeKeseredy, 1997). Fernandez and Lizotte (1995) find that the number of students enrolled on campus is positively correlated with the reported sexual assault rate on campus. This phenomenon can likely be attributed to the college setting creating a geographical clustering of potential victims. Additionally, an increased number of leisure activities, especially during the nighttime, has been found to be a significant determinant of the victimization risks of sexual assault for college females due to the increased chance of the females being exposed to likely offenders when there is minimal effective guardianship (Mustaine & Tewksbury, 2002). Female college students who are highly involved in campus life through participation in numerous clubs or organizations have a higher level of exposure to others who may be potential offenders (Mustaine & Tewksbury, 2002) than women who are less involved; for instance, females who are involved in fraternity activities (i.e., college Greek membership) have a higher likelihood of being in close proximity to Greek men who hold attitudes supportive of sexual assault, particularly in settings with alcohol (Boeringer, 1996; Martin & Hummer, 1993).

The college "culture of alcohol" – regular public alcohol consumption and drug use – is also likely to increase the risk of victimization (Abbey, Ross, & McDuffie, 1996; Felson, 1997; Fisher, Cullen, & Turner, 2000; Mustaine & Tewksbury, 2002; Sampson & Lauritsen, 1990; Schwartz & Pitts, 1995; Schwartz et al., 2001; Sherley, 2005; Testa & Livingston, 2000; Tewksbury & Mustaine, 2001; Tewksbury et al., 2008; Vogel & Himelein, 1995). College students who are in a lower state of awareness due to alcohol and/or drug consumption are likely to be perceived as vulnerable targets by would-be offenders. Specifically, while intoxicated, engaging in self-protective behaviors is difficult. In the case of sexual victimization, intoxicated individuals are perceived as sexually available (Tyler, Hoyt, & Whitbeck, 1998). Alternatively, Mustaine and Tewksbury (1998) find that college students who use extra protective measures (e.g., extra locks on doors, owning a dog) are less likely to be victimized.

4.3   Single Theory Explanations of Sexual Homicide

As noted by Chan and colleagues (2011), the tenets of both the social learning theory and the routine activity theory can be used independently to explain the occurrence of sexual homicide.[1] However, similar to other studies that criticize the applicability of a single theoretical model in explaining crime and delinquency (Cohen, 1962; Elliott, Huizinga, & Ageton, 1985; Glueck, 1956; Glueck & Glueck, 1950; Hirschi & Selvin, 1967; Sutherland, 1924; Tittle, 1985, 1989), Chan and colleagues argue that the application of only one theory to explain sexual homicide limits the potential to offer a complete depiction of this type of incident (see Bernard,, 2001; Bernard & Ritti, 1990; Bernard & Snipes, 1996; Gibbs, 1972 for a discussion on the limitations of the presence of multiple single theories that undermine the role of theory as a way of organizing theoretical ideas to advance research).[2]

According to Tittle (1995), the causal processes of crime and delinquency may be more complicated than the explanations offered by a single criminological theory (see also Elliott, 1985). The causes of crime and delinquency are too complex and diverse to fit within a single theoretical perspective, much less a single theory (Bernard & Snipes, 1996). Elliott (1985) asserts that a large number of tests of theories document small statistical significance with uncertain substantive meaning. Hence, it is not unexpected to find that many of these theories account for only a little of the crime and delinquency variance they explain (Elliott, 1985; Tittle, 1995).

For decades, scholars have posited that an integrative theoretical approach can better elucidate the causation mechanisms of delinquent or criminal conduct by combining different theories at either a single level or different levels (e.g., Agnew, 2003; Elliott, Ageton, & Canter, 1979; Thornberry, 1987). The objective of theory integration is to unify theory into comprehensive explanations that have greater explanatory power than individual constituent theories (Farnworth, 1989). Integrated theories generally involve only a single-level (micro-level or macro-level) explanation of crime and delinquency. Nevertheless, cross-level integration that offers explanations that incorporate both micro-level (individual process) and macro-level (social structural process) social influences on crime and delinquency is not uncommon (Akers, 1968, 1973, 1992, 1998; Bernard & Snipes, 1996; Elliott, 1985; Groves & Lynch, 1990; Hagan, 1989; Pearson & Weiner, 1985; Reiss, 1986; Sampson, 1985; Short, 1979, 1985, 1989; Sutherland, 1939, 1947; Tittle, 1985).

With regard to theoretical integration, the social learning theory is one of the widely used theories integrated with or incorporated into other theoretical concepts or propositions to provide more comprehensive explanations of crime and delinquency (Verill, 2005). Over the years, there have been numerous attempts to integrate other theoretical elements with social learning theoretical concepts; these theoretical elements include integrated elements from such theories as social learning and control theories (Akers & Lee, 1999; Krohn, 1986; Thornberry, 1987); social learning, control, and labeling theories (Braithwaite, 1989); social learning, control, and rational choice theories (Tittle, 1995); and social learning, control, and strain theories (Akers & Cochran, 1985; Elliott et al., 1985; Hoffman, 2003).

In addition, some scholars claim that the concepts of social learning theory overlap with several other theories and that these alternative theories' concepts and propositions are special cases of the social learning concepts. The examples of such theories are control, self-control, deterrence, labeling, anomie or strain, normative conflict, economic, rational choice, routine activity, neutralization, and relative deprivation theories (Akers, 1973, 1977, 1985, 1989, 1990, 1998; Pearson & Weiner, 1985). It is interesting to note that in most of the integrated theories that incorporate social learning concepts, the social learning constructs typically yield the strongest effect (Conger, 1976; Elliott et al., 1985; Johnson, Marcos, & Bahr, 1987; Lanza-Kaduce & Klug, 1986; Lewis, Sims, & Shannon, 1989; Marcos, Bahr, & Johnson, 1986; Thornberry, Lizotte, Krohn, Farnworth, & Jang, 1994; White & LaGrange, 1987; see also Kaplan, Martin, & Robbins, 1984; Michaels & Miethe, 1989).

In light of the support for the aforementioned theoretical integration, Chan et al. (2011) adopt an integrative theoretical approach by combining all of the factors explicated in both the social learning and the routine activity theories to explain the offending perspective of sexual homicide. Chan et al. (2011) assert that the use of an integrative approach to comprehend the sexual homicide offending phenomenon is likely to explain more of the offending variance than any one theory on its own (see Barak, 1998; Hirschi, 1989). Prior to discussing

Chan et al.'s (2011) integrative model, a review of the existing literature on sexual homicide and related topics using the tenets of the social
learning and the routine activity theories, respectively, is provided in
the following sections.

4.3.1   Explanations of Sexual Homicide from the Social Learning Perspective

Consistent with the literature on the behavioral learning process of
sexual offenders, SHOs consistently grow up in abusive domestic environments. This literature indicates that SHOs usually either suffer from
childhood or adolescence physical and/or sexual abuse by their parents
and/or primary caregivers or witness such incidents (Beauregard,
Stone, Proulx, & Michaud, 2008; Burgess, Hartman, Ressler, Douglas,
& McCormack, 1986; Chan & Heide, 2009; Cicchett & Lynch, 1995;
Dent & Jowitt, 2003; Heide, Beauregard, & Myers, 2009; Hickey,
2002; Langevin, Ben-Aron, Wright, Marchese, & Handy, 1988; Lussier,
Beauregard, Proulx, & Nicole, 2005; Meloy, 2000; Myers, 2004; Myers,
Burgess, & Nelson, 1998; Ressler, Burgess, & Douglas, 1988; Ressler,
Burgess, Douglas, Hartman, & D'Agostino, 1986; Ressler, Burgess,
Hartman, Douglas, & McCormack, 1986; Stone, 2001). Accordingly, this
unhealthy parent-child relationship often leads to insecure parent-child
attachment (Cicchetti & Lynch, 1995; Hickey, 2002; Meloy, Gacono,
& Kenney, 1994). Similarly, the studies on stalkers – offenders whose
common behaviors share similarities with those of sexual killers – also
report that early childhood trauma associated with insecure parent-child
attachment, parental rejection, and/or domestic violence is common
(Bartholomew, 1990; Kienlen, Birmingham, Solberg, O'Regan, & Meloy,
1997; Main, 1996; Meloy, 1996, 1997; Spitzberg & Cupach, 2003).

Generally, the parents of violent offenders who are involved in
deviant sexual and homicidal conduct often have histories of violent
behavior, alcohol and/or drug abuse, and psychiatric and sexual problems (Burgess et al., 1986; Dent & Jowitt, 2003; Ressler et al., 1988; Stone,
2001). Particularly, the inadequate sexual behavior of parents or other
caretakers has largely been linked with the aggressive acts of abused and
psychologically unhealthy children who experience or witness domestic
violence (Burgess et al., 1986) through *differential associations*. Burgess
and colleagues (1986) confirm that most of the deviant sexual attitudes
(or *definitions* from the social learning theoretical perspective) in their
sample of 36 sexual murderers are initially introduced through modeling by either their parents or primary caregivers during childhood. The
literature is consistent in finding that the percentage of sexual killers

who experience childhood or adolescence physical and/or sexual abuse and other types of family violence is very high, ranging from 86% to 94% (Ressler, Burgess, Hartman, et al., 1986; Myers, 2004; Myers et al., 1998). According to Ressler et al. (1986), the physical and/or sexual victimization experienced at home is strongly correlated with the development of sexual deviations or traits of psychosexual disorders. The examples of such sexual deviations are deviant and sadistic fantasies (Dietz, Hazelwood, & Warren, 1990; Eth & Pynoos, 1985; Jackson, Lee, Pattison, & Ward, 2002) and paraphilic behaviors (Arrigo & Purcell, 2001; Hickey, 2002; Stone, 2001).

On the basis of the literature, the SHOs who indulge in deviant fantasies are more likely to premeditate their offense. In most cases, the SHOs' primary motives for perpetrating sexual offenses include obtaining sadistic psychological gratification or sexual euphoria via their expression of power and/or anger as a need to dominate, punish, control, humiliate, degrade, and torture their victims (Chan & Heide, 2009; Cook & Hinman, 1999; Hazelwood & Warren, 2000; Hickey, 2002; Langevin et al., 1988; McNamara & Morton, 2004; Meloy, 2000; Myers, 2002; Myers, Eggleston, & Smoak, 2003; Myers, Husted, Safarik, & O'Toole, 2006; Ressler, Burgess, Hartman, et al., 1986; Salfati, James, & Ferguson, 2008). From the *differential reinforcement* viewpoint, positive reinforcement results from the acting out of deviant sexual fantasies that culminates in sexual orgasm. This operant conditioning process increases behavioral habituation and escalation, which, in turn, leads to the repetitive behavior of sexual killing.

It is noteworthy that the experience of abuse and the development of deviant sexual fantasies during childhood or adolescence are congruent with the attachment model of the development of sexual deviance (Marshall, 1993; Ward, Hudson, Marshall, & Siegert, 1995). According to Marshall (1993), attachment refers to the parent-child bonding that provides the necessary security and confidence a child needs to explore his/her social world. The experience of negative childhood disturbances such as physical and/or sexual abuse may thwart the development of a secure parent-child attachment (Cicchetti & Lynch, 1995; Heide & Solomon, 2006, 2009). Consequently, the psychosocial deficits such as low self-esteem and the lack of the essential social skills required to establish a healthy relationship with peers may develop (Marshall, Hudson, & Hodkinson, 1993).

As a result of the difficulty in relating to peers, individuals seek alternative ways to fulfill emotional and sexual needs that do not challenge these psychosocial deficits. Among these alternative ways, sexually assaultive behavior seems appealing because it requires little self-confidence and social skill and can offer the illusion of intimacy without the fear of being rejected (Marshall & Eccles, 1993; see, for example, Bushman, Baumeister, Thomaes, Ryu, Begeer, & West, 2009; Diamantopoulou, Rydell, & Henricsson, 2008 for discussions on where both low and high self-esteem can be related to aggressive behavior). According to Law and Marshall (1990), this behavior can be "learned" through a social learning process by being exposed to, or being a victim of, sexual abuse. Deviant sexual fantasies can be paired with orgasm to create a conditioning process, and these scripted sexual deviant actions can then be used during masturbatory activities for sexual gratification (Abel & Blanchard, 1974; McGuire, Carlisle, & Young, 1965).

The research also indicates that alcohol is a disinhibiting factor in a sexual assault (Barbaree, Marshall, Yates, & Lightfoot, 1983; Marshall & Barbaree, 1990). On the basis of their state-disinhibition model, Barbaree and Marshall (1991) posit that situational and contextual factors (i.e., consumption of alcohol and the viewing of pornography) may enhance the sexual aggressors' rape arousal, thus facilitating sexual assaultive actions. These circumstantial constructs may influence the occurrence of a sexual assault through the disruption of stimulus inhibition. Put differently, situational constructs are able to temporarily disrupt an individual's level of self-control over sexual and aggressive propensities and accentuate the risk of a sexual assault. Consistent with the state-disinhibition model, a number of recent sexual offender studies also find a positive relationship between the use of alcohol and (a) the level of force exerted by the offender and (b) the level of injury inflicted on the victim (Beauregard, Lussier, & Proulx, 2005; Ouimet, Guay, & Proulx, 2000).

According to the *imitation* tenet from the social learning standpoint, sexually aggressive parents or primary caregivers are the key role models for their children in terms of shaping their sexually deviant attitudes and behavioral patterns into future sexual homicides. Additionally, sadistic pornography is likely to have an impact on those who sexually assault and murder. Studies report that a high percentage of SHOs (ranging from 39% to 81%), both sadistic and nonsadistic, collect and consume violent pornographic materials (Brittain, 1970; Grubin, 1994; Langevin, 2003; Ressler, Burgess, Hartman, et al., 1986). These high percentages indicate the devastating impact of sexual killers imitating the sadistic acts depicted in violent pornography.

Broadly speaking, the developmental risk factors discussed in this section from the social learning standpoint are not limited to sexual murderers. According to Heide (1992, 1999, 2003, 2013), family dysfunction and parental pathology are also frequently reported in studies examining violent offenders and nonsexual murderers. Even more notably, homicidal and nonhomicidal sex offenders, in general, share many characteristics with respect to poor parenting. In a Canadian comparative study of 101 sexual aggressors and 40 SHOs, for example, no significant differences between the two groups are found in terms of exposure to deviant and antisocial models of attitudes and behaviors (Proulx, Beauregard, Cusson, & Nicole, 2007). More than half of the offenders in each group report to having been exposed to psychological violence and abusive alcohol consumption prior to the age of 18. In addition, approximately half of the offenders in both groups experienced physical violence as juveniles.

Even though both homicidal and nonhomicidal sex offenders do not present diametrically opposed developmental trajectories, it is logical to assume that they can be distinguished from one another on the basis of the degree of the severity of their developmental disturbance (Nicole & Proulx, 2007). A question remains: Why did some of the offenders in the Canadian study murder, whereas others did not? It seems that the social learning perspective of criminal behavior is able to offer part of the answer, and the routine activity theory also helps to explain the differences between the lethal and nonlethal outcomes in crimes committed by sex offenders.

4.3.2 Explanations of Sexual Homicide from the Routine Activity Perspective

Most of the routine activity theoretical studies on sex-related offenses focus on the victimization risks; no study has attempted to examine the offending process from this theoretical perspective (Chan et al., 2011). This is partly because the routine activity theory has traditionally been viewed as a "victimization" theory. However, Chan et al. (2011) argued that this theoretical model is versatile and can be used to explain offending behavior as well as victimization. It can be used to elucidate both why certain victims are selected and why certain offenders target certain victims at particular places and times (Graney & Arrigo, 2002). Put differently, the routine activity theory can be useful in understanding both the offenders' and the victims' perspectives.

It is imperative to note that the routine activity model assumes a motivated offender without offering further explanation on how an individual learns to become a motivated offender. For decades, researchers who examined the sexual fantasy of SHOs believed that sexual fantasy plays a vital role in the motivation to kill in many sexual murders (e.g.,

Britain, 1970; Chan & Heide, 2009; Grubin, 1994; Prentky et al., 1989). The routine activity point of view does not address the development of sexual fantasy, mainly because it is beyond the scope of this theoretical framework.

Broadly speaking, the sexual fantasies of sexual murderers usually involve repetitive acts of sexual violence (Burgess et al., 1986; Warren, Hazelwood, & Dietz, 1996), which primarily serve to fulfill or alleviate sexual frustration (Langevin, Lang, & Curnoe, 1998). For sexual murderers, sexual fantasy is a frequent resource for sexual arousal. Studies find that many SHOs who are *motivated* to sexually assault and murder their victims fulfill their deviant sexual fantasies through highly planned sex killings (Burgess et al., 1986; Langevin, 2003; Warren et al., 1996) once their inhibitions about executing their sexual fantasies no longer exist (e.g., techniques of neutralization; Prentky et al., 1989).

The fantasies are apt to strengthen over time, and as they do, the urge to fulfill them in reality becomes more likely and driven (Hill, Habermann, Berner, & Briken, 2007; Prentky et al., 1989; MacCulloch, Snowden, Wood, & Mills, 1983). The findings suggest that the acting out of deviant sexual fantasies is probably due to the locating of an outlet for unexpressed emotional states such as humiliation, rage, and suffering (Myers et al., 2006; Proulx, McKibben, & Lusignan, 1996). The acting out of deviant sexual fantasies is likely to happen after an extended period of emotional retreat into a fantasy world. This retreat results in emotional loneliness and social isolation due to the lack of healthy intimate heterosexual relationships (Arrigo & Purcell, 2001; Grubin, 1994; Harbot & Mokros, 2001; Marshall, 1989; Ressler et al., 1988).

According to the second tenet, *target suitability and attractiveness*, an offense is less likely to occur if there is no suitable target for the motivated offender. In sexual homicides, sexually motivated offenders often initiate their "hunt" for suitable targets (Amir, 1971) who satisfy the "goodness of fit" with their deviant sexual fantasies (Meloy, 2000). Often, these motivated offenders create a "mental map" of neighborhoods when they spot potentially suitable targets (Rossmo, 1999). Engaging in stalking and/or voyeuristic behavior during their hunt for suitable targets is a vital component in mental mapping among sexual killers.

Aside from repetitively assessing their would-be targets' accessibility and vulnerability in the course of their daily routines (Boudreaux et al., 2001), the search for a perpetration opportunity in the absence of detection and deterrence is also another important factor for sexually motivated murderers in planning their sex killings. In their study, Chan and

Heide (2008) find that among the four types of victims (children, adolescents, adults, and elderly victims), children and elderly victims appear to be the most vulnerable targets because of their less advantaged physical build or makeup and their physical strength in comparison to the perpetrator. Elderly female victims, especially those who are widows, are more likely to live alone and away from any immediate capable guardian. Therefore, this living arrangement increases their risk of becoming suitable targets (Safarik, Jarvis, & Nussbaum, 2002). The sex killers of children, on the other hand, are likely to prey on their victims in locations where the would-be targets gather (e.g., schools, playgrounds, convenience stores, and shopping centers). In most situations, these motivated offenders patiently wait for an abduction opportunity when their targets' *guardianship is weak or reduced* (i.e., parents or school teachers walk away and leave the children alone for a short moment; Beauregard et al., 2008; Beauregard, Proulx, & St-Yves, 2007).

Nevertheless, both child and elderly victims may also be perceived as the least vulnerable targets according to the routine activity theoretical standpoint. Due to the nature of their age and common lifestyle, children and elderly individuals are less likely than average adults to be exposed to would-be perpetrators during the nighttime because these individuals are less likely to leave their homes (Chan et al., 2011). Rather, adolescent and adult males and females who routinely go out at night and those who frequent bars or nightclubs would appear to be at greater risk of being victimized than children and elderly individuals.

4.3.3 Limitations of Single Theory Explanations of Sexual Homicide

The routine activity theoretical perspective of criminal behavior is able to explicate the dynamics of the offending process of sexual murderers. Simply put, the routine activity theory focuses on the situational opportunity created from the structural relationships of different social groups. The primary emphasis of this theoretical model is placed on the situational opportunity for a motivated offender to come into contact with a suitable target in the absence of a capable guardian or guardianship.

However, from the sexual homicide study viewpoint, this theoretical framework limits itself to the situational constructs that fail to address the important issues on an individual basis (micro-level). No proposition is given in this theoretical model to elucidate how an individual becomes motivated to commit a sexual offense and to murder (Chan et al., 2011). According to Chan and colleagues (2011), the applicability of the routine activity theory in explaining the offending perspective of sexual homicide can be strengthened by combining it with another more micro-based theory that could account for the missing piece of the puzzle.

In this sense, the social learning theory has great potential to fill the gap by offering justification for the core element of the "motivated offender" proposition in the routine activity theory. The social learning perspective is capable of predicting the type of behavioral learning atmosphere that is conducive to crime commission. In addition, this theory is also able to answer the question of why one individual might become more likely than another to commit a sexual murder, particularly against a vulnerable target in unprotected surroundings, in the presence of certain conditions (Chan et al., 2011).

The social learning theory by itself is incapable of predicting under what circumstances sexually deviant individuals will or will not commit a sexual homicide. The routine activity perspective is able to overcome this deficiency by explicating the situational opportunity piece of the puzzle. To illustrate, the routine activity model is useful for clarifying the odds of a sexual homicide being committed by a motivated offender upon weighing up the pros and cons of the opportunities to offend (Chan et al., 2011). On the one hand, a motivated offender's opportunities to commit an offense on an attractive target in the absence of an effective guardian or guardianship are likely to yield higher rewards than costs. Conversely, in the absence of a suitable target or in the presence of a capable guardian or guardianship, the commission of an offense, even by a motivated offender, would probably result in higher costs than rewards.

5
Sexual Homicide Offending: Toward an Integrative Theoretical Explanation

5.1 Chan, Heide, and Beauregard's integrated theory of the offending perspective of sexual homicide

With extensive support from the literature on sexual homicide and sex-related offenses, Chan and colleagues (2011) propose arguably the first integrated criminological theory of the offending perspective of sexual homicide by applying the tenets of both the social learning and the routine activity theories. According to Chan et al. (2011), the individual-level view of sexual murderers is elucidated by the social learning principles, while the situational-level view of the offending process is complemented by the routine activity propositions to provide a better model of offending for understanding sexual homicide. Simply put, this theoretical framework proposes to explain the processes whereby an individual becomes motivated to sexually murder; decides to sexually murder; and acts on that desire, intention, and opportunity.

5.1.1 The pre-dispositional factors: the motivated offender

According to this integrative model, psychologically unhealthy development during childhood and adolescence plays a vital role in shaping a future road to murder, both sexual and nonsexual (Chan et al., 2011). More importantly, a large majority of SHOs are reported to have grown up in a dysfunctional home environment.

5.1.1.1 Differential Association, Definitions, Differential Reinforcement or Punishment, and Imitation

Childhood and adolescence experiences of physical and/or sexual abuse or witnessing domestic violence are common within this sexual predator population. Through their direct and/or indirect associations with individuals with whom they have shared close and intimate relationships since childhood, these SHOs become involved in a strong process of learning deviant behavior. Over an extended period of time of frequent and intense exposure to various deviant and aggressive attitudes, these pro-offending values and attitudes are embedded into their minds and become part of their own belief system. The attitudes and behaviors conducive to sexual offending are typically learned via two primary ways: (a) through interaction with primary social groups and (b) through the emulation of the primary role models' behavior. Remarkably, in terms of sexually deviant behaviors and attitudes, parents and primary caregivers are potentially the most important sources of role modeling for these individuals, especially during childhood and adolescence. Interestingly, according to the literature, most sexual murderers' parents have criminal backgrounds and/or previous sexual violence experiences (Chan et al., 2011). As long as these deviant sexually conducive behaviors are positively reinforced and promote positive feelings, they are likely to be repeated, with the potential for escalation and habituation.

In addition to direct behavioral imitation of those in their primary social groups during childhood and adolescence, SHOs are also tremendously influenced by reference groups such as the media. Amongst others, the consumption of violent (and sadistic) pornographic materials is a factor in sex killings, especially prior to the offense (Chan et al., 2011). It is noteworthy that according to the literature, a large number of SHOs admit to having a great interest in violent (and sadistic) pornography, which appears in part to compensate for their emotional loneliness and social isolation rooted in their domestically abusive environment. To illustrate, because these individuals suffer violence at home during their childhood and adolescence, they are likely to retreat into their own deviant sexual fantasy world to achieve some degree of control and mood regulation. These probable outcomes of deviant sexual fantasies are likely to function as positive reinforcers, which in turn encourage them to return to their fantasy world for pleasure.

5.1.2 The situational factors: an attractive and suitable target and the absence of a capable guardian

However, once the mere indulgence in deviant sexual fantasies is insufficient to produce the expected sexual euphoria, these individuals begin to seek alternatives. The acting out of their deviant sexual fantasies is one of the best methods for these individuals to achieve anticipated outcomes to satisfy their psychological desires. Prior to perpetrating their crime, they are likely to develop a set of criteria in their search for suitable targets. During their hunt for suitable and attractive targets, they may mentally map their targeted neighborhood by way of their stalking and voyeuristic behavior in order to maximize the probability of capturing and abducting their targeted victims successfully. These offenders wait for the opportunity to perpetrate their crime against their targets when the guardianship of the immediate surroundings is weak or absent.

The mental mapping associated with the search for suitable targets is typically carried out via the routine activities of the offender. Commonly, the offender is constantly on the lookout for potential targets as he/she goes to and from work and as he/she engages in leisure activities. The probability of a victim being targeted and ultimately captured increases when the offender's routine activities intersect with those of this potential victim. Here is a scenario provided by Chan et al. (2011):

> An individual drinks to quell social anxiety that he feels because of negative childhood experiences. Drinking helps him to feel more powerful, to interact more easily with women, and to feel more sexual. If this individual regularly frequent bars because he is a regular drinker, he is more likely to select a victim at a bar. Many scenarios are possible. Perhaps, the encounter starts off as flirting and the woman eventually leaves the bar with the offender to go to a quieter, more secluded area "to talk." The man wants sex; the woman does not. The man becomes aggressive in his pursuit of sex. The violence escalates. Whether intended from the onset of the exchange or not, the man kills the woman. (p. 239)

Once their targets are captured, if the offenders are so motivated, various paraphilic and ritualistic behaviors (e.g., necrophilia, genitalia mutilation) may be performed on their victims prior to and/or after the killing in order to achieve maximum sexual gratification. Most of these paraphilic and ritualistic behaviors, in conjunction with their deviant sexual fantasies, are repetitive behaviors that reinforce reoffending unless these offenders are stopped by the legal authorities (Arrigo & Purcell, 2001; Holmes & Holmes, 2001). Provided that situational factors permit, serial offending is not uncommon in sexual murderers.

5.2   A revised model of Chan et al.'s integrated theory

The integrated model proposed by Chan and colleagues (2011) is a preliminary one. Their theoretical framework is primarily developed by using the findings from empirical studies on sexual homicide. No empirical test has been attempted on this model; therefore, its validity and reliability in explaining the offending process of SHOs have yet to be established. In light of the potential for unexplained variance, a revised theoretical model with the inclusion of pre-crime precipitating factors is proffered to better explain the sexual homicide offending phenomenon.

5.2.1   The additional motivating factors: the pre-crime precipitators

Recent empirical studies on sexual homicide, mostly conducted by Beauregard and colleagues, demonstrate that pre-crime precipitating factors, especially within the 48 hours prior to the offense, influence sexual offenders, including HSOs (i.e., SHOs), to commit a sexual offense (e.g., Beauregard & Proulx, 2002, 2007; Beauregard, Proulx, et al., 2007; Beauregard, Stone, et al., 2008; Mieczkowski & Beauregard, 2010). These pre-crime precipitators, similar to the criminal event perspective proposed by Mieczkowski and Beauregard (2010), include drug and/or alcohol consumption, pornography consumption, indulgence in deviant sexual fantasies, conflicts related to interpersonal relationships, and sexual problems. Simply put, in addition to the pre-dispositional and situational factors hypothesized in Chan et al.'s (2011) theoretical framework, the pre-crime precipitators are posited to have an effect on making the offender become (more) "motivated" to commit a sexual homicide.

5.3   Empirical evidence: tests of Chan et al.'s original and revised integrative theoretical models

An empirical test of Chan et al.'s (2011) original model examines the effects of social learning (individual-level) and routine activity (situational-level) elements on the offending process in sexual homicide. Drawing on the above discussion, despite the lack of conclusive findings, three key hypotheses are proposed:

1. Sexual homicide offenders[1] who grow up in an abusive domestic environment (i.e., experienced physical and/or sexual abuse by their parents and/or primary caregivers or witnessed domestic violence) are more likely to be *differentially associated*, directly or indirectly, with sexually deviant *definitions* (attitudes, beliefs, values, and norms) that later influence their behavioral learning process than non-homicidal sexual offenders with a similar background.

2. Compared with those of non-homicidal sexual offenders, the sexually deviant *definitions* (i.e., learned through behavioral conditioning of *differential reinforcement or punishment* for sexual responses to any stimulus that promotes positive feelings and *imitation* of inappropriate and culturally prohibited sexual role models) of sexual homicide offenders long embedded since adolescence are more likely to subsequently increase their likelihood of becoming *motivated offenders* predisposed to committing sexual offenses.

3. Sexual homicide offenders who are motivated to commit a sexual offense are more likely than non-homicidal sexual offenders to perpetrate their crime in the presence of an *attractive and suitable target*, coupled with *the absence of an effective and capable guardian or guardianship* in the immediate surroundings to protect against a violation.

As aforementioned and displayed in Figure 5.1, Point (A) reflects the principal social learning theoretical concept that sexually deviant behavior is expected to be learned through differential association, definitions, differential reinforcement or punishment, and imitation (Akers, 1985, 2001), which explains how an individual becomes motivated to commit sexual offenses, especially sexual homicide, as posited by Chan et al. (2011). Point (B) signifies the theoretical assumptions set forth in the routine activity theory (Cohen & Felson, 1979; Felson, 2008), whereby the probability of an offense occurring in a given community or society is strongly influenced by the convergence in space and time of a motivated offender, an attractive and suitable target, and the absence of a capable guardian.

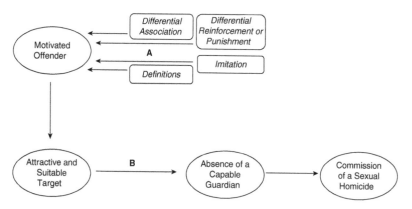

Figure 5.1 Chan et al.'s (2011) social learning-routine activity integrative model of the offending process in sexual homicide

Besides examining Chan et al.'s (2011) original integrative theoretical model, a revised model with the inclusion of the pre-crime precipitating factors as potential motivators for the offender to commit sexual homicide is tested. This revised model is presented in Figure 5.2. In addition to Chan et al.'s (2011) proposed integrative model, Point (B) indicates the potential effect that the pre-crime precipitating factors have on the motivated offender in hunting for an attractive and suitable target for a sex killing (Beauregard & Proulx, 2007; Beauregard, Proulx, et al., 2007; Beauregard, Stone, et al., 2008; Mieczkowski & Beauregard, 2010). Despite the lack of conclusive comparative findings in the literature, a directional hypothesis is set forth in the present empirical test:

1. The pre-crime precipitating factors are more likely to accelerate the motivation of sexual homicide offenders to commit a sexual offense than to accelerate the motivation of non-homicidal sexual offenders.

5.3.1   Research methodology

An empirical test is conducted to examine the suitability of the proposed integrative model theorized by Chan, Heide, and Beauregard (2011). In addition, the effects of the pre-crime precipitating factors in further motivating the offender to commit sexual homicide and to search for a suitable and attractive target, as hypothesized in the revised theoretical model, are also explored. This study uses a data set of homicidal and non-homicidal sexual offenders (NHSOs) who victimized adult females

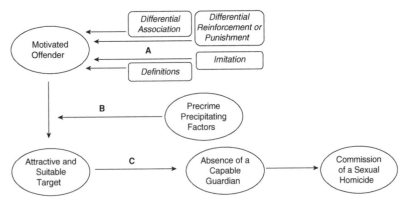

Figure 5.2   A revised model of Chan et al.'s (2011) social learning-routine activity integrative model of the offending process in sexual homicide

collected by a group of Canadian researchers (e.g., Beauregard & Field, 2008; Beauregard & Proulx, 2002, 2007; Beauregard, Proulx, et al., 2007; Beauregard, Stone, et al., 2008; Mieczkowski & Beauregard, 2010). Most importantly, this data set is selected because it contains both the individual-level (social learning theory) and situational-level (routine activity theory) variables required to test Chan et al.'s (2011) theoretical model.

5.3.1.1 *Sampling population*

This study performs a secondary analysis of the data on 230 sexual offenders who target female victims (55 homicidal and 175 non-homicidal sexual offenders). These offenders were incarcerated in a maximum security correctional institution operated by the Correctional Service of Canada in the province of Quebec between 1995 and 2005 (e.g., Beauregard & Field, 2008; Beauregard & Proulx, 2002, 2007; Beauregard, Proulx, et al., 2007; Beauregard, Stone, et al., 2008; Mieczkowski & Beauregard, 2010). The HSOs were all murderers (i.e., no individuals convicted of attempted murder were included), while the NHSOs were primarily sexual aggressors against women. For the purpose of this study, only sexual offenders who committed a murder were categorized as HSOs.

In order to qualify for this research project (e.g., Beauregard & Field, 2008; Beauregard & Proulx, 2002, 2007; Beauregard, Proulx, et al., 2007; Beauregard, Stone, et al., 2008; Mieczkowski & Beauregard, 2010), subjects who had been convicted of a homicidal sexual offense had to meet at least one of the six criteria of the definition of sexual homicide offered by Ressler et al. (1988): (a) victim's attire or lack of attire; (b) exposure of the sexual parts of the victim's body; (c) sexual positioning of the victim's body; (d) insertion of foreign objects into the victim's body cavities; (e) evidence of sexual intercourse (oral, anal, vaginal); and (f) evidence of substitute sexual activity, interest, or sadistic fantasy. All of the subjects (homicidal and non-homicidal) were males, and they had all been convicted of offenses that were non-serial in nature. The NHSOs had all been convicted of sexual assaults or sex-related crimes other than sexual homicide.

The subjects who are identified as suitable are contacted by the researchers following institutional approval. Informed consent for their participation in the research project is obtained from the subjects, and the response rate is 93%. In order to reduce the potential response distortion due to exaggeration (e.g., drug and/or alcohol use prior the offense) or minimization (e.g., consumption of pornography prior to the offense) of certain behaviors related to the offense, the subjects are promised complete confidentiality, and a guarantee is given that their information will only be used for research purposes and could not be used against them by the Correctional Service of Canada (Beauregard & Proulx, 2002; Mieczkowski & Beauregard, 2010).

5.3.1.2 Data collection procedures used by the original research team

Prior to the semi-structured interview, the institutional records of the consenting subjects were reviewed. These institutional records contain the results of the subjects' psychological and psychiatric evaluation reports and specialized tests (e.g., psychometric and phallometric assessments); their disciplinary reports, information on programs they participated in while incarcerated, their criminal records, and court transcripts (Beauregard, Proulx, et al., 2007). The reports provided by all of the police agencies are also reviewed to aid the reconstruction of the offense; some reports contain the surviving victim's statement. The autopsy reports and crime scene photographic materials provided by the homicide unit of the Montreal Urban Community Police Service (now the City of Montreal Police Service), the major crime unit of the Sûreté du Québec, and the homicide unit of the City of Quebec Police Service are also consulted (Beauregard, Proulx, et al., 2007). These reviews allow the researchers to corroborate the information given by the subjects during their semi-structured interview.

A semi-structured interview is conducted in a closed room with each subject for a period of between three to five hours, and the subjects are encouraged to talk freely. Occasionally, some interviews last for more than five hours because the subjects wish to talk about topics that are not part of the interview protocol (Beauregard, Proulx, et al., 2007). According to Mieczkowski and Beauregard (2010), a semi-structured interview is selected over other data collection methods because it allows the subjects to converse freely and at length using their own terminology and concepts. In addition, it provides the researcher the opportunity to foster a relationship of trust and confidence with the subjects in a very informal and nonthreatening environment (Bennett & Wright, 1984).

During the interview, the Computerized Questionnaire for Sexual Aggressors (CQSA; Proulx, St-Yves, & McKibben, 1994) is used to gather information on different aspects of the subject's life and criminal activities such as correctional information; pre-crime, crime, and postcrime factors; and attitudes regarding their offense, apprehension, victimology, developmental factors, and psychopathological diagnostics. Each of the subjects is interviewed by two male criminologists on the following topics: emotions (e.g., affect before, during, and after the offense), attitudes toward their offenses (e.g., admit all acts committed, negative consequences for victim, and responsibility), disinhibitors (e.g., deviant sexual fantasies, alcohol, drugs, and pornography consumption), relationship difficulties (e.g., loneliness, separation, and familial problems), occupational problems (e.g., compulsive work and loss of employment), crime phase constructs (e.g., crime scene variables and acts committed while committing the offense), and victim's characteristics.

Where a discrepancy is found between the official and the self-report data, official records are relied on due to their legitimacy and socially unbiased information. The inter-rater reliability is measured jointly by two raters (interviewers) on the basis of 16 randomly selected interviews combined with consultations of the official records. The ratings are performed independently following the interviews, which are conducted by one rater in the presence of the other. The mean kappa obtained is 0.87, indicating a very strong inter-rater agreement (Beauregard & Field, 2008; Beauregard, Proulx, et al., 2007; Mieczkowski & Beauregard, 2010).

5.3.1.3 *statistical measures*

The items selected for examination in this study as measures for (a) *a motivated offender*, (b) *an attractive and suitable target*, (c) *the absence of a capable guardian*, and (d) *pre-crime precipitating factors* are extracted from the original research project. The observed indicators for each measure are assessed using a scale format.

5.3.1.3.1   Scale 1: A motivated offender (0–19 points)

The research indicates that sexual murderers' deviant sexual and violent behavioral patterns and attitudes are learned, in part, from observations of parental aggressive attitudes and behavior and their personal experiences with family violence (i.e., physical and sexual abuse; Beauregard, Stone, et al., 2008; Heide, Beauregard, & Myers, 2009). In most cases, the parents of sexual murderers are reported as having criminal backgrounds or past experiences of committing sexual violence (Chan et al., 2011). In addition, the behaviors of close family members, such as siblings' past violent sexual and nonsexual criminal history, may also have an influence on the behaviors of sexual murderers. These familial violent and sexual victimization experiences, in turn, might encourage sexual killers to learn to use violence (sexual and/or nonsexual deviance) as their coping mechanism to promote positive feelings (Burgess, Hartman, & McCormack, 1987; Flowers, 2006; Ellis, 1989).

Because of their familial exposure to violence and sexual (and/or nonsexual) deviance since childhood, the SHOs are likely to indulge in deviant sexual fantasies and to consume violent (and sadistic) pornography as ways of compensating for their social isolation and emotional loneliness, which further strengthen their sexually deviant behaviors and attitudes (Dietz, Hazelwood, & Warren, 1990; Jackson, Lee, Pattison, & Ward, 2002). Studies report that when the mere indulgence in deviant sexual fantasies is insufficient to produce the expected sexual euphoria, sexual killers are motivated to seek a suitable target(s) to act out their deviant sexual fantasies in a set of planned actions in order to satiate their psychological gratification (Chan et al., 2011; Hill, Habermann, Berner, & Briken, 2007). Ressler et al. (1988) assert that it is the SHOs' deviant sexual fantasies that motivate them to sexually murder. Taken together, the sexual murderers' violent and deviant sexual behavioral learning since childhood or adolescence in a familial environment might play an important role in shaping their subsequent motivation to commit sexual violence, including sexual homicide.

However, several comparative studies of homicidal and non-homicidal sexual offenders (e.g., Oliver et al., 2007; Proulx et al., 2002) find no significant differences pertaining to their dysfunctional family background; specifically, both types of sex offenders are similarly likely to have been physically and sexually abused during childhood. Despite these findings, it seems to be premature to offer any conclusion at this stage on the basis of the limited empirical studies on this topic area. Nonetheless, as hypothesized in this study, it is expected that deviant domestic influences play a more critical role in motivating HSOs to commit a sexual offense than they do in motivating their non-homicidal counterparts.

The observed indicators of the motivated offender latent variable[2] are based on responses to 16 items that ask each subject about his exposure to inappropriate model(s) of sexually deviant and violent behavior at home during childhood and adolescence, experiences as a victim of family violence, consumption of pornographic materials, and sexually deviant behaviors and attitudes. Of particular note, the specific elements of social learning theory (i.e., differential association, definitions, differential reinforcement, and imitation) are not readily available in the data. Instead, there were a variety of familial factors that may reasonably represent the different aspects of the social learning theory. To reiterate, these 16 observed indicators as a measure of *a motivated offender* are not used to explicitly assess the elements of the social learning theory. There are five subscales for measuring this latent variable.

5.3.1.3.1.1   Subscale 1.1: Parental or familial aggressive and deviant sexual behaviors and attitudes (0–5 points)

(a) "Before reaching 18 years of age, the offender had been exposed to inappropriate models of psychological violence at home."

(b) "Before reaching 18 years of age, the offender had been exposed to inappropriate models of physical violence at home."

(c) "Before reaching 18 years of age, the offender had been exposed to inappropriate models of sexual promiscuity at home."

(d) "Before reaching 18 years of age, the offender had been exposed to inappropriate models of pedophilic (i.e., erotic interest in prepubescent children) or hebephilic (i.e., erotic interest in pubescent children) sexual abuse at home."

(e) "Before reaching 18 years of age, the offender had been exposed to inappropriate models of sexual attack on adult women at home."

5.3.1.3.1.2   Subscale 1.2: Parental or sibling past sexual and nonsexual criminal background (0–4 points)

(f) "One or several persons in the offender's close family (parents or siblings) had served one or several sentences for violent and nonsexual offense(s)."

(g) "One or several persons in the offender's close family (parents or siblings) had served one or several sentences for nonviolent and nonsexual offense(s)."

(h) "One or several persons in the offender's close family (parents or siblings) had served one or several sentences for sexual offense(s) with contact(s)."

(i) "One or several persons in the offender's close family (parents or siblings) had served one or several sentences for sexual offense(s) without contact but including sexual nuisance(s)."

5.3.1.3.1.3   Subscale 1.3: Victim of family violence (0–6 points)

(j) "Before reaching 18 years of age, the offender had been a victim of psychological violence at home."

(k) "Before reaching 18 years of age, the offender had been a victim of physical violence at home."

(l) "Before reaching 18 years of age, the offender had been a victim of sexual assault(s) and/or sexual contact(s) at home."

5.3.1.3.1.4   Subscale 1.4: Personal consumption of pornography (0–1 point)

(m) "The offender's consumption of pornographic movies and magazines had started at least a year prior to the index offense."

5.3.1.3.1.5   Subscale 1.5: Personal sexually deviant behaviors and attitudes (0–3 points)

(n) "The offender had indulged in deviant sexual fantasies started at least a year prior to the index offense."

(o) "The offender had engaged in compulsive masturbation."

(p) "The offender had engaged in sexual paraphilia (e.g., coprophilia, fetishism, partialism, masochism, sexual sadism, transvestism, urophilia, zoophilia)."

"No" is coded "0" and "yes" is coded "1" for subscales 1.1, 1.2, 1.4, and 1.5; and "no" is coded "0" and "yes" is coded "2" for subscale 1.3 to demonstrate the severity of personal experience as a victim of traumatic events as a motivating factor to commit a sexual offense. The *motivated offender* latent variable is measured by using a scale format (0–19 points), with more points indicating a greater motivation for the offender to commit a sexual offense.

5.3.1.3.2   Scale 2: An attractive and suitable target (0–5 points)

As shown in Figure 5.1, the *attractive and suitable target* latent variable is specified from four observed indicators regarding the homicidal and nonhomicidal sexual offenders' perception of the attractiveness and suitability of the target. A targeted victim usually meets a set of distinct criteria that hold special significance for the particular sex killer (Bourdreaux, Lord, & Jarvis, 2001; Canter 1989). Therefore, it is hypothesized that HSOs are more likely than their non-homicidal counterparts to hunt for an attractive and suitable target.

The first item, which is based on a dichotomous response format ("no" is coded "0" and "yes" is coded "1"), is "The victim had one or several distinctive characteristics the offender looked for." The other two items are "The offender's physical attraction to the victim at time of the offense" and "The offender's attraction to the victim's personality at time of the offense." For the purpose of this study, which is to create a consistent categorical response format for items measuring the attractive and suitable target latent variable and to classify the level of the offender's interest in the victim, the latter two items, which were initially based on a continuous scale ranging from 0 (no interest) to 10 (extreme interest), were recoded into three ordinal levels. These three levels are no or low level of interest (scored 0 to 3 points; coded "0"), moderate level of interest (scored 4 to 7 points; coded "1"), and a high level of interest (scored 8 to 10 points; coded "2"). Similarly, the *attractive and suitable target* latent variable is measured using a scale format with a point range of 0 to 5, with more points indicating the greater attractiveness and suitability of a target to the offender.

5.3.1.3.3 Scale 3: the absence of a capable guardian or guardianship (0–3 points)

According to Cohen and Felson (1979), a guardian or guardianship is basically an individual social control mechanism, formal or informal, that limits the availability and accessibility of an attractive target. Essentially, a capable guardian is someone who is watching and could detect untoward behaviors, which is likely to deter a potential offender from committing a criminal act (Felson, 1995). However, Felson (1995, 2006, 2010) revisits the guardianship concept in his later work and defines a guardian as an individual who "keeps an eye on the potential *target* of crime," a definition which "potentially includes anybody passing by or anybody assigned to look after people or property... [and] usually refers to ordinary citizens, not police or private guards" (Felson, 2006, p. 80, emphasis in original work). In Felson's (2010) latest work, he defines a guardian as "someone whose mere presence serves as a gentle reminder that someone is looking" (p. 28) or an individual who engages in natural surveillance, including "ordinary citizens going about their daily lives but providing by their presence some degree of security" (p. 37).

However, recent developments have expanded the operationalization of the guardianship concept into self-protective behaviors and measures (Mustaine & Tewksbury, 1998; Tewksbury & Mustaine, 2003; Wilcox, Madensen, & Tillyer, 2003). Self-protective and personal protective behaviors measure target hardening (i.e., efforts made to make the target difficult to be targeted). These protective measures aim to decrease the suitability of the targets for crime by making changes to them to make them less attractive to the potential offender (Hollis-Peel et al., 2011). Recent studies find that alcohol and drug use, especially during the time of the attack, lower the likelihood of using self-protective guardianship behaviors or measures, which thus increases the likelihood of victimization (e.g., Mustaine & Tewksbury, 1998; Schwartz, DeKeserdery, Tait, & Alvi, 2001; Spano & Freilich, 2009; Tewksbury & Mustaine, 2003).

According to Cohen et al. (1981), individuals who live alone are likely to be perceived by offenders as more suitable targets and also to lack capable guardians. Hindelang et al. (1978) also posit that individuals who live alone are more likely than individuals who live with someone else to spend their free time involved in recreational activities away from home, which increases their exposure to motivated offenders and their victimization risk. In addition, formal or informal social control measures (e.g., security devices, self-protective behaviors) or guardians (e.g., police, informal guardians [handlers, managers, and target-guardians]) are capable of disrupting, directly or indirectly, the offending behavior and conduct of the offender (Hollis-Peel et al., 2011; Sampson et al., 2010). Simply put, a lack of a capable guardian/guardianship decreases the likelihood of an offender being arrested or interrupted during the offense.

Hence, the observed indicators of an ineffective guardian/guardianship are based on responses to three items indicative of the failure of self-protective behavior as a result of alcohol and/or drug consumption, the negative consequences of living alone, and the absence of a capable guardian/guardianship to intervene or to stop the occurrence of the offense. This latent variable is measured by using a scale format with a point range of 0 to 3, with more points indicating the low effectiveness of a guardian/guardianship in the immediate surroundings. This study hypothesizes that the victims of HSOs are more likely to be targeted in the absence of effective guardian/guardianship than the victims of NHSOs. The three items based on the individual level are as follows:

(a)   "The victim was an alcoholic or a drug addict at the time of the attack."
(b)   "At the time of the attack, the victim was living alone."
(c)   "Was there a probability of the offender being arrested or interrupted when the offense occurred?"

"No" is coded "0" and "yes" is coded "1" for the first two items, whereas "no" is coded "1" and "yes" is coded "0" for the final item.

5.3.1.3.4   Scale 4: Pre-crime precipitating factors (0–7 points)

In the revised model, in order to better understand the offending perspective of SHOs, the observed indicators of pre-crime precipitating dynamics are based on responses to seven items. These factors are not included in Chan et al.'s (2011) original integrated theoretical framework of the social learning and routine activity theories. Generally speaking, the pre-crime precipitating factors refer to the events that occur prior to a crime and accelerate the offender's decision to commit the crime. The research supports the argument that the pre-crime precipitators, especially 48 hours prior to the commission of the offense, have an accelerating effect in sexual offenses. For instance, studies find that drug and alcohol are disinhibiting factors in sexual assaults (Barbaree, Marshall, Yates, & Lightfoot, 1983; Marshall & Barbaree, 1990), particularly before the crime (Beauregard & Proulx, 2002, 2007; Mieczkowski & Beauregard, 2010). Drug consumption is much higher among HSOs than among NHSOs who target adult women (Beauregard, Proulx, et al., 2007). However, Koch et al. (2011) find that NHSOs are more likely than their homicidal counterparts to have abuse illegal drugs prior to their offense. The disinhibitory role of drug and alcohol consumption prior to the offense among both homicidal and non-homicidal sexual offenders is possibly due to their attempt to justify their acts.

Similarly, the consumption of pornographic materials and indulgence in deviant sexual fantasies prior to the offense are evidenced in the completion of a sexual assault, especially among those who sexually kill (Beauregard & Proulx, 2002, 2007). The immediacy to act out their deviant sexual fantasies in order to gratify their psychological urges is perhaps an accelerating factor for sexual murderers to commit their offense moments after indulging in their fantasies. In the 48 hours preceding the crime, most SHOs experience significantly more problematic issues related to their interpersonal relationships (e.g., loneliness, idleness, separation, and marital difficulties) and sexual problems (Beauregard, Proulx, et al., 2007; Beauregard, Stone, et al., 2008). Unfortunately, no comparative studies have been attempted to test the differences between homicidal and non-homicidal sexual offenders in terms of the effect of pre-crime precipitators during the immediate period (i.e., 48 hours, 24 hours) prior to the offense on accelerating their motivation to commit a sexual offense. Essentially, precipitating factors, especially within 48 hours prior to crime, are disinhibitors that favor the commission of sexual offenses (Proulx, McKibben, & Lusignan, 1996). But because killing is more extreme than a sex offense alone, it is hypothesized that the effect of pre-crime precipitating factors would be higher for HSOs than for their non-homicidal counterparts.

The seven items for measuring the latent variable of the *pre-crime precipitating factors* are measured using a scale format (0–7 points), with more points indicating more pre-crime precipitators. Using a dichotomous response format ("no" is coded "0" and "yes" is coded "1"), these items are designed to obtain information from the subject about his pre-crime precipitating factors:

(a)   "Alcohol consumption during the hours before the offense."
(b)   "Drug consumption during the hours before the offense."
(c)   "Use of pornographic material during the hours before the offense."
(d)   "Occurrence of deviant sexual fantasies featuring or regarding the victim within 48 hours before the sexual offense."
(e)   "Occurrence of deviant sexual fantasies (scenarios excluding the victim) within 48 hours before the sexual offense."
(f)   "One or several relational/interpersonal problems occurred within 48 hours before the sexual offense."
(g)   "One or several accelerating/precipitating sexual problems occurred within 48 hours before the sexual offense."

5.3.1.3.5   Commission of a sexual homicide

The observed indicator of *commission of a sexual homicide* is dichotomous ("no" is coded "0" and "yes" is coded "1"), with official information (e.g., institutional records, presentence reports, tribunal files, police reports, and professional evaluations) documenting whether the subjects committ "a murder with a sexual nature" (this term is coined in the original study). Simply put, a sexual assault or other sex-related crimes that result in the death of the victim are referred to as sexual homicides. In this study, an attempted murder by the offender on or after the sexual assault is not counted as a commission of a sexual homicide.

5.3.1.4   *Analytic strategy*

In addition to outlining the descriptive statistics of the sample subjects on a number of demographic characteristics, chi-square analyses are also performed in this study to explore the differences between homicidal and non-homicidal sexual offenders on the observed indicators of different theoretical measures. The significance of the chi-square models is set at the 0.05 level. In light of the small sample size and the exploratory nature of this study, the decision was made to note the findings that suggested a tendency towards significance in cases where the probability of the event occurring is between greater than 0.05 and less than 0.10. Given the nominal nature of the variables, measures of association (Phi and Cramer's *V*) are used to analyze significant findings for *meaningful* patterns. Using Cohen's standards for the interpretation of the size of the chi-square's effect, a value of 0.20 and below is regarded as weak, between 0.21 and 0.79 as moderate, and 0.80 and above as strong in terms of the size of the effect (Cohen, 1988, 1992; Gravetter & Wallnau, 2008).

The logistic regression approach is used to examine the two different theoretical models of sexual homicide presented in Figure 5.1 and Figure 5.2: (a) Chan et al.'s (2011) original integrative model (without pre-crime precipitators) and (b) the revised model (with pre-crime precipitators). Using the present data, these tests are conducted to explore which theoretical model (with or without the addition of pre-crime factors) better explains the offending perspective of sexual homicide. On the basis of the observed indicators, scales and subscales are generated for each of the four measures (i.e., *a motivated offender, an attractive and suitable target, the absence of a capable guardian or guardianship*, and *pre-crime precipitating factors*). Reliability analyses are computed to examine the internal consistency of these scale and subscales. Essentially, two different testing models are designed to test each theoretical model, with one model consisting of five subscales of the *motivated offender* measure and another model combining all of the observed indicators into a single motivated offender scale. In total, four testing models are tested in this study.

Due to the dichotomous nature of the dependent/outcome variable, a logistic regression statistical approach is used in this study as the key method of analysis rather than the ordinary least square (OLS) technique. The basic concepts fundamental to a multiple regression analysis are similar to those of a logistic regression analysis, although "the meaning of the resultant regression equation is considerably different" for these two analytical techniques, according to Mertler and Vannatta (2005: p. 313).Of particular note, the multiple regression models assume that (1) a linear relationship between the independent and outcome variables exists in the model, (2) the data are measured at the interval or ratio level, and (3) the error terms are independent, normally distributed, and have constant variance across the independent variables (Bachman & Paternoster, 2004).

Another distinction between the two statistical approaches is that the linear relationships between the independent and outcome variables are assumed in the OLS approach, whereas the logistic regression approach allows for a more flexible type of sigmoidal relationship between the independent and outcome variables. Furthermore, as opposed to OLS equations that use the total weighted and actual values of the predictor variables in estimating the values of the outcome variables, the logistic regression's equations are based on probabilities, odds, and log-odds in the estimation of the value of the outcome variable. According to Mertler and Vannatta (2005), "probabilities are simply the number of outcomes of a specific type [that are] expressed as a proportion of the total number of possible outcomes" (p. 317). The probabilities that are estimated in the logistic regression are limited to a range of zero to one, as opposed to the continuous values that may fall below zero or above one for independent variables in the linear probability models. Clearly, the assumptions of multiple regression models are violated by a binary dependent variable as the distribution, and the standard deviation of this outcome variable produces a sigmoidal response (Agresti & Finlay, 1997).

Although the probabilities that are generated by using the logistic regression may not be greater than one, the odds can be larger than a value of one. According to Mertler and Vannatta (2005), the odds are the chance of an event occurring divided by the chance of an event not occurring, as expressed by the following formula:

$$\text{Odds} = \frac{p(X_1)}{1 - p(X_1)}$$

In this formula, $p(X_1)$ is the chance of the event happening and $1 - p(X_1)$ is the chance of the event not happening. In order to interpret the relative difference between the category of interest and the reference category, the odds ratios (OR) are used in the logistic regression model [Exp(B)] to explain these odds. To further illustrate, an OR of one is interpreted as the exact same odds or probability of the events representing both the category of interest and the reference category occurring. An OR value above one demonstrates higher odds or probability that the event representing the category of interest will happen, while an OR value under one means that the event of interest is less likely to happen.

It is worth noting that the logistic regression is eventually based upon the logit or log-odds, which are both defined as the natural logarithm of the odds (Mertler & Vannatta, 2005). Put differently, a change in the natural logarithm of the odds of the outcome variable is associated with a one-unit increase in the independent variable (Miller, 2005). However, in order to facilitate easier comprehension, the ORs are used in this study to interpret the logistic regression findings; specifically, percentages are used to explicate the ORs (OR – 1 X 100%).

5.3.2 Empirical findings

Different statistical analyses are conducted on the data. First, the demographic characteristics (i.e., the age, ethnic origin, and marital status of the offenders and the age and ethnic origin of the victims) of the sample are presented, with statistical differences between homicidal and non-homicidal sex offenders noted where applicable. Next, the chi-square analyses are performed to explore the differences between homicidal and non-homicidal sex offenders and are based on the observed indicators of the different measures in this study. On the basis of the theoretical model suggested by Chan et al. (2011) and the revised model, the descriptive statistics of the different measures (scales and subscales) that comprise the relevant observed indicators are generated.[3] The mean differences between homicidal and non-homicidal sexual offenders on different scales and subscales are also examined. Finally, the logistic regression is employed to explore the different theoretical constructs, as described in Chan et al. (2011) and the revised model, used in predicting the lethal outcome of a sexual offense. Four different regression models are computed, with the *motivated offender* measure being examined in two models (five-subscale model and a single-scale model) for both theoretical frameworks. Step-wise logistic regressions are employed in both theoretical models in order to examine the proposed offending pathways of HSOs (see Figure 5.1 and Figure 5.2).

5.3.2.1   Demographic characteristics of the sample

Table 5.1 presents the demographic characteristics of the non-serial homicidal (N = 55) and the non-homicidal (N = 175) sexual offenders of female adults that are examined in this study. The average age of the sexual offenders when they are first incarcerated for their index offense is 34.35 years old (SD = 9.29), with 77% of them being between 18 and 40 years old when they commit the offense. When this sample is further explored in terms of the lethality of their sexual offenses, no significant age difference is found between the homicidal (M = 32.96, SD = 8.45) and the non-homicidal (M = 34.75, SD = 9.50) sexual offenders.

In this study, the sexual offenders are primarily whites (86%). Comparing homicidal and non-homicidal sexual offenders, nearly 93% of the sexual offenders who killed were white, as opposed to only 84% of their non-homicidal counterparts. A chi-square analysis finds that this difference has a tendency towards significance ($\chi^2[2]$ = 5.09, Cramer's V = .15, p = 0.09). When the ethnic origins of the sexual offenders are divided into white and non-white categories, no significant difference between homicidal and non-homicidal sexual offenders is found.

In terms of these sexual offenders' marital status, approximately 68% of them are single, separated, divorced, or widowed at the time of their offense. Interestingly, in the total sample, more HSOs than NHSOs are

Table 5.1 Sample demographic characteristics of non-serial homicidal and non-homicidal sexual offenders who target female adults

Variables	Whole sample		Non-serial HSOs against Female Adult Victims (Sexual Murderers)		Non-serial NHSOs against Female Adult Victims	
	# of Cases	Percentage	# of Cases	Percentage	# of Cases	Percentage
	(N = 230)	(100)	(N = 55)	(100%)	(N = 175)	(100%)
Types of sexual offenders	(N = 230)					
Homicidal sexual offenders (HSOs)	55	23.9				
Non-homicidal sexual offenders (NHSOs)	175	76.1				
Offender's age (when first incarcerated)	(N = 226)		(N = 51)		(N = 175)	
18 to 40 years	175	77.4	44	86.3	131	74.9
41 to 60 years	48	21.2	6	11.8	42	24.0
61 years and above	3	1.3	1	2.0	2	1.1
Offender's ethnic origin (multi-group)	(N = 230)		(N = 55)		(N = 175)	
White	198	86.1	51	92.7	147	84.0
Black	15	6.5	4	7.3	15	8.6
Others (e.g., Hispanic, Arab, Native American)	17	7.4	–	–	13	7.4
Offender's ethnic origin (white/non-white)	(N = 230)		(N = 55)		(N = 175)	
White	198	86.1	51	92.7	147	84.0
Non-white	32	13.9	4	7.3	28	16.0

	(N = 229)		(N = 54)		(N = 175)	
Offender's marital status (multi-group)						
Single	122	53.3	36	66.7	86	49.1
Unmarried partnership	60	26.2	8	14.7	52	29.7
Married	14	6.1	5	9.3	9	5.2
Separated/divorced/widowed	33	14.4	5	9.3	28	16.0
Offender's marital status (single/nonsingle)	(N = 229)		(N = 54)		(N = 175)	
Single	155	67.7	41	76.0	114	65.1
Nonsingle	74	32.3	13	24.0	61	34.9
Victim's age (when the offense occurred)	(N = 227)		(N = 54)		(N = 173)	
17 years and under	18	7.9	3	5.6	15	8.7
18 to 40 years	165	72.7	39	72.2	126	72.8
41 to 60 years	37	16.3	9	16.7	28	16.2
61 years and above	7	3.1	3	5.6	4	2.3
Victim's ethnic origin (multi-group)	(N = 228)		(N = 55)		(N = 173)	
White	206	90.4	51	92.7	155	89.6
Black	7	3.1	1	1.8	6	3.5
Others (e.g., Hispanic, Arab, Native American)	15	6.6	3	5.5	12	6.9
Victim's ethnic origin (white/non-white)	(N = 228)		(N = 55)		(N = 173)	
White	206	90.4	51	92.7	155	89.6
Non-white	22	9.6	4	7.3	18	10.4

reported as having no intimate partner (76% versus 65%), and this difference is statistically significant ($\chi^2[3]$ = 8.32, Cramer's V = 0.19, $p < 0.05$). However, when the sexual offenders' marital status is divided into single and non-single categories, no statistical difference is found between the two types of offenders.

Of the total of 230 sexual offenders, 114 were convicted of a sexual assault and the remaining 116 were found guilty of a minor sexual offense that included a sexual component (e.g., indecent action, illegal acts regarding obscene material, exhibitionism, or frotteurism). Of those who were convicted of a sexual assault, 24% committed their offense with a weapon. More NHSOs than HSOs admit to engaging in some form of premeditation (unstructured or structured premeditation) prior to the attack (68% versus 56%); however, this difference is not significant. In this study, significantly more NHSOs than HSOs admit to having performed sexual penetration (oral, vaginal, or anal) against their victims (76.6% versus 58.2%; t = -2.33, $p < 0.05$). Interestingly, significantly more HSOs than NHSOs mutilate the sexual body parts of their victims (18.2% versus 3.4%, t = 3.68, $p < 0.001$).

Regarding the victims of the sexual offenders in this study, nearly 73% of them are aged between 18 and 40 years when the offense occurs ($M = 30.30$, $SD = 13.70$). This victim portrait in terms of the victim's age is relatively similar for both the homicidal and non-homicidal sexual offenders who targeted adult female victims. The victims of the NHSOs are younger on average ($M = 29.54$, $SD = 13.67$) compared with the victims of their homicidal counterparts ($M = 32.74$, $SD = 13.63$); however, this difference is not statistically significant. In terms of the victim's ethnic background, a large portion of the victims (90%) in this study are white (93% of the HSOs' victims; 90% of the NHSOs' victims). No statistically significant difference is found with regard to the victim's ethnic origin for either type of sexual offender. Similarly, no significant difference is found between the homicidal and the non-homicidal sexual offenders in terms of ethnic background when they are grouped into white and non-white categories.

5.3.2.2 *The scale of the observed indicators in the chi-square analyses*

In this study, four different measures/independent variables (i.e., *a motivated offender, an attractive and suitable target, the absence of a capable guardian or guardianship*, and *precrimepre-crime precipitating factors*) were examined. Each of these independent variables wasis assessed using a scale format which consisted of a number of observed indicators. For the *motivated offender* measure, five subscales (i.e., *parental or familial aggressive and deviant sexual behavior and attitudes, parental or sibling past sexual and nonsexual criminal background, victim of family violence, personal consumption of pornography,* and *personal sexually deviant behaviors and attitudes*) were created with different numbers of observed indicators for each subscale. Chi-square analyses were performed to explore the differences between homicidal and nonhomicidal sexual offenders in these observed indicators of different measures. Only findings with significant differences between the two types of sexual offender are discussed in this section. Overall, although several significant chi-square analyses are conducted, the size of the effect in these chi-square models is rather weak (ranged from 0.13 to 0.24).

Among the 16 observed indicators that measure *a motivated offender,* only two are significantly different for homicidal and nonhomicidal sexual offenders (see Table 5.2). Both of these items measure *personal sexually deviant behaviors and attitudes.* A chi-square analysis shows that

Table 5.2 Sexual offenders' sexually deviant behaviors and attitudes by offender type

| Variables | Offender type | | Total |
	Homicidal sexual offender	Nonhomicidal sexual offender	
Indulgence in deviant sexual fantasies			
No	31	127	158
Row %	19.6	80.4	100.0
Column %	58.5	74.7	70.9
Yes	22	43	65
Row %	33.8	66.2	100.0
Column %	41.5	25.3	29.1
Total	53	170	223
Row %	23.8	76.2	100.0
$\chi^2(1) = 5.14$, Phi = 0.15, $p < 0.05$			
Paraphilia			
No	40	164	204
Row %	19.6	80.4	100.0
Column %	78.4	94.8	91.1
Yes	11	9	20
Row %	55.0	45.0	100.0
Column %	21.6	5.2	8.9
Total	51	173	224
Row %	22.8	77.2	100.0
$\chi^2(1) = 12.98$, Phi = 0.24, $p < 0.001$			

significantly more HSOs than NHSOs report indulgence in deviant sexual fantasies that start at least a year prior to their index offense (42% versus 25%; $\chi^2[1]$ = 5.14, Phi = 0.15, p < 0.05). Similarly, more sexual offenders who killed admit to having engaged in paraphilia than those who did not kill (22% versus 5%; $\chi^2[1]$ = 12.98, Phi = 0.24, p < 0.001).

With regard to *the absence of a capable guardian or guardianship* measure, there appears to be a difference between the homicidal and the nonhomicidal sexual offenders with regard to one of the four observed indicators, although this difference does not reach statistical significance (see Table 5.3). The victims of the HSOs have a greater tendency to live alone at the time of the attack than the victims of the NHSOs (35% versus 22%; $\chi^2[1]$ = 3.03, Phi = 0.13, p = 0.08).

Among the seven pre-crime precipitating factors, a significant difference is found between sexual offenders who killed and those who did not kill in two observed indicators (see Table 5.4). More HSOs than NHSOs are intoxicated by alcohol during the hours before their offense (80% versus 61%; $\chi^2[1]$ = 6.60, Phi = 0.17, p < 0.01). In addition, compared with their nonhomicidal counterparts, more of the HSOs admit to engaging in deviant sexual fantasies that do not involve their victim within the 48-hour period prior to committing their sexual offense (31% versus 18%), and this difference is statistically significant ($\chi^2[1]$ = 4.00, Phi = 0.14, p < 0.05).

Table 5.3 Absence of a capable guardian or guardianship at the time of the offense by offender type

Variables	Offender type		
	Homicidal sexual offender	Nonhomicidal sexual offender	Total
Victim living alone at time of the attack			
No	28	121	149
Row %	18.8	81.2	100.0
Column %	65.1	78.1	75.3
Yes	15	34	49
Row %	30.6	69.4	100.0
Column %	34.9	21.9	24.7
Total	43	155	198
Row %	21.7	78.3	100.0
$\chi^2(1)$ = 3.03, Phi = 0.13, p = 0.08			

Table 5.4 Sexual offenders' pre-crime precipitating factors by offender type

| Variables | Offender type | | Total |
	Homicidal sexual offender	Nonhomicidal sexual offender	
Alcohol consumption during the hours before the offense			
No	11	68	79
Row %	13.9	86.1	100.0
Column %	20.0	38.9	34.3
Yes	44	107	151
Row %	29.1	70.9	100.0
Column %	80.0	61.1	65.7
Total	55	175	230
Row %	23.9	76.1	100.0
$\chi^2(1) = 6.60$, Phi $= 0.17$, $p < 0.01$			
Deviant sexual fantasies (victim excluded) within 48 hours before the offense			
No	36	138	174
Row %	20.7	79.3	100.0
Column %	69.2	82.1	79.1
Yes	16	30	46
Row %	34.8	65.2	100.0
Column %	30.8	17.9	20.9
Total	52	168	220
Row %	23.6	76.4	100.0
$\chi^2(1) = 4.00$, Phi $= 0.14$, $p < 0.05$			

5.3.2.3 *Descriptive Statistics of Different Theoretical Components*

As aforementioned, the theoretical components of Chan et al.'s (2011) original model and the revised model are tested by using measures that consist of relevant observed indicators. Prior to any statistical analyses of the different measures, reliability analyses are conducted on the different measurement scales and subscales to examine their internal consistency (see Table 5.5). Five subscales are created for the *motivated offender* measure. The Cronbach's alpha for the *victim of family violence* subscale (three items) is 0.65, which is approaching the 0.70 acceptable level (see Cronbach, 1951). Similarly, the five items of the *parental or familial aggressive and deviant sexual behavior and attitudes* subscale yields a Cronbach's alpha of 0.60. The subscales of *personal sexually deviant behaviors and attitudes* (three items) and *parental or sibling past sexual and nonsexual criminal background* (four items) only reach the alpha coefficients of 0.53 and 0.44, respectively.

Table 5.5 Means and standard deviations for the observed variables of homicidal and non-homicidal sexual offenders (N = 230)

Variables	Homicidal sexual offenders (N = 55)		Nonhomicidal sexual offenders (N = 175)		
	M	SD	M	SD	t value
Cronbach's alpha = 0.60 (0.70 for homicidal and 0.56 for nonhomicidal sexual offenders) Motivated offender (subscale 1): Parental and familial aggressive and deviant sexual behaviors and attitudes (5 items; 0–5 points)	0.91	1.16	0.97	1.01	−0.33
Cronbach's alpha = 0.44 (0.52 for homicidal and 0.41 for nonhomicidal sexual offenders) Motivated offender (subscale 2): Parental or sibling past sexual and nonsexual criminal background (4 items; 0–4 points)	0.60	0.58	0.64	0.84	0.27
Cronbach's alpha = 0.65 (0.72 for homicidal and 0.62 for nonhomicidal sexual offenders) Motivated offender (subscale 3): Victim of family violence (3 items; 0–6 points)	1.85	2.03	1.76	1.88	0.31
Motivated offender (subscale 4): Personal consumption of pornography (1 item; 0–1 point)	0.78	0.42	0.69	0.47	1.33
Cronbach's alpha = 0.53 (0.59 for homicidal and 0.48 for nonhomicidal sexual offenders) Motivated offender (subscale 5): Personal sexually deviant behaviors and attitudes (3 items; 0–3 points)	0.94**	1.01	0.54	0.79	2.70
Cronbach's alpha = 0.72 (0.76 for homicidal and 0.71 for nonhomicidal sexual offenders) Motivated offender (overall scale; 16 items; 0–19 points)	5.00	3.59	4.57	3.22	−0.79
Cronbach's alpha = 0.57 (0.74 for homicidal and 0.52 for nonhomicidal sexual offenders) Attractive and suitable target (overall scale; 3 items; 0–5 points)	1.33	1.49	2.15**	1.45	3.58
Cronbach's alpha = 0.11 (0.40 for homicidal and −0.16 for nonhomicidal sexual offenders) Absence of a capable guardian or guardianship (overall scale; 3 items; 0–3 points)	1.18*	0.98	0.90	0.75	−2.23
Cronbach's alpha = 0.39 (0.33 for homicidal and 0.40 for nonhomicidal sexual offenders) Pre-crime precipitators (overall scale; 7 items; 0–7 points)	2.38[a]	1.24	2.06	1.38	1.62

Note: [a] $p = 0.09$, *$p < 0.05$, **$p < 0.01$.

Most of the scales used in this study have a low internal consistency. Of particular note, the low internal consistency may be due to the highly skewed distributions of the included items because this reduces "the size of the correlation between items and therefore also the alpha" (Straus & Kantor, 2005, p. 25). Additionally, the alpha coefficient is "dependent not only on the magnitude of the correlations among items, but also on the number of items" (Streiner & Norman, 1989, p. 64). Many of the subscales used in this analysis consist of less than four items, which likely influence the alpha coefficients. No Cronbach's alpha is computed for the single-item *personal consumption of pornography* subscale. Overall, the *motivated offender* scale yields an internal consistency estimate of 0.72 (16 items), which is above the acceptable level.

As regards the internal consistency of the *attractive and suitable target* scale, the scale yields an alpha coefficient of 0.57 for this 3-item scale. Unexpectedly, an internal consistency estimate of only 0.11 is found for the *absence of a capable guardian or guardianship* scale (three items). Although the alpha coefficient of this scale is low, the items that are included in this scale in examining the domain of interest are supported by the literature; therefore, these items are retained. The limitation of this scale, partly due to the issue of data availability, will be discussed in the section on the limitations of this study.

Finally, the 7-item scale measuring the *pre-crime precipitating factors* yields a Cronbach's α of 0.39. The items that are included in this scale are also selected mainly because of the support from the current literature. Besides the internal consistency estimates computed from the total sample, Table 5.3 also presents the alpha coefficients of homicidal and non-homicidal sexual offenders that are found in different scales and subscales.

Subsequently, the descriptive statistics (e.g., means and standard deviations) of these different measures are computed for both homicidal and nonhomicidal sexual offenders. Table 5.5 presents the mean differences between these two types of sexual offenders in different measurement scales and subscales. Although HSOs ($M = 5.00$, $SD = 3.59$), in general, are more motivated to commit a sexual offense than the NHSOs ($M = 4.57$, $SD = 3.33$), this difference (based on the combined 16 items with a possible maximum score of 19 points) is not statistically significant. When the *motivated offender* measure is assessed in five different subscales, only one subscale yields a significant difference between sexual offenders who killed and those who did not. HSOs ($M = 0.94$, $SD = 1.01$) have significantly more sexually deviant behaviors and attitudes (a possible maximum score of three points) compared with the NHSOs ($M = 0.54$, $SD = 0.79$; $t = 2.70$, $p < 0.01$).

In contrast to Chan et al.'s (2011) theoretical proposition, the NHSOs' (M = 2.15, SD = 1.45) victim selection is significantly more selective in terms of the victim's attractiveness and suitability (with a possible maximum score of five points) compared with their homicidal counterparts (M = 1.33, SD = 1.49; t = 3.58, p < 0.01). However, in terms of the *absence of a capable guardian or guardianship* measure (with a possible maximum score of three points), HSOs (M = 1.18, SD =0.98) yield a higher mean score than the NHSOs (M = 0.90, SD = 0.75), and the direction of this finding is consistent with Chan et al.'s (2011) theoretical proposition. In other words, compared with the sexual offenses committed by their nonhomicidal counterparts, the sexual offenses committed by are significantly more likely to be successfully completed without the offender being arrested or without the intervention of others; this difference is significant (t = -2.23, p < 0.05).

Finally, the mean difference of the pre-crime precipitating factors between homicidal and non-homicidal sexual offenders in terms of their motivation to commit a sexual offense is examined. As a whole, sexual offenders who killed (M = 2.38, SD = 1.24) yield a significantly higher mean score than those who did not kill (M = 2.06, SD = 1.38) in terms of their pre-crime precipitators. This difference is not significant at conventional levels but does approach significance (t = 1.62, p = 0.09).

5.3.2.4   Multivariate Analyses of Chan, Heide, and Beauregard's Theoretical Model

As described in Chan et al.'s (2011) model, step-wise logistic regressions are employed to explore the various theoretical constructs that are used in predicting the lethal outcome of a sexual offense. The types of sexual offender serve as the binary outcome variable (e.g., 0 = NHSO, 1 = SHO). Two separate theoretical models are estimated; in this estimation, the *motivated offender* construct is first analyzed in five dimensions and subsequently examined in a single construct. Simply put, the step-wise approach is selected over the enter approach because it permits the testing of the effect of each predictor variable on the dependent variable. In this study, the adjusted odds ratios are computed (exp(B) – 1 X 100 = adjusted odds ratio) to report the percentage change in odds for the statistically significant effects. The percentages are used to explicate the ORs (OR – 1 X 100%).

Surprisingly, only one dimension of the *motivated offender* measure – *personal sexually deviant behaviors and attitudes* – is a significant predictor in Model II (χ^2 = 16.94, p < 0.01) and Model III (χ^2 = 23.65, p < 0.001) of Chan et al.'s original model (see Table 5.6; Model I is not significant). When the sexual offender possesses sexually deviant behaviors and attitudes, the odds of him murdering his victim increased by 55% in Model II when the *attractive and suitable target* construct is added to the model. Unexpectedly, the effect of the *attractive and suitable target* construct in predicting the lethal outcome of a sexual offense is incompatible with Chan et al.'s (2011) theoretical proposition. Every one-unit increase in the target's attractiveness and suitability results in decreasing the odds of being murdered by 29%.

Model III presents the empirical test of the complete theoretical model as proffered by Chan et al. (2011). When the sexual offender possesses sexually deviant behaviors and attitudes, the odds of him murdering his victim increases by 77%. In addition, the odds of the offender killing his victim increases by 73% when his sexual offense is committed in the absence of a capable guardian or guardianship. However, inconsistent with Chan et al.'s (2011) theoretical proposition, every one-unit increase in the target's attractiveness and suitability results in decreasing the odds of the victim being killed by 27%.

In the second theoretical model, the *motivated offender* measure is assessed in a single construct (see Table 5.7). Only Model II (χ^2 = 13.64, p < 0.001) and Model III (χ^2 = 17.58, p < 0.001) are significant. Overall, the effect of the *motivated offender* construct is not statistically significant in predicting the lethal outcome of a sexual offense in all of the models. Unexpectedly, every one-unit increase in target attractiveness and suitability results in decreasing the odds of the victim being murdered by 33% in both Models II and III. The *absence of a capable guardian or guardianship* construct is added to Model III, and the results indicate that the odds of the offender murdering his victim when no interference occurs from a third party increases by 48%.

The receiver operating characteristics (ROC) curve is used to examine the diagnostic value of the two different models, with one model tested with five *motivated offender* subscales and another with a single (combined) *motivated offender* scale. The results indicate that the values of the area under the curve (AUC) are 0.53 for Model I, 0.46 for Model II, and 0.49 for Model III (see Table 5.7 and Table 5.8). Although Model I yields the highest AUC value compared with the AUC values in Models II and III, an area of approximately 0.50 represents chance, with no accuracy in terms of prediction or discrimination (Kleinbaum & Klein, 2010).

Table 5.6 Logistic regressions of Chan, Heide, and Beauregard's theoretical model (a five-subscale *motivated offender* model)

Predictor variable	Model I			Model II			Model III		
	B	SE	Odds ratio	B	SE	Odds ratio	B	SE	Odds ratio
Parental aggressiveness[a]	-0.12	0.22	0.88	-0.12	0.22	0.88	-0.12	0.23	0.89
Parental criminal history[b]	0.03	0.21	1.03	0.05	0.21	1.06	0.04	0.22	1.04
Family violence[c]	-0.01	0.12	0.99	-0.02	0.12	0.99	-0.02	0.12	0.98
Pornography[d]	0.27	0.40	1.30	0.20	0.41	1.22	0.16	0.41	1.18
Sexually deviant behavior[e]	0.46	0.18	1.59**	0.44	0.19	1.55*	0.57	0.21	1.77**
Attractive target				-0.34	0.12	0.71**	-0.31	0.12	0.73**
Absence of a guardian							0.55	0.22	1.73**
Constant	-1.63	0.37	0.20	-0.93	0.43	0.40	-1.61	0.52	0.20
-2 log likelihood	230.70			218.63			211.92		
Model chi-square	8.59			16.94**			23.65***		
Hosmer-Lemeshow test	$\chi^2(8) = 6.16, p = 0.63$			$\chi^2(8) = 2.70, p = 0.95$			$\chi^2(8) = 9.61, p = 0.29$		
Nagelkerke R^2	0.06			0.11			0.16		
N	222			215			215		
AUC	0.53			0.46			0.49		

Note: [a] motivated offender subscale 1, [b] motivated offender subscale 2, [c] motivated offender subscale 3, [d] motivated offender subscale 4, and [e] motivated offender subscale 5. AUC = the area under the curve. * $p < 0.05$, ** $p < 0.01$, *** $p < 0.001$.

Table 5.7 Logistic regressions of Chan, Heide, and Beauregard's theoretical model (a single-scale *motivated offender* model)

Predictor variable	Model I			Model II			Model III		
	B	SE	Odds ratio	B	SE	Odds ratio	B	SE	Odds ratio
Motivated offender	0.04	0.05	1.04	0.03	0.05	1.03	0.04	0.05	1.04
Attractive target				−0.41	0.12	0.67***	−0.39	0.12	0.67***
Absence of a guardian							0.39	0.20	1.48*
Constant	−1.34	0.27	0.26	−0.54	0.34	0.58	−1.00	0.42	0.37
−2 log likelihood	252.37			234.36			230.42		
Model chi-square	0.67			13.64***			17.58***		
Hosmer-Lemeshow test	$\chi^2(8) = 13.96, p = 0.08$			$\chi^2(8) = 18.74, p = 0.02$			$\chi^2(8) = 12.35, p = 0.14$		
Nagelkerke R^2	0.01			0.09			0.11		
N	230			221			221		
AUC	0.53			0.46			0.49		

Note: AUC = area under the curve.
* $p < 0.05$, ** $p < 0.01$, *** $p < 0.001$

5.3.2.5   *Multivariate Analyses of the Revised Chan et al.'s Theoretical Model*

Similar to the empirical tests of Chan et al.'s (2011) theoretical model described above, the effect of the revised theoretical propositions with the inclusion of pre-crime precipitating factors in terms of predicting the lethal outcome of a sexual offense is investigated. Step-wise logistic regressions are used to examine two separate theoretical models, with one assessing the five dimensions of the *motivated offender* measure and the second model examining the combined measure of the *motivated offender* in a single construct. In this revised theoretical model, the construct of the *pre-crime precipitators* is added to the theoretical models with the rationale that these precipitators have a motivating effect on the offender in committing a sexual offense against an attractive and suitable target in the absence of a capable guardian or guardianship.

In general, only two of the four theoretical models are statistically significant (χ^2 = 17.48, p < 0.05 for Model III and χ^2 = 23.93, p < 0.01 for Model IV; Models I and II are not significant; see Table 5.8). Overall, when the construct *of the pre-crime precipitators* is added to Models III and IV), the construct of the *sexually deviant behaviors and attitudes* is the only dimension that measures the *motivated offender* and yields statistically significant findings. In Model III, a one-unit increase in sexually deviant behaviors and attitudes increases the odds of the offender murdering his victim by 48%. Unexpectedly, the construct of the *pre-crime precipitators* fails to yield any statistically significant findings in any of the models. In the presence of the construct of the *pre-crime precipitators* in Model III, the construct of the *attractive and suitable target* is inconsistent with the theoretical proposition; every one-unit increase in target attractiveness and suitability results in decreasing the odds of being killed by 29%.

Model IV provides the empirical test of the completely revised theoretical model. The odds of a sexual offense resulting in a lethal outcome increases by 71% both when the sexual offender possesses sexually deviant behaviors and attitudes and when the offense is committed without any third party interference. Inconsistent with the theoretical proposition, every one-unit increase in the target's attractiveness and suitability results in decreasing the odds of being murdered by 27%.

Table 5.8 Logistic regressions of the revised Chan, Heide, and Beauregard's theoretical model (a five-subscale *motivated offender* model)

Predictor variable	Model I			Model II			Model III			Model IV		
	B	SE	Odds ratio	B	SE	Odds ratio	B	SE	Odds ratio	B	SE	Odds ratio
Parental aggressiveness[a]	-0.12	0.22	0.88	-0.12	0.22	0.89	-0.13	0.22	0.88	-0.12	0.23	0.89
Parental criminal history[b]	0.26	0.21	1.03	0.01	0.21	1.00	0.25	0.22	1.03	0.01	0.22	1.01
Family violence[c]	-0.01	0.12	0.99	-0.01	0.12	1.00	-0.01	0.12	0.99	-0.01	0.12	0.99
Pornography[d]	0.27	0.40	1.30	0.24	0.40	1.27	0.16	0.41	1.18	0.13	0.42	1.14
Sexually deviant behavior[e]	0.46	0.18	1.59**	0.43	0.19	1.54*	0.39	0.20	1.48*	0.54	0.21	1.71**
Pre-crime precipitators				0.08	0.13	1.08	0.10	0.13	1.10	0.07	0.14	1.08
Attractive target							-0.35	0.12	0.71**	-0.32	0.12	0.73**
Absence of a guardian										0.54	0.22	1.71**
Constant	-1.63	0.37	0.20	-1.75	0.42	0.17	-1.06	0.47	0.35	-1.69	0.55	0.19
–2 log likelihood	230.70			230.35			218.09			211.65		
Model chi-square	8.59			8.94			17.48 *			23.93**		
Hosmer-Lemeshow test	$\chi^2(8) = 13.96, p = 0.08$			$\chi^2(8) = 4.71, p = 0.79$			$\chi^2(8) = 7.78, p = 0.46$			$\chi^2(8) = 17.71, p = 0.02$		
Nagelkerke R^2	0.06			0.06			0.08			0.16		
N	222			222			215			215		
AUC	0.53			0.55			0.49			0.52		

Note. [a]motivated offender subscale 1, [b]motivated offender subscale 2, [c]motivated offender subscale 3, [d]motivated offender subscale 4, and [e]motivated offender subscale 5. AUC = area under the curve. * $p < 0.05$, ** $p < 0.01$, *** $p < 0.001$

Table 5.9 presents the second revised theoretical model with the *motivated offender* measure being measured in a single construct. Only Model III ($\chi^2 = 15.93$, $p < 0.001$) and Model IV ($\chi^2 = 19.71$, $p < 0.001$) are statistically significant. The construct of the *pre-crime precipitators* has a tendency toward significance in both Model III ($p = 0.08$) and Model IV ($p = 0.09$). In contrast, every one-unit increase in target attractiveness and suitability results in decreasing the odds of being murdered by 34%.

With the exception of the constructs for the *motivated offender* and the *pre-crime precipitators*, all of the other constructs described in the revised theoretical model, as tested in Model IV, are statistically significant for predicting the lethal outcome of a sexual offense. To illustrate, the odds of a sexual offense resulting in the killing of the victim increases by 47% when the offense is committed in the absence of a capable guardian or guardianship. In contrast to the revised theoretical proposition, every one-unit increase in target attractiveness and suitability results in decreasing the odds of being killed by 34%.

In testing the revised theoretical model of Chan et al. (2011), the AUC values of 0.49 for Model III and 0.52 for Model IV are obtained (see Table 5.8 and Table 5.9). These AUC values indicated that both models are equally likely to be no different than chance.

Table 5.9 Logistic regressions of the revised Chan, Heide, and Beauregard's theoretical model (a single-scale *motivated offender* model)

Predictor variable	Model I			Model II			Model III			Model IV		
	B	SE	Odds ratio	B	SE	Odds ratio	B	SE	Odds ratio	B	SE	Odds ratio
Motivated offender	0.04	0.05	1.04	0.02	0.05	1.03	0.01	0.05	1.01	0.02	0.05	1.02
Pre-crime precipitators				0.16	0.12	1.17	0.19	0.12	1.21[a]	0.19	0.13	1.20[b]
Attractive target							−0.42	0.12	0.66***	−0.41	0.12	0.66***
Absence of a guardian										0.38	0.20	1.47*
Constant	−1.34	0.27	0.26	−1.63	0.35	0.20	−0.85	0.40	0.43	−1.30	0.47	0.27**
−2 log likelihood	252.37			250.45			232.07			228.29		
Model chi-square	0.67			2.58			15.93***			19.71***		
Hosmer-Lemeshow test	$\chi^2(8) = 13.96, p = 0.08$			$\chi^2(8) = 15.59, p = 0.05$			$\chi^2(8) = 9.16, p = 0.33$			$\chi^2(8) = 8.64, p = 0.37$		
Nagelkerke R^2	0.01			0.02			0.10			0.13		
N	230			230			221			221		
AUC	0.53			0.55			0.49			0.52		

Note: AUC = the area under the curve.
[a] $p = 0.08$, [b] $p = 0.09$* $p < 0.05$, ** $p < 0.01$, *** $p < 0.001$

6
Implications and Conclusions

6.1 Overview

Ever since the screening of the blockbuster movie *The Silence of the Lambs* and the like in the late 1980s and early 1990s, the public's interest in and the media's portrayal of sexual homicide cases have been high. Regardless of the substantial public attention to this type of violent offense, sexual homicide remains an understudied research area, primarily due to its rarity. To date, less than 50 empirically based studies on sexual homicide have been published. Hence, it is not surprising that many of the research topics on sexual homicide remain unexplored.

The focal point of this study is the offending process in sexual homicide. More specifically, the purpose of the study is to examine the theoretical model of Chan, Heide, and Beauregard (2011) in explaining the offending process of (SHOs) by using an integrated approach that combines the social learning and routine activity theories. To further enhance the explanatory power of Chan et al.'s (2011) model, a revised framework with the inclusion of pre-crime precipitating factors during the offending process is proposed; this approach is supported by the recent findings in sexual homicide studies. This study has at least two merits worth mentioning.

Prior to Chan et al.'s (2011) theoretical model of the sexual homicide offending process, no effort had been made to offer a criminological and theoretical framework for understanding the offending process of sexual homicide offenders. The present study is the first to empirically test their theoretical model. Secondly, despite the fact that the present study is a secondary analysis of the existing data that were collected by using a Canadian sample, the depth of information on pre-crime, crime, and post-crime factors; victimology; and the offender's psychological, sociological, and developmental background in the data enabled the analysis of all of the theoretical constructs in Chan et al.'s (2011) model. Most importantly, few data sets currently exist that offer such a richness of data on sexual homicide cases. To illustrate, although a number of recently published studies on SHOs use a nationally representative sample of this type of offender (e.g., Chan & Beauregard, 2014; Chan & Frei, 2013; Chan & Heide, 2008; Chan, Frei, & Myers, 2013; Chan, Heide, & Myers, 2013; Chan, Myers, & Heide, 2010; Myers & Chan, 2012; Myers, Chan, & Mariano, 2014; Myers, Chan, Vo, & Lazarou, 2010), their data are nevertheless limited to basic offender, victim, and incident-related information. Therefore, this study is potentially an important contribution to the research on sexual homicide.

The present study specifically tests four theory based and interrelated hypotheses that frame both Chan et al.'s (2011) framework and the proposed alternative Chan et al. model. The first three hypotheses are based on Chan et al.'s model. First, relative to non-homicidal sexual offenders with a similar background, homicidal sex offenders who grow up in an abusive environment are expected to be either directly or indirectly exposed to or to have learned (to be *differentially associated* with) sexually deviant attitudes, beliefs, values, and norms (deviant *definitions*) that influence their later behavioral learning process. Second, in response to their long-embedded sexually deviant attitudes, beliefs, values, and norms learned through behavioral conditioning (of *differential reinforcement or punishment* and *imitation*) since adolescence, it is anticipated that these factors would affect homicidal sex offenders more than their non-homicidal counterparts with similar backgrounds in terms of increasing their propensity to commit a sexual offense. This theorized pathway predicts the shaping of *an offender that is motivated* to commit a sexual offense. Third, it is expected that homicidal sex offenders would be more likely than their non-homicidal counterparts to commit a sexual offense against *an attractive and suitable target* in the absence of *an effective and capable guardian or guardianship* in the immediate crime scene surroundings. Lastly, in the proposed alternative model, the fourth hypothesis is set forth to better explain the offending process in sexual homicide. Because killing is more extreme, the effect of *pr-ecrime precipitating factors* on the commission of a sexual offense is anticipated to have a more influential impact on homicidal sex offenders than on non-homicidal sexual offenders.

In essence, the primary goal of this study is to empirically test two criminological theoretical frameworks in explaining the offending process in sexual homicide: (1) Chan et al.'s (2011) integrated model of the social learning theory and the routine activity theories and (2) the proposed alternative model of Chan et al.'s (2011) framework. Using non-serial homicidal (N = 55) and non-homicidal (N = 175) sexual offenders who victimize females, the present study examines four step-wise logistic regression models to determine the different theoretical constructs (i.e., a motivated offender [measured using a five-subscale model and a single-scale model], an attractive and suitable target, the absence of a capable guardian or guardianship, and pre-crime precipitating factors) in the prediction of a lethal outcome of a sexual offense. While the primary focus of this study is to determine if the theoretical model proposed by Chan et al. (2011) is able to explain the offending process in sexual homicide, a comparison is made with the proposed alternative model that includes the theoretical construct of pre-crime precipitating factors.

To facilitate easier comprehension of the key findings of this study, these findings are organized in two sections. First, the univariate and bivariate analytical findings are presented in the following order: (1) significant differences in demographic characteristics between homicidal and non-homicidal sexual offenders, (2) significant differences between both types of sexual offenders in the observed indicators of different theoretical constructs, and (3) significant mean differences between both types of sexual offenders in different theoretical scales and subscales that are constructed on the basis of the relevant observed indicators. Subsequently, this study outlines the significant findings resulting from the four different step-wise logistic regression models.

The homicidal (M = 32.96) and non-homicidal (M = 34.75) sexual offenders in this study are not significantly different in age. However, more homicidal sex offenders than non-homicidal offenders are white (93% versus 84%), and this difference has a tendency toward significance (p = 0.09). Supporting the previous findings (e.g., Firestone et al., 1998b; Grubin, 1994; Milsom et al., 2003; Oliver et al., 2007), significantly more homicidal (76%) than non-homicidal (65%) sexual offenders have no intimate partner (i.e., married or unmarried partnership) at the time of their offense. Although significantly fewer homicidal sex offenders admit having sexually penetrated (oral, vaginal, and/or anal) their victims than their non-homicidal counterparts (58% versus 77%), they are nevertheless more likely to report having engaged in mutilation of their victim's sexual body parts than their non-homicidal counterparts (18% versus 3%).

In terms of the psychological characteristics of homicidal and non-homicidal sexual offenders, sex offenders who kill are reported to have indulge significantly more in deviant sexual fantasies starting at least a year prior to their sexual offense than their non-homicidal counterparts (42% versus 25%). This finding is consistent with the findings in the previous studies (e.g., Langevin et al., 1988; Proulx et al., 2002). On a similar note, significantly more sexual murderers than non-homicidal sexual offenders (NHSOs) (22% versus 5%) are found to have engaged in at least one paraphilia (e.g., coprophilia, fetishism, partialism, masochism, sexual sadism, tranvestism, urophilia, and zoophilia). This finding is consistent with the previous findings that indicate that sexual killers are particularly more likely to be diagnosed with sexual sadism and fetishism than nonhomicidal sex offenders (Chan & Beauregard, 2015; Firestone et al., 1998b; Koch et al., 2011; Langevin et al., 1988).

Of particular note, more of the homicide victims of sexual murderers live alone at the time of the attack compared with the victims of sex offenders who do not murder (35% versus 22%), and this difference tends toward significance ($p = 0.08$). This finding is novel as none of the past studies have tested for this difference. In terms of the pre-crime precipitators, significantly more sex offenders who killed (80%) than those who did not kill (61%) are intoxicated by alcohol during the hours prior to their sexual offense. The previous studies also report a similar trend, namely that homicidal sex offenders use and/or abuse alcohol and/or drugs more frequently than their nonhomicidal counterparts (Chene & Cusson, 2007; Koch et al., 2011; Langevin, 2003). Importantly, this study is the first to find that significantly more sexual murderers (31%) than nonhomicidal sex offenders (18%) engage in deviant sexual fantasies featuring scenarios that exclude their eventual victim within the 48-hour period prior to their sexual offense.

Different measurement scales and subscales are constructed on the basis of 29 observed indicators. Although there is no significant mean difference between homicidal and nonhomicidal sexual offenders in terms of their overall propensity to become *an offender motivated* to commit a sexual offense, the sex offenders who kill have significantly more *sexually deviant behaviors and attitudes* than those who do not kill (0.94 versus 0.54 out of 3 possible points). Additionally, the study finds that there is a significantly higher probability of the sexual murderers committing their sexual offense in *the absence of a capable guardian or guardianship* than the nonhomicidal sex offenders (1.18 versus 0.90 out of 3 possible points). Sexual homicide offenders also report having higher *pre-crime precipitator* scores than their non-homicidal counterparts (2.38 versus 2.06 out of 7 possible points). Although this last finding is not statistically significant ($p < 0.05$), it nevertheless approaches this statistical mark ($p = 0.09$). In contrast to the expected offending pattern theorized by Chan et al. (2011), nonhomicidal sex offenders are significantly more likely than homicidal sexual offenders to perpetrate an offense against a victim whom they perceived as *attractive and suitable* (2.15 versus 1.33 out of 5 possible points).

In order to examine the theoretical pathway of the sexual homicide offending process as outlined in Chan et al. (2011) and the proposed alternative models, the step-wise logistic regressions are used. As aforementioned, the measure of *a motivated offender* is assessed in two ways: a five-subscale model and a single-scale model. When the construct of the motivated offender is measured with the five-subscale model, it yields somewhat similar effects for the models with (i.e., proposed alternative model) and without (i.e., Chan et al.'s model) the inclusion of the *pre-crime precipitators*. As one of the subscales of the *motivated offender* construct, the odds of the offender killing his victim increase by 77% in the model without the *pre-crime precipitators* when the sexual offender possesses *sexually deviant behaviors and attitudes*; however, the odds reduce to 71% when the construct of the *pre-crime precipitators* is included in the model. Supporting the previous findings (e.g., Chan & Beauregard, 2015; Firestone et al., 1998a, 1998b, 2000; Koch et al., 2011; Langevin et al., 1988; Proulx et al., 2002), sexual murderers have more sexually deviant behaviors and attitudes (e.g., paraphilias, deviant sexual fantasies) than their nonhomicidal counterparts.

When the offense is committed in the *absence of a capable guardian or guardianship*, the odds of a sexual offense resulting in a lethal outcome increase by 73%, but the odds drop to 71% when the *pre-crime precipitators* construct is added to the model. Interestingly, with and without the *pre-crime precipitators*, the odds of the victim being murdered decrease by 27% when the victim is deemed an *attractive and suitable target*. These findings are novel in the literature. It is important to note that the inclusion of the *pre-crime precipitators* into the offending model fail to yield any significant effect on the odds of the offender's victim being murdered. Simply put, the inclusion of the *pre-crime precipitators* construct in the model fails to enhance the theoretical model in terms of explaining the offending process in sexual homicide by using the five-subscale *motivated offender* model.

Besides the five-subscale model, a single-scale model is used to test the *motivated offender* measure. When the *motivated offender* measure is assessed in the single-scale model, no significant effect is found in the models with and without the construct of the *pre-crime precipitators*. In the model without the *pre-crime precipitators*, the odds of the offender murdering his victim increase by 48% when the offense is committed in the *absence of any capable guardian or guardianship*. However, the odds of the offender killing his victim is only slightly reduced to 47% in the model that includes the construct of the *pre-crime precipitators* as the offender's motivation accelerator. Similar to the findings previously discussed in relation to both models (with and without the construct of the *pre-crime precipitators*), the odds of the offender not killing the victim who he regards as attractive and suitable increases by 49% in the model without this construct by using the five-subscale *motivated offender* measure. However, the odds increase to 52% when the *pre-crime precipitators* are considered as the factors that further motivate the offender to commit a sexual offense.

As proposed in the alternative model of Chan et al.'s (2011) framework, the construct of *pre-crime precipitators* only yields a tendency toward significance ($p = .09$) in terms of motivating the offender to commit a sexual homicide when tested in the model. Even when this construct is tested independently without any other constructs, a significant finding is not obtained ($p = .11$). Compared with the previous findings (e.g., Chene & Cusson, 2007; Koch et al., 2011; Langevin, 2003) where homicidal sex offenders have more *pre-crime precipitators* (e.g., use and/or abuse drugs and alcohol prior to and/or at the time of the offense) than nonhomicidal sex offenders, this study fails to find a significant difference between these two types of sexual offenders. The insignificant results for the *pre-crime precipitators* that are found in this study could possibly be due to the limited number of observed indicators in measuring this construct. For instance, although the offender's angry feelings are argued to be a predisposing factor in several studies (e.g., Beauregard & Proulx, 2002, 2007; Beauregard, Proulx et al., 2007; Beauregard, Stone, et al., 2008; Mieczkowski & Beauregard, 2010), this pre-crime factor is not included as one of the observed indicators of the construct of the *pre-crime precipitators* in this study. Clearly, more research is warranted.

Of interest are the additional regression analyses performed by removing female victims aged 17 years old and below, which results in a sample of 209 offenders with valid cases based on the victim's age (51 HSOs and 158 NHSOs). These additional analyses are conducted to investigate if a different offense trend could be found among offenders who victimize only adult females. It is noteworthy that the findings in this sample of offenders remain the same as those found in the originally designed study (230 valid cases of homicidal and nonhomicidal sexual offenders who perpetrated offenses against females of all ages).

Overall, the findings in this study indicate that the theoretical constructs measuring the propositions of the social learning theory are better supported than the propositions of the routine activity theory. Nevertheless, both Chan et al.'s (2011) theoretical framework and the proposed alternative model are not empirically well supported in this study. There are two possible reasons for this lack of support. First, the measures of the theoretical constructs in this study may have had a critical impact on the findings. It is possible that the observed indicators that are selected to test the different theoretical constructs are not good measures of the proposed theoretical propositions. This is not unexpected given that the data set used in this study is not initially collected for the purpose of this research.

Another possible reason is that both theoretical models are not good at explaining the offending process in sexual homicide. Of particular note, in this study, the *attractive and suitable target* proposition of the routine activity theory is not a good theoretical proposition in predicting the lethal outcome of a sexual offense. Clearly, sexual homicide is a rare event. Furthermore, each individual is unique in terms of the manifestation of their personality and behavior. Therefore, it may be difficult to theoretically explain the behavioral patterns of such a distinctive offending behavior. Specifically, both theoretical models fail to incorporate other determining factors that are difficult to measure, particularly with the data set used in this study, such as the offender's psychopathological factors (e.g., personality disorder, sexual sadism, paraphilias, and psychopathy). As such, it is not unreasonable that this study generates findings that are inconsistent with the previous findings, especially with regard to the effect of the pre-crime precipitating factors in explaining the offender's motivation to commit a sexual murder. As an alternative, an offender's typology with distinctive criminal profiles may be a better way to comprehend the offending process and behavior of sexual murderers. As evidenced, different typologies, both clinical and empirical, have been developed over the years as ways to better explain the different types of sexual murderers.

6.2   The integrative explanation: theoretical and practical implications

Although the findings presented in this study fail to confirm the theoretical predictions outlined in both Chan et al.'s (2011) framework and the proposed alternative model, the results contribute to the literature in two key areas: (1) theoretical implications and (2) practical implications in the areas of crime prevention measures and offender profiling. Clearly, this empirical research is designed to substantively advance our knowledge in terms of understanding the offending process in sexual homicide. As such, the empirical findings of this study could provide scholars, researchers, and law enforcement agents with insights into the phenomenon of sexual homicide offending. Specifically, the findings of this study may prove valuable in assisting law enforcement agents to ascertain persons of interest in their investigative efforts.

6.2.1   Theoretical implications

Notably, the most direct implication of this study is the empirical testing of Chan et al.'s (2011) integrated criminological theory of sexual homicide offending. Although this theoretical model is only marginally supported by the findings of this study, the study nevertheless paves the path for future informative research by using Chan et al.'s model. Further empirical investigations of this theoretical model that use different methodological and statistical strategies are warranted. For example, data collection methods should be tailored to the purpose of the study, with measures that are developed for specific theoretical constructs. Additionally, the statistical strategies that are used specifically for theory testing or development should be adopted. More elaboration on suggestions for future research is given in the following section. Further comparative research could be conducted to assess whether Chan et al.'s model or the proposed alternative model substantially explains the offending process of SHOs.

6.2.2   Practical implications

Besides contributing to the sexual homicide literature from the theoretical standpoint, the findings of this study have practical implications, especially from the perspective of crime prevention and offender profiling. Taken as a whole, consistent with Chan et al.'s theoretical propositions, the findings of this study suggest that the sexual offender's sexually deviant behaviors and attitudes as a motivating factor and the presence/absence of a capable guardian or guardianship in the immediate crime scene surroundings are significant and critical factors in deciding the survival rate of the victim.

Specifically from the perspective of offender profiling, if the victim of a sexual offense is killed, the likelihood of the murderer being someone who possesses sexually deviant behaviors and attitudes and engages in deviant sexual fantasies, paraphilias, and compulsive masturbation is significantly high, the odds ranging from 71% to 77% (approximately four out of five cases). Of particular note, the predicting effect of deviant sexual fantasies depends not only on the frequency of such behavior but also on the degree of severity or deviance of these sexual fantasies. Nonetheless, more research is needed to further distinguish the differences in type and frequency of sexual fantasies between homicidal and non-homicidal sexual offenders. Drawing from this finding, sexual homicides can potentially be prevented from the outset. In order to attempt to lessen the occurrence of sexual homicides and sexual offenses, crime prevention measures should be undertaken as early as possible in at-risk populations. As reflected in this study, sexually deviant behaviors and attitudes are a significant predictor of a sexual offense resulting in a lethal outcome. Thus, sexually deviant behaviors and attitudes should be discouraged at the domestic level, where such behaviors and attitudes can be learned via differential association and/or imitation (as tested in this study) within a family setting.

As supported by previous studies, healthy parent-child bonding and secure attachment from birth are crucial in shaping positive and constructive behavioral and attitude patterns (Chan & Chui, 2012; Chan, Lo, Zhong, & Chui, 2015; Chui & Chan, 2011a, 2012a, 2012b, 2013a, 2013b, 2013c; 2014a), especially toward sex and the avoidance of violence (Heide & Solomon, 2006). Programs and activities designed to prepare individuals to become good parents and caregivers, such as parenting classes, support groups for parents and caregivers, and child development and parenting courses in high schools, are called for (Heide, 1999; Wong, Chan, & Cheng, 2014). The involvement of a third party such as professionally trained social service personnel not only could build bridges between parents and children, especially to parents who are less confident in rearing their children adequately (Chan & Chui, 2013, 2015a, 2015b; Chan & Wong, 2015; Chui & Chan, 2012c), but also to provide other effective social services tailored to the needs of individual family units that gear toward the development of pro-social attitudes and behavior (Chui & Chan, 2011b, 2012d, 2013d). The findings of this study address the importance of a healthy parent-child relationship in preventing the involvement of offspring in delinquent conduct, including sexually deviant acts that may result in a lethal outcome. With healthy and prosocial behavioral and attitude patterns embedded since early childhood, the probability of learning deviant behaviors and adopting negative attitudes, particularly those sexual in nature (e.g., indulgence in deviant sexual fantasies, engaging in paraphilias, consumption of pornography, and compulsive masturbation), from other influential individuals such as close friends and intimate partners later in life would likely be greatly diminished. This notion is recently empirically supported by a study of the influence of childhood maltreatment on subsequent adult sexual offending (Reckdenwald, Mancini, & Beauregard, 2014). This influence could even be exacerbated in the case of near fatal childhood maltreatment (Mariano, Chan, & Myers, 2014).

At the individual level, sexual offenses, both homicidal and non-homicidal, can be prevented through self-protective measures. In this study, the results indicate that the likelihood that the victim of a sexual offense is killed significantly increases when the victim is being victimized in the absence of effective self-guardianship or a capable guardian. Certainly, this finding addresses the importance of appropriate self-guardianship in avoiding a sexual offense ending with a lethal outcome. For instance, extra self-protection measures (e.g., installing extra locks on entrance doors, owning a dog, or having an alarm monitoring system) if living alone are likely to reduce the likelihood of being victimized (Mustaine & Tewksbury, 1998). In addition, alcohol and/or drug use or abuse is related to a lower probability of using self-protective measures (Tewksbury & Mustaine, 2003). Most importantly, intoxicated individuals are perceived to be more vulnerable than those who are not intoxicated (Abbey, 1987, 1991; George, Gournic, & McAfee, 1988; Mustaine & Tewksbury, 2002). Hence, individuals would be wise to curtail using alcohol or drugs, particularly to excess, in outdoor surroundings, especially when not accompanied by trusted individuals.

Taken as a whole, this study clearly offers an important implication for the practice in the area of notification policies on sexual offenders. Recent studies (Hill, Habermann, Klussman, Berner, & Briken, 2008; Khachatryan, Heide, Hummel, & Chan, 2014; Myers et al., 2010) also show that the recidivism rates (violent recidivism, sexual, or nonsexual) of sex offenders who killed, especially those who commit their first sexual homicide as adolescents or young adults, are substantially higher than those of nonhomicidal sex offenders in general (see Proulx, Beauregard, Lussier, & Leclerc, 2014 for a review). Certainly, more efforts should be made to reduce the reoffending risk of HSOs. One such effort would be to enhance the sexual offender notification system by allocating more monitoring resources if sexual offenders who previously have killed their victims are going to be released.

6.3 Conclusion

Sexual homicides are rare events. Even in a country where violent offenses are rampant, like in the US, sexual homicide arrestees accounted for only about 0.6% of the homicide arrestees over the 32-year period from 1976 to 2007 (Chan, Frei, et al., 2013). In view of the rarity of this offense, much remains to be studied in the field of sexual homicide. To date, fewer than 50 empirical studies have been published on topics related to sexual homicide (Chan & Heide, 2009).

Although this study furthers our understanding of the offenders and victims of sexual homicide and the offense itself, its findings should be interpreted cautiously given the shortcomings of the data. First, the sample of this study comprises a total of 230 valid cases of homicidal and non-homicidal sexual offenses against females. Although this sample is arguably a representative sample of the population of male HSOs and NHSOs incarcerated in the province of Quebec, Canada, during the period of 1995 to 2005,[1] who sexually offended against females, the size of the sample might prevent some findings from reaching a significance level. In addition, the unequal number of valid cases of homicidal ($N = 55$) and non-homicidal ($N = 175$) sexual offenders in this study might have prevented some differences from reaching statistical significance. Future studies should consider recruiting a sizeable sample with an equal number of HSOs and NHSOs in order to increase the likelihood of producing convincing and robust findings. Another noteworthy point is that this sample of 230 cases consisted of HSOs and NHSOs who committed either a sexual assault or a minor sexual offense. This study includes cases of sexual assault and other minor sexual offenses to increase the sample size of both groups of sexual offenders. Perhaps the results might have been different if the samples of homicidal SHOs and nonhomicidal sexual offenders were limited to offenders who sexually assaulted their victim. Therefore, future research should consider re-examining both theoretical models by controlling for the types of sexual offenses committed by both offenders.

As evidenced in this study, it is possible to argue that these models are simply not good theoretical models to distinguish the offense process of HSOs from that of NHSOs. Thus, because of the less supported univariate and bivariate findings in terms of differentiating these two offender samples, the analytic strategies that are used in this study restrict the range and sophistication of the multivariate statistical analyses that could be performed. In future research, other comparison groups such as nonsexual homicide offenders (NSHOs) could be used as another comparison sample to further test the suitability of both Chan et al.'s theoretical framework and the proposed alternative model in explaining the offending perspective of sexual homicide. Additionally, if significant findings are found in univariate and bivariate analyses in future studies, more advanced statistical analytic strategies might be possible. More advanced techniques might produce findings with greater depth. Among the other possible advanced analytic strategies, the structural equation modeling (SEM) approach is an option to consider. Broadly speaking, SEM is a statistical modeling approach that is functional for theory testing or development (Asparouhov & Muthén, 2008; Kline, 2005). According to Garson (2009) and Kline (2005), SEM can be utilized to test or develop a theoretical model in several ways: (1) in a strictly confirmatory way with one model proposed and tested; (2) in an exploratory way by examining alternative models, with several theoretical models being examined and compared to determine the best fitting model; or (3) in a model development approach with a preliminary model tested and subsequent modifications made to improve the model fit. Simply put, the SEM approach is able to measure if the hypothesized model will adequately project the actual observed relationship pattern in the data (see Kline, 2005).

Secondly, the data collection methodology adopted by the original research team has some limitations. As noted by the original research team, the external validity of the findings generated from the data, especially on nonhomicidal sex offenders, is questionable (Beauregard & Proulx, 2007; Beauregard, Deslauriers-Varin, & St-Yves, 2010; Beauregard, Rossmo, & Proulx, 2007; Beauregard et al., 2007, 2008; Deslauriers-Varin & Beauregard, 2010). The data only samples incarcerated sexual offenders who had been charged and convicted. Sexual offenders, both homicidal and non-homicidal, such as those who are initially apprehended by the police but later released or acquitted by the court are not part of the sample of this study. In addition, it is likely that the offending patterns of homicidal and non-homicidal sexual offenders who have avoided detection are different from the offending patterns of those who have been detained. It is hypothesized that the former are likely to be more sophisticated in their offending patterns in order to avoid being apprehended (Beauregard, Rebocho, & Rossmo, 2010; Beauregard et al., 2007). Replication of this study with other samples of SHOs and NSHOs is desirable. The generalizability of the findings produced using this Canadian data to sexual offenders in other countries is unknown. If possible, future studies should include both incarcerated and non-incarcerated sexual offenders of both types so that the findings produced are capable of being generalizing to the entire population of SHOs and NSHOs. Non-incarcerated sexual offenders, such as those who are arrested and/or charged but not convicted, might be considered for inclusion in future studies. Additionally, comparative research on sexual offenders from different countries is desirable.

In addition, the data collection methodology used by the original research team consisted of both official data and self-reported responses. Retrospective self-report methods are used to obtain information that is not recorded in the official records (Beauregard & Lecler, 2007; Beauregard et al., 2007; Deslauriers-Varin & Beauregard, 2010). This type of data collection method may suffer from retrospective distortion, both intentional and unintentional, even if adequate interviewing techniques are used to enhance the level of detail (Polascheck, Hudson, Ward, & Siegert, 2001). Of particular note, the responses provided by the sexual offenders only reflect their perception of the offense. To safeguard against this concern, self-reported information that is used in future research should be compared with the official data (e.g., police reports) when such data are available. In the case of discrepancy, information from the official data should be prioritized, because it is in the data set developed by the Canadian researchers and used in the current study (see also Deslauriers-Varin & Beauregard, 2010).

Another possible drawback of the data collection method is the restriction of responses to dummy-coded options. This method clearly restricts the variability of the sample's responses. Consequently, the low alpha coefficients of the theoretical measures in this study are not surprising. In future research, the subject's responses should not be restricted to dummy-coded options. Instead, more variability of responses should be considered in order to capture a wide range of possible responses from the subjects.

Most importantly, this study performs a secondary analysis of the data collected on both incarcerated homicidal and non-homicidal sexual offenders by a group of Canadian researchers. Thus, the variable selection for the constructs that is included in the current study is limited by the availability of variables in the data set. For example, there is a lack of data measuring *the absence of a capable guardian or guardianship*. No information is available in the data set to permit analyses at the structural level of this theoretical proposition (e.g., environmental conditions, geographical locations, and formal or informal social control mechanisms). Consequently, only the constructs at the individual level of this theoretical proposition (i.e., self-guardianship measures) are assessed. Therefore, it is not surprising to find that the internal consistency of *the absence of a capable guardian or guardianship* measure is low. Nevertheless, the previous studies have acknowledged the importance of self-protective measures in preventing individuals from becoming the victims of violent offenses, especially crimes that are sexual in nature (e.g.,

Mustaine & Tewksbury, 1998, 2002; Schwartz & Pitts, 1995; Schwartz et al., 2001; Tewksbury & Mustaine, 2001, 2003).

Future research should ideally focus on first-hand data collection in the sample population of interest (i.e., homicidal and non-homicidal sexual offenders) by targeting the specific data required to comprehensively examine both theoretical models (i.e., Chan et al.'s model and the proposed alternative framework) discussed in this study. Particularly, the responses regarding the structural level of *the absence of a capable guardian or guardianship* measure should be obtained. If such findings support Chan et al.'s theoretical propositions, the practical implications, specifically crime prevention measures, would not be limited to the individual level only, as in the present study. For instance, enhanced ecological guardianship and human guardianship, such as increasing formal (e.g., actively monitored closed-circuit televisions [CCTVs] and police surveillance cameras) and informal (e.g., neighborhood watch groups, urban citizen patrols, and security guards) social control mechanisms (Hollis-Peel et al., 2011; Smallbone, Marshall, & Wortley, 2008), may effectively discourage potential sexual offenders from executing their offending plan in these highly guarded surroundings.

Additionally, social control efforts to curtail sexual offenses, and sexual homicides in particular, should not only be limited to the physical world. Guardianship in cyberspace is clearly an area worth paying extra attention to. Even though the data are anecdotal, cases of SHOs hunting for victims through online chats or forums have been reported (Chan et al., 2011). The utility of the cyber world to potential sex killers in searching for their prey should not be overlooked. Online guardians in the form of law enforcement and regulatory agencies, website personnel, and netizens (i.e., individuals who frequently surf the Internet) are needed to reduce the probability that a motivated offender will troll the virtual world for his next prey. Therefore, with the use of first-hand data, the future research should not be limited to the individual level but should also explore the structural level of the guardianship measure theorized by Chan and colleagues (2011).

Taken together, although the theoretical propositions of both Chan et al.'s model and the proposed revised framework are partially supported by the findings produced in this study, different results may be generated from a more finely tuned test of the models. The inclusion of more precise variables would answer more convincingly whether Chan et al.'s theoretical model is able to explain the offending process in sexual homicide with data collected specifically for this purpose. In addition, and particularly relevant to the present study, further empirical examination might help to determine whether Chan et al.'s theoretical model or the proposed alternative framework produces a stronger and more comprehensive criminological theory of the sexual homicide offending process.

Notes

2   Sexual Homicide Offending: Offender Classifications

1. The victims of the non-serial SHOs were 89% female and 8% male. The remaining 3% of the victims were murdered by serial SHOs whose victims included both females and males.

3   Sexual Homicide Offending: Theoretical Explanations

1. Although Hickey's (1997, 2002) trauma-control model initially offers a theoretical explanation for serial murder, this model can also be applied to the theoretical study of sexual homicide, particularly serial sexual homicide.

4   Sexual Homicide Offending: In Search of a Criminological Explanation

1. The potential of other mainstream criminological theories, such as self-control, social bonding, strain, and social disorganization, to explain the offending perspective of sexual homicide, although not examined in this work, should not be overlooked.
2. Proponents of theoretical integration argue that this method reduces the number of theories and offers a more powerful explanation of crime and delinquency. There are scholars (e.g., Hirschi, 1979, 1989; Short, 1979) who believe in combining two or more theories. However, is this either an undesirable goal or a formidable task (Bernard & Snipes, 1996)? Hirschi (1979), for example, argue that most theories are contradictory in nature and their assumptions are incompatible. Theories can only be integrated if they are basically arguing the same thing. Integration may ultimately misrepresent individual theories (Hirschi, 1989).

5   Sexual Homicide Offending: Toward an Integrative Theoretical Explanation

1. Homicidal sexual offenders (HSOs), sexual homicide offenders (SHOs), sexual murderers, and sex killers are used interchangeably in referring to the same group of sexual offenders – those who sexually killed their victim.
2. A latent variable is referred to as an unobservable or immeasurable concept that helps to explain the association among two or more observed constructs (Bollen, 2002).
3. For the *motivated offender* measure, five subscales with a total of 16 items (a possible maximum score of 19 points) are created: (1) *parental or familial*

aggressive and deviant sexual behaviors and attitudes (five items; 0–5 points), (2) *parental or sibling past sexual and nonsexual criminal background* (four items; 0–4 points), (3) *personal experience with family violence* (three items; 0–6 points), (4) *personal consumption of pornography* (one item; 0–1 point), and (5) *personal sexually deviant behaviors and attitudes* (three items; 0–3 points). The *attractive and suitable target* scale was measured using three items with a possible maximum score of five points, while the *absence of a capable guardian or guardianship* scale was assessed using three items with a possible maximum score of three points. Lastly, the *precrime precipitating factors* scale was assessed using seven items with a possible maximum score of seven points.

6   Implications and Conclusions

1. The sample of nonhomicidal sex offenders in this study was noted to represent 85% of the sexual murderers convicted and imprisoned in correctional institutions in the Quebec region of Canada (Beauregard et al., 2008).

References

Abbey, A. (1987). Misperceptions of friendly behavior as sexual interest: A survey of naturally occurring incidents. *Psychology of Women Quarterly*, 11, 173–194.

Abbey, A. (1991). Acquaintance rape and alcohol consumption on college campuses: How are they linked? *Journal of American College Health*, 39, 165–169.

Abbey, A., Ross, L. T., & McDuffie, D. (1996). Alcohol and dating risk factors for sexual assault among college women. *Psychology of Women Quarterly*, 20, 147–169.

Abel, G. G., Becker, J. V., Cunningham-Rather, J., Muttleman, M., & Rouleau, J. L. (1988). Multiple paraphilic diagnoses among sex offenders. *Bulletin of the American Academy of Psychiatry and the Law*, 16(2), 153–168.

Abel, G. G., & Blanchard, E. B. (1974). The role of fantasy in the treatment of sexual deviation. *Archives of General Psychiatry*, 30, 467–475.

Adjorlolo, S., & Chan, H. C. O. (2014). The controversy of defining serial murder: Revisited. *Aggression and Violent Behavior*, 19(5), 486–491.

Agnew, R. (2003). An integrated theory of the adolescent peak in offending. *Youth and Society*, 34(3), 263–299.

Agresti, A., & Finlay, B. (1997). *Statistical methods for the social sciences*. Upper Saddle River, NJ: Prentice Hall.

Akers, R. L. (1968). Problems in the sociology of deviance: Social definitions and behavior. *Social Forces*, 46(4), 455–465.

Akers, R. L. (1973). *Deviant behavior: A social learning approach*. Belmont, CA: Wadsworth Publishing Company.

Akers, R. L. (1977). *Deviant behavior: A social learning approach* (2nd edition). Belmont, CA: Wadsworth Publishing Company.

Akers, R. L. (1985). *Deviant behavior: A social learning approach* (3rd edition). Belmont, CA: Wadsworth Publishing Company.

Akers, R. L. (1989). A social behaviorist's perspective on integration of theories of crime and deviance. In S. F. Messner, M. D. Krohn, & A. E. Liska (eds), *Theoretical integration in the study of deviance and crime* (pp. 23–36). Albany, NY: State University of New York Press.

Akers, R. L. (1990). Rational choice, deterrence, and social learning theory in criminology: The path not taken. *Journal of Criminal Law and Criminology*, 81(3), 653–676.

Akers, R. L. (1992). *Drugs, alcohol, and society: Social structure, process, and policy*. Belmont, CA: Wadsworth Publishing Company.

Akers, R. L. (1997). *Criminological theories: Introduction and evaluation* (2nd edition). Los Angeles, CA: Roxbury.

Akers, R. L. (1998). *Social learning and social structure: A general theory of crime and deviance*. Boston, MA: Northeastern University Press.

Akers, R. L. (2001). Social learning theory. In R. Paternoster & R. Bachman (eds), *Explaining criminals and crime: Essays in contemporary criminological theory* (pp. 192–210). Los Angeles, CA: Roxbury.

Akers, R. L., & Cochran, J. K. (1985). Adolescent marijuana use: A test of three theories of deviant behavior. *Deviant Behavior, 6,* 323–346.

Akers, R. L., & Jensen, G. F. (2003). Editors' introduction. In R. L. Akers & G. F. Jensen (Vol. eds), *Social learning theory and the explanation of crime: Advances in criminological theory* (Vol. 11) (pp. 1–8). New Brunswick, NJ: Transaction.

Akers, R. L., & Jensen, G. F. (2006). The empirical status of social learning theory of crime and deviance: The past, present, and future. In F. T. Cullen, J. P. Wright, & K. R. Blevins (Vol. eds), *Taking stock: The status of criminological theory, advances in criminological theory* (Vol. 15) (pp. 37–76). New Brunswick, NJ: Transaction.

Akers, R. L., & Lee, G. (1996). A longitudinal test of social learning theory: Adolescent smoking. *Journal of Drug Issues, 26*(2), 317–343.

Akers, R. L., & Sellers, C. (2009). *Criminological theories: Introduction, evaluation, and application* (5th edition), New York: Oxford University Press.

Amir, A. (1971). *Patterns of forcible rape.* Chicago, IL: University of Chicago Press.

Anderson, A. L., & Meier, R. F. (2004). Interactions and the criminal event perspective. *Journal of Contemporary Criminal Justice, 20,* 416–440.

Arnold, R., Keane, C., & Baron, S. (2005). Assessing risk of victimization through epidemiological concepts: An alternative analytic strategy applied to routine activities theory. *Canadian Review of Sociology and Anthropology, 42,* 345–364.

Arrigo, B. A., & Purcell, C. E. (2001). Explaining paraphilias and lust murder: Toward an integrated model. *International Journal of Offender Therapy and Comparative Criminology, 45,* 6–31.

Asparouhov, T., & Muthén, B. (2008). Exploratory structural equation modeling. *Structural Equation Modeling, 16,* 397–438.

Bachman, R., & Paternoster, R. (2004). *Statistics for criminology and criminal justice.* Boston, MA: McGraw Hill.

Balemba, S., Beauregard, E., & Martineau, M. (2014). Getting away with murder: A thematic approach to solved and unsolved sexual homicides using crime scene factors. *Police Practice and Research,* 15(3), 221–233.

Bandura, A. (1977). *Social learning theory.* Englewood Cliffs, NJ: Prentice Hall.

Bandura, A. (1978). Social learning theory of aggression. *Journal of Communication, 28,* 12–29.

Barack, G. (1998). *Integrating criminologies.* Boston: Allyn and Bacon.

Barbaree, H. E., & Marshall, W. L. (1991). The role of male sexual arousal in rape: Six models. *Journal of Consulting and Clinical Psychology, 59,* 621–630.

Barbaree, H. E., Marshall, W. L., Yates, E., & Lightfoot, L. O. (1983). Alcohol intoxication and deviant sexual arousal in male social drinkers. *Behavior Research and Therapy, 21,* 365–373.

Baron, L., & Straus, M. A. (1989). *Four theories of rape in American society: A state-level analysis.* New Haven, CT: Yale University Press.

Batton, C., & Ogle, R. S. (2003). "Who's it gonna be – you or me?" The potential of social learning for integrated homicide-suicide theory. In R. L. Akers & G. F. Jensen (eds), *Social learning theory and the explanation of crime* (pp. 85–108). New Brunswick, NJ: Transaction Publishers.

Beauregard, E., & Field, J. (2008). Body disposal patterns of sexual murderers: Implications for offender profiling. *Journal of Police and Criminal Psychology,* 23(2), 81–89.

Beauregard, E. & Lecler, B. (2007). An application of the rational choice approach to the offending process of sex offenders: A closer look at the decision-making. *Sexual Abuse: A Journal of Research and Treatment, 19,* 115–133.

Beauregard, E., & Proulx, J. (2002). Profiles in the offending process of nonserial sexual murderers. *International Journal of Offender Therapy and Comparative Criminology,* 46(4), 386–399.

Beauregard, E., & Proulx, J. (2007). A classification of sexual homicide against men. *International Journal of Offender Therapy and Comparative Criminology,* 51(4), 420–432.

Beauregard, E., Deslauriers-Varin, N., & St-Yves, M. (2010). Interactions between factors related to the decision of sex offenders to confess during police interrogation: A classification-tree approach. *Sexual Abuse: A Journal of Research and Treatment,* 22(3), 343–367.

Beauregard, E., Lussier, P., & Proulx, J. (2005). The role of sexual interests and situational factors on rapists' modus operandi: Implications for offender profiling. *Legal and Criminological Psychology,* 10, 265–278.

Beauregard, E., Proulx, J., & St-Yves, M. (2007). Angry and sadistic: Two types of sexual murderers. In J. Proulx, E. Beauregard, M. Cusson, & A. Nicole (eds), *Sexual murderers: A comparative analysis and new perspectives* (pp. 123–141). Chichester: John Wiley and Sons.

Beauregard, E., Rebocho, M. F., & Rossmo, D. K. (2010). Target selection patterns in rape. *Journal of Investigative Psychology and Offender Profiling,* 7, 137–152.

Beauregard, E., Rossmo, D. K., & Proulx, J. (2007). A descriptive model of the hunting process of serial sex offenders: A rational choice perspective. *Journal of Family Violence,* 22, 449–463.

Beauregard, E., Stone, M. R., Proulx, J., & Michaud, P. (2008). Sexual murderers of children: Developmental, precrime, crime, and postcrime factors. *International Journal of Offender Therapy and Comparative Criminology,* 52(3), 253–269.

Beauregard, E., Proulx, J., Rossmo, K., Leclerc, B., & Allaire, J. -F. (2007). Script analysis of hunting process in serial sex offenders. *Criminal Justice and Behavior,* 34, 1069–1084.

Beech, A., Robertson, D., & Clarke, J. (2001). *Towards a sexual murder typology.* Paper presented at the 20th annual conference of the Association of the Treatment of Sexual Abusers, San Antonio, Texas.

Beech, A., Oliver, C., Fisher, D., & Beckett, R. C. (2006). *STEP 4: The sex offender treatment program in prison: Addressing the needs of rapists and sexual murderers.* Birmingham, UK: University of Birmingham.

Belknap, J. (1987). Routine activities theory and the risk of rape: Analyzing ten years of national crime survey data. *Criminal Justice Policy Review,* 2, 337–356.

Bellair, P. E., Roscigno, V. J., & Velez, M. B. (2003). Occupational structure, social learning, and adolescent violence. In R. L. Akers & G. F. Jensen (eds), *Social learning theory and the explanation of crime* (pp. 197–225). New Brunswick, NJ: Transaction Publishers.

Benda, B. B., & DiBlasio, F. A. (1994). An integration of theory: Adolescent sexual contacts. *Journal of Youth and Adolescence,* 23(3), 403–420.

Bennell, C., Bloomfield, S., Emeno, K., & Musolino, E. (2013). Classifying serial sexual murder/murderers: An attempt to validate Keppel and Walter's (1999) model. *Criminal Justice and Behavior,* 40(1), 5–25.

Bennett, T., & Wright, R. (1984). *Burglars on burglary: Prevention and the offender.* Aldershot: Gower.

Bernard, T. J. (2001). Integrating theories in criminology. In R. Paternoster & R. Bachman (eds), *Essays in contemporary criminological theory: Explaining criminals and crime* (pp. 335–346). Los Angeles: Roxbury Publishing.

Bernard, T. J., & Ritti, R. (1990). The role of theory in scientific research. In K. Kempf (ed.), *Measurement issues in criminology* (pp. 1–20). New York: Springer-Verlag.

Bernard, T. J., & Snipes, J. B. (1996). Theoretical integration in criminology. In M. Tonry (ed.), *Crime and justice: A review of the research, volume 20* (pp. 301–348). Chicago, IL: University of Chicago Press.

Bernburg, J., & Thorlindsson, T. (2001). Routine activities in social context: A closer look at the role of opportunity in deviant behavior. *Justice Quarterly*, 18, 543–567.

Birkbeck, C., & LaFree, G. (1993). The situational analysis of crime and deviance. *Annual Review of Sociology*, 19, 113–137.

Blackburn, R. (1993). *The psychology of criminal conduct: Theory, research, and practice*. Chichester: John Wiley and Sons, Ltd.

Boeringer, S. B. (1996). Influences of fraternity membership, athletics, and male living arrangements on sexual aggression. *Violence and Victims*, 2, 134–147.

Boeringer, S. B., Shehan, C. L., & Akers, R. L. (1991). Social context and social learning in sexual coercion and aggression: Assessing the contribution of fraternity membership. *Family Relations*, 40(1), 58–64.

Bollen, K. B. (2002). Latent variables in psychology and the social sciences. *Annual Review of Psychology*, 53, 605–634.

Bossler, A. M., Holt, T. J., & May, D. C. (2012). Predicting online harassment victimization among a juvenile population. *Youth & Society*, 44(4), 500–523.

Boudreaux, M. C., Lord, W. D., & Jarvis, J. P. (2001). Behavioral perspectives on child homicide: The role of access, vulnerability, and routine activities theory. *Trauma, Violence, and Abuse*, 2, 56–78.

Braithwaite, J. (1989). *Crime, shame, and reintegration*. New York: Cambridge University Press.

Brittain, R. P. (1970). The sadistic sexual murderers. *Medicine, Science, and the Law*, 10, 198–207.

Burgess, A. W., Hartman, C. R., & McCormack, A. (1987). Abused to abuser: Antecedents of socially deviant behaviors. *American Journal of Psychiatry*, 144(11), 1431–1436.

Burgess, A. W., Hartman, C. R., Ressler, R. K., Douglas, J. E., & McCormack, A. (1986). Sexual homicide: A motivational model. *Journal of Interpersonal Violence*, 1, 251–272.

Burgess, R. L., & Akers, R. L. (1966). A differential association-reinforcement theory of criminal behavior. *Social Problems*, 14, 128–147.

Bushman, B. J., Baumeister, R. F., Thomaes, S., Ryu, E., Begeer, S., & West, S. G. (2009). Looking again, and harder, for a link between low self-esteem and aggression. *Journal of Personality*, 77(2), 427–446.

Campos, E., & Cusson, M. (2007). Serial killers and sexual murderers. In J. Proulx, E. Beauregard, M. Cusson, & A. Nicole (eds), *Sexual murderers: A comparative analysis and new erspectives* (pp. 99–105). Chichester: John Wiley and Sons.

Canter, D. (1989). Offender profiles. *The Psychologist*, 2(1), 12–16.

Canter, D. V., Alison, L. J., Alison, E., & Wentink, N. (2004). The organized/disorganized typology of serial murder: Myth or model? *Psychology, Public Policy, and Law*, 10(3), 293–320.

Carter, A. J., & Hollin, C. R. (2010). Characteristics of non-serial sexual homicide offenders: A review. *Psychology, Crime, and Law*, 16(1–2), 25–45.

Cass, A. I. (2007). Routine activities and sexual assault: An analysis of individual- and school-level factors. *Violence and Victims, 22*(3), 350–366.

Casten, J. A., & Payne, B. K. (2008). The influence of perceptions of social disorder and victimization on business owners' decisions to use guardianship strategies. *Journal of Criminal Justice, 36,* 396–402.

Chan, H. C. O., & Beauregard, E. (2014). Choice of weapon or weapon of choice? Examining the interactions between victim characteristics in single-victim male sexual homicide offenders. *Journal of Investigative Psychology and Offender Profiling.* Advance online publication. doi: 10.1002/jip.1432.

Chan, H. C. O., & Beauregard, E. (2015). Nonhomicidal and homicidal sexual offenders: Prevalence of maladaptive personality traits and paraphilic behaviors. *Journal of Interpersonal Violence.* Advance online publication. doi: 10.1177/0886260515575606.

Chan, H. C. O., & Chui, W. H. (2012). Psychological correlates of violent and non-violent Hong Kong juvenile probationers. *Behavioral Sciences and the Law, 30*(2), 90–102.

Chan, H. C. O., & Chui, W. H. (2013). Social bonds and school bullying: A study of Macanese male adolescents on bullying perpetration and peer victimization. *Child and Youth Care Forum, 42*(6), 599–616.

Chan, H. C. O., & Chui, W. H. (2015a). The influence of low self-control on violent and nonviolent delinquencies: A study of male adolescents from two Chinese societies. *Journal of Forensic Psychiatry and Psychology.* Advance online publication. doi: 10.1080/14789949.2015.1012534.

Chan, H. C. O., & Chui, W. H. (2015b). Social bond and self-reported nonviolent and violent delinquency: A study of traditional low risk, at-risk, and adjudicated male Chinese adolescents. *Child and Youth Care Forum.* Advance online publication. doi: 10.1007/s10566-015-9303-4.

Chan, H. C. O., & Frei, A. (2013). Female sexual homicide offenders: An examination of an under-researched offender population. *Homicide Studies, 17*(1), 95–118.

Chan, H. C. O., & Heide, K. M. (2008). Weapons used by juveniles and adult offenders in sexual homicides: An empirical analysis of 29 years of US data. *Journal of Investigative Psychology and Offender Profiling, 5*(3), 189–208.

Chan, H. C. O., & Heide, K. M. (2009). Sexual homicide: A synthesis of the literature. *Trauma, Violence, and Abuse, 10*(1), 31–54.

Chan, H. C. O., & Wong, D. S. W. (2015). The overlap between school bullying perpetration and victimization: Assessing the psychological, familial, and school factors of Chinese adolescents in Hong Kong. *Journal of Child and Family Studies.* Advance online publication. doi: 10.1007/s10826-015-0125-7.

Chan, H. C. O., Beauregard, E., & Myers, W. C. (2014). Single-victim and serial sexual homicide offenders: Differences in crime, paraphilias, and personality traits. *Criminal Behaviour and Mental Health.* Advance online publication. doi: 10.1002/cbm.1925.

Chan, H. C. O., Frei, A. M., & Myers, W. C. (2013). Female sexual homicide offenders: An analysis of the offender racial profiles in offending process. *Forensic Science International, 233*(1–3), 265–272.

Chan, H. C. O., Heide, K. M., & Beauregard, E. (2011). What propels sexual murderers: A proposed integrated theory of social learning and routine activities theories. *International Journal of Offender Therapy and Comparative Criminology, 55*(2), 228–250.

Chan, H. C. O., Heide, K. M., & Myers, W. C. (2013). Juvenile and adult offenders arrested for sexual homicide: An analysis of victim-offender relationship and weapon used by race. *Journal of Forensic Sciences, 58*(1), 85–89.

Chan, H. C. O., Myers, W. C., & Heide, K. M. (2010). An empirical analysis of 30 years of U.S. juvenile and adult sexual homicide offender data: Race and age differences in the victim-offender relationship. *Journal of Forensic Sciences, 55*(5), 1282–1290.

Chan, H. C. O., Lo, T. W., Zhong, L. Y., & Chui, W. H. (2015). Criminal recidivism of incarcerated male nonviolent offenders in Hong Kong. *International Journal of Offender Therapy and Comparative Criminology, 59*(2), 121–142.

Chene, S., & Cusson, M. (2007). Sexual murderers and sexual aggressors: Intention and situation. In J. Proulx, E. Beauregard, M. Cusson, & A. Nicole (Eds.), *Sexual murderers: A comparative analysis and new perspective* (pp. 71–97). Chichester: Wiley.

Chui, W. H., & Chan, H. C. O. (2011a). Social bonds and male juvenile delinquency while on probation: An exploratory test in Hong Kong. *Children and Youth Services Review, 33*(11), 2329–2334.

Chui, W. H., & Chan, H. C. O. (2011b). Baseline findings of a prospective study on pro-offending attitudes and self-reported problems among juvenile probationers. *The Hong Kong Journal of Social Work, 45*(1–2), 13–26.

Chui, W. H., & Chan, H. C. O. (2012a). Criminal recidivism among Hong Kong juvenile probationers. *Journal of Child and Family Studies, 21*(5), 857–868.

Chui, W. H., & Chan, H. C. O. (2012b). An empirical investigation of social bonds and juvenile delinquency in Hong Kong. *Child and Youth Care Forum, 41*(4), 371–386.

Chui, W. H., & Chan, H. C. O. (2012c). Outreach social workers for at-risk youth: A test of their attitudes towards crime and young offenders in Hong Kong. *Children and Youth Services Review, 34*(12), 2273–2279.

Chui, W. H., & Chan, H. C. O. (2012d). The Chinese Youth Attitudes toward Young Drug Users scale: An initial scale development and refinement. *Drug and Alcohol Review, 31*(4), 477–482.

Chui, W. H., & Chan, H. C. O. (2013a). Association between self-control and school bullying behaviors among Macanese adolescents. *Child Abuse & Neglect, 37*(4), 237–242.

Chui, W. H., & Chan, H. C. O. (2013b). The gendered analysis of self-control on theft and violent delinquency: An examination of Hong Kong adolescent population. *Crime & Delinquency.* Advance online publication. doi: 10.1177/0011128712470992.

Chui, W. H., & Chan, H. C. O. (2013c). Self-control and the fear of death among adolescents in Hong Kong. *Journal of Youth Studies, 16*(1), 70–85.

Chui, W. H., & Chan, H. C. O. (2013d). Psychological characteristics of male 14- to 20-year-olds on probation and in a residential home in Hong Kong. *Criminal Behaviour and Mental Health, 23*(1), 41–55.

Chui, W. H., & Chan, H. C. O. (2014a). Self-control, school bullying perpetration, and victimization among Macanese adolescents. *Journal of Child and Family Studies.* Advance online publication. doi: 10.1007/s10826-014-9979-3.

Chui, W. H., & Chan, H. C. O. (2014b). Juvenile offenders' perceptions of probation officers as social workers in Hong Kong. *Journal of Social Work, 14*(4), 398–418.

Cicchetti, D., & Lynch, M. (1995). Failures in the expectable environment and their impact on individual development: The case of child maltreatment. In D. Cicchetti & D. J. Cohen (eds), *Development psychopathology, vol. 2: Risk, disorder, and adaptation* (pp. 32–71). New York: John Wiley.

Clarke, J. & Carter, A. J. (2000). Relapse prevention with sexual murderers. In D. R. Laws, S. M. Hudson, & T. Ward (eds), *Remaking Relapse Prevention with Sex Offenders* (pp. 389–401). London: Sage.

Cohen, A. K. (1962). Multiple factor approaches. In M. E. Wolfgang, L. Savitz, & N. Johnston (eds), *The sociology of crime and delinquency* (pp.77–80). New York: John Wiley.

Cohen, L. E., & Felson, M. (1979). Social change and crime rate trends: A routine activity approach. *American Sociological Review*, 44, 588–608.

Cohen, L. E., Kluegel, J. R., & Land, K. C. (1981). Social inequality and criminal victimization. *American Sociological Review*, 46, 505–524.

Cohen, J. (1988). *Statistical power analysis for the behavioral sciences* (2nd edition). Hillsdale, NJ: Lawrence Earlbaum Associates.

Cohen, J. (1992). A power primer. *Psychological Bulletin*, 112(1), 155–159.

Commission on Obscenity and Pornography. (1970). *The report of the commission on obscenity and pornography*. New York: Bantam.

Conger, R. D. (1976). Social control and social learning models of delinquent behavior: A synthesis. *Criminology*, 14(1), 17–40.

Cook, P. E., & Hinman, D. L. (1999). Serial murder. In H. V. Hall (ed.), *Lethal violence: A sourcebook on fatal, domestic, acquaintance, and stranger violence* (pp. 363–382). Boca Raton, FL: CRC Press.

Cronbach, L. (1951). Coefficient alpha and the internal structure of tests. *Psychometrika*, 16, 297–334.

Danto, B. (1982). A psychiatric view of those who kill. In J. Bruhns, K. Bruhns, & H. Austin (eds), *The human side of homicide* (pp. 3–20). New York: Columbia University Press.

De Coste, S., Estes, S. B., & Mueller, C. W. (1999). Routine activities and sexual harassment in the workplace. *Work and Occupations*, 26, 21–49.

Dent, R. J., & Jowitt, S. (2003). Homicide and serious sexual offenses committed by children and young people: Findings from the literature and a serious case review. *Journal of Sexual Aggression*, 9(2), 85–96.

Deslauriers-Varin, N., & Beauregard, E. (2010). Victims' routine activities and sex offenders' target selection scripts: A latent class analysis. *Sexual Abuse: A Journal of Research and Treatment*, 22(3), 315–342.

Diamantopoulou, S., Rydell, A-. M., & Henricsson, L. (2008). Can both low and high self-esteem be related to aggression in children? *Social Development*, 17(3), 682–698.

Dietz, P. E., Hazelwood, M. S., & Warren, D. S. W. (1990). The sexually sadistic criminal and his offenses. *Bulletin of the American Academy of Psychiatry and the Law*, 16, 163–178.

Donnerstein, E., & Linz, D. (1995). The media. In J. Q. Wilson & J. Petersilia (eds), *Crime* (pp. 237–266). Oakland, CA: ICS Press.

Donnerstein, E., Linz, D., & Penrod, S. (1987). *The questions of pornography*. New York: Free Press.

Dworkin, A. (1979). *Pornography: Men possessing women*. New York: G.P. Putnam's Sons.

Elliott, D. S. (1985). The assumption that theories can be combined with increased explanatory power. In R. F. Meier (ed.), *Theoretical methods in criminology* (pp. 123–149). Beverly Hills, CA: Sage.

Elliott, D. S., Ageton, S. S., & Canter, R. J. (1979). An integrated theoretical perspective on delinquent behavior. *Journal of Research in Crime and Delinquency,* 16, 3–27.

Elliott, D. S., Huizinga, D., & Ageton, S. S. (1985). *Explaining delinquency and drug use.* Beverly Hills, CA: Sage Publications.

Ellis, L. (1989). *Theories of rape: Inquiries into the causes of sexual aggression.* New York: Hemisphere Publishing Corporation.

Fagan, J., & Wexler, S. (1987). Family origins of violent delinquents. *Criminology,* 24, 439–471.

Farnworth, M. (1989). Theory integration versus model building. In S. F. Messner, M. D. Krohn, & A. E. Liska (eds), *Theoretical integration in the study of deviance and crime* (pp. 93–100). Albany, NY: State University of New York Press.

Felson, M. (1986). Linking criminal choices, routine activities, informal social control, and criminal outcomes. In D. Cornish & R. Clarke (eds), *The reasoning criminal* (pp. 119–128). New York: Springer-Verlag.

Felson, M. (1995). Those who discourage crime. In J. E. Eck & D. Weisburd (eds), *Crime and place: Crime prevention studies, Vol. 4* (pp. 53–66). Monsey: Criminal Justice.

Felson, M. (2006). *Crime and nature.* Thousand Oaks, CA: Sage.

Felson, M. (2008). Routine activity theory. In R. Wortley & L. Mazerolle (eds), *Environmental criminology and crime analysis* (pp. 70–77). Cullompton, UK: Willan Publishing.

Felson, M., & Boba, R. (2010). *Crime and everyday life: Insight and implications for society.* Thousand Oaks, CA: Pine Forge.

Felson, M., & Cohen, L. (1980). Human ecology and crime: A routine activity approach. *Human Ecology,* 8, 389–406.

Felson, R. (1997). Routine activities and involvement in violence as actor, witness, or target. *Violence and Victims,* 12, 209–221.

Felson, R. B., & Messner, S. F. (1996). To kill or not to kill? Lethal outcomes in injurious attacks. *Criminology,* 34, 519–545.

Fernandez, A., & Lizotte, A. (1995). An analysis of the relationship between campus crime and community crime: Reciprocal effects? In J. Sloan & B. Fisher (eds), *Campus crime: Legal, social, and policy perspectives* (pp. 79–102). Springfield, IL: Charles Thomas.

Feshbach, S. (1964). The function of aggression and the regulation of aggressive drive. *Psychological Review,* 71(4), 257–272.

Firestone, P., Bradford, J. M., Greenberg, D. M., & Larose, M. R. (1998a). Homicidal sex offenders: Psychological, phallometric, and diagnostic features. *Journal of American Academy of Psychiatry and Law,* 26(4), 537–552.

Firestone, P., Bradford, J. M., Greenberg, D. M., & Nunes, K. L. (2000). Differentiation of homicidal child molesters, nonhomicidal child molesters, and nonoffenders by phallometry. *American Journal of Psychiatry,* 157(11), 1847–1850.

Firestone, P., Bradford, J. M., Greenberg, D. M., Larose, M. R., & Curry, S. (1998b). Homicidal and nonhomicidal child molesters: Psychological, phallometric, and criminal features. *Sexual Abuse: A Journal of Research and Treatment,* 10(4), 305–323.

Fisher, D., & Beech, A. R. (2007). Identification of motivations for sexual murder. In J. Proulx, E. Beauregard, M. Cusson, & A. Nicole (eds), *Sexual murderers: A comparative analysis and new perspectives* (pp. 175–190). Chichester, West Sussex: John Wiley and Sons Ltd.

Fisher, B., Cullen, F., & Turner, M. (2000). *The sexual victimization of college women.* Washington, DC: National Institute of Justice.

Flowers, R. B. (2006). *Sex crimes, predators, perpetrators, prostitutes, and victims: An examination of sexual criminality and victimization* (2nd edition). Springfield, IL: Charles C Thomas.

Folino, J. O. (2000). Sexual homicide and their classification according to motivation: A report from Argentina. *International Journal of Offender Therapy and Comparative Criminology,* 44, 740–750.

Fox, J. G., & Sobol, J. J. (2000). Drinking patterns, social interaction, and barroom behavior: A routine activities approach. *Deviant Behavior,* 21(5), 429–450.

Gacono, C. B., & Meloy, J. R. (1994). *The Rorschach investigation of aggressive and psychopathic personalities.* Mahwah, NJ: Erlbaum.

Gacono, C. B., Meloy, J. R., & Bridges, M. R. (2000). A Rorschach comparison of psychopaths, sexual homicide perpetrators, and nonviolent pedophiles: Where angels fear to tread. *Journal of Clinical Psychology,* 56, 757–777.

Gaetz, S. (2004). Safe streets for whom? Homeless youth, social exclusion, and criminal victimization. *Canadian Journal of Criminology and Criminal Justice,* 46, 423–455.

Garson, G. D. (2009). Structural equation modeling. Retrieved 23 August 2011 from http://faculty.chass.ncsu.edu/garson/PA765/structur.htm

Geberth, V. (1996). *Practical homicide investigation: Tactics, procedures, and forensic techniques* (3rd edition). Boca Raton, FL: CRC Press.

George, W. H., Gournic, S. J., & McAfee, M. P. (1988). Perceptions of postdrinking female sexuality: Effects of gender, beverage choice, and drink payment. *Journal of Applied Social Psychology,* 18, 1295–1317.

Gerard, F., Mormont, C., Kocsis, R. N. (2007). Offender profiles and crime scene patterns in Belgian sexual murders. In R. N. Kocsis (ed.), *Criminal profiling: International theory, research, and practice* (pp. 27–47). Totowa, NJ: Humana Press.

Gibbs, J. P. (1972). *Sociological theory construction.* Hinsdale, IL: Dryden Press.

Glueck, S. (1956). Theory and fact in criminology. *British Journal of Delinquency,* 7, 92–109.

Glueck, S., & Glueck, E. (1950). *Unraveling juvenile delinquency.* Cambridge, MA: Harvard University Press.

Goodwin, G. M. (1998). Reliability, validity, and utility of extant serial murder classifications. *The Criminologist,* 22, 194–210.

Goodwin, G. M. (2000). *Hunting serial predator: A multivariate classification approach to profiling violent behavior.* Boca Raton, FL: CRC Press.

Gover, A. R., Park, M., Tomsich, E. A., & Jennings, W. G. (2011). Dating violence perpetration and victimization among South Korean college students: A focus on gender and childhood maltreatment. *Journal of Interpersonal Violence,* 26(6), 1232–1263.

Graney, D. J., & Arrigo, B. A. (2002). *The power serial rapist: A criminology-victimology typology of female victim selection.* Springfield, IL: Charles C. Thomas.

Gratzer, T., & Bradford, J. (1995). Offender and offense characteristics of sexual sadists: A comparative study. *Journal of Forensic Sciences,* 40, 450–455.

Gravetter, F. J., & Wallnau, L. B. (2008). *Essentials of statistics for the behavioral sciences* (6th edition). Belmont, CA: Wadsworth, Cengage Learning.

Gray, S. H. (1982). Exposure to pornography and aggression toward women: The case of the angry male. *Social Problems, 29,* 389–397.

Greenall, P. V., & Richardson, C. (2014). Adult male-on-female stranger sexual homicide: A descriptive (baseline) study from Great Britain. *Homicide Studies.* Advance online publication. doi: 10.1177/1088767914530555.

Groth, A. N., & Birnbaum, H. J. (1979). *Men who rape: The psychology of the offender.* New York: Plenum.

Groth, A. N., Burgess, A. W., & Holmstrom, L. L. (1977). Rape: Power, anger, and sexuality. *American Journal of Psychiatry, 134,* 1239–1243.

Groves, W. B., & Lynch, M. J. (1990). Reconciling structural and subjective approaches to the study of crime. *Journal of Research in Crime and Delinquency, 27*(4), 348–375.

Grubin, D. (1994). Sexual murder. *British Journal of Psychiatry, 165,* 624–629.

Hagan, J. (1989). Micro and macro structures of delinquency causation and a power-control theory of gender and delinquency. In S. F. Messner, M. D. Krohn, & A. E. Liska (eds), *Theoretical integration in the study of deviance and crime* (pp. 213–227). Albany, NY: State University of New York Press.

Harbot, S., & Mokros, A. (2001). Serial murd erers in Germany from 1945 to 1995: A descriptive study. *Homicide Studies, 5,* 311–334.

Hare, R. D. (2003). *The Hare psychopathy checklist-revised.* Toronto, Canada: Multi Health Systems.

Harris, D. A., Mazerolle, P., & Knight, R. A. (2009). Understanding male sexual offending: A comparison of general and specialist theories. *Criminal Justice and Behavior, 36,* 1051–1069.

Harris, G. T., Rice, M. E., & Lalumière, M. L. (2001). Criminal violence: The roles of psychopathy, neurodevelopmental insults, and antisociality. *Criminal Justice and Behavior, 28,* 402–426.

Hawley, A. (1950). *Human ecology.* New York: The Ronald Press Company.

Hazelwood, R. R., & Burgess, A. N. (1987). *Practical aspects of rape investigation: A multidisciplinary approach.* New York: Elsevier North-Holland.

Hazelwood, R. R., & Douglas, J. D. (1980, April). The lust murderer. *FBI Law Enforcement Bulletin, 16,* 18–22.

Hazelwood, R. R., & Warren, J. (2000). The sexually violent offender: Impulsive or ritualistic? *Aggression and Violent Behavior, 5*(3), 267–279.

Heide, K. M. (1992). *Why kids kill parents: Child abuse and adolescent homicide.* Thousand Oaks, CA: Sage Publications.

Heide, K. M. (1999). *Young killers: The challenge of juvenile homicide.* Thousand Oaks, CA: Sage Publications.

Heide, K. M. (2003). Youth homicide: A review of the literature and a blueprint for action. *International Journal of Offender Therapy and Comparative Criminology, 47*(1), 6–36.

Heide, K. M. (2013). *Understanding parricide: When sons and daughters kill parents.* New York: Oxford University Press.

Heide, K. M. & Solomon, E. P. (2006). Biology, childhood trauma, and murder: Rethinking justice. *International Journal of Law & Psychiatry, 29,* 220–233.

Heide, K. M. & Solomon, E.P. (2009). Female juvenile murderers: Biological and psychological factors leading to homicide. *International Journal of Law & Psychiatry,* 32(4). 244–252.

Heide, K. M., Beauregard, E., & Myers, W. C. (2009). Sexually motivated child abduction murders: Synthesis of the literature and case illustration. *Victims & Offenders,* 4(1), 58–75.

Heide, K. M., Roe-Sepowitz, D., Solomon, E. P., & Chan, H. C. O. (2012). Male and female juveniles arrested for murder: A comprehensive analysis of U.S. data by offender gender. *International Journal of Offender Therapy and Comparative Criminology,* 56(3), 356–384.

Heide, K. M., Solomon, E. P., Sellers, B.G., & Chan, H. C. O. (2011). Male and female juvenile homicide offenders: An empirical analysis of U.S. arrests by offender age groups. *Feminist Criminology,* 6(1), 3–31.

Henry, T. (2010). Characteristics of sex-related homicides in Alaska. *Journal of Forensic Nursing,* 6, 57–65.

Hickey, E. W. (1997). *Serial murderers and their victims* (2nd edition). Belmont, CA: Wadsworth.

Hickey, E. W. (2002). *Serial murderers and their victims* (3rd edition). Belmont, CA: Wadsworth.

Hill, A., Habermann, N., Berner, W., & Briken, P. (2007). Psychiatric disorders in single and multiple sexual murderers. *Psychopathology,* 40, 22–28.

Hill, A., Habermann, N., Klussman, D., Berner, W., & Briken, P. (2008). Criminal recidivism in sexual homicide perpetrators. *International Journal of Offender Therapy and Comparative Criminology,* 52(1), 5–20.

Hindelang, M., Gottfredson, M., & Garofalo, J. (1978). *Victims of personal crime: An empirical foundation for a theory of personal victimization.* Cambridge, MA: Ballinger.

Hirschi, T. (1979). Separate but unequal is better. *Journal of Research in Crime and Delinquency,* 16, 34–38.

Hirschi, T. (1989). Exploring alternatives to integrated theory. In S. F. Messner, M. D. Krohn, & A. E. Liska (eds), *Theoretical integration in the study of deviance and crime: Problems and prospects* (pp. 37–49). Albany: State University of New York Press.

Hirschi, T., & Selvin, H. C. (1967). *Delinquency research: An appraisal of analytic methods.* New York: Free Press.

Hoffman, J. P. (2003). A contextual analysis of differential association, social control, and strain theories of delinquency. *Social Forces,* 81(3), 753–785.

Hollis-Peel, M. E., Reynald, D. M., van Bavel, M., Elffers, H., & Welsh, B. C. (2011). Guardianship for crime prevention: A critical review of the literature. *Crime, Law, and Social Change.* Available Online. Doi: 10.1007/s10611-011-9309-2.

Holmes, R. (1991). *Sex crimes.* Newsbury Park, CA: Sage.

Holmes, R. M., & Holmes, S. T. (2001). *Murder in America* (2nd edition). Thousand Oaks, CA: Sage Publications.

Holt, T., & Bossler, A. (2009). Examining the applicability of lifestyle-routine activities theory for cyber crime victimization. *Deviant Behavior,* 30, 1–25.

Hough, M. (1987). Offenders' choice of target: Findings from victim surveys. *Journal of Quantitative Criminology,* 3, 355–369.

Huprich, S. K., Gacono, C. B., Schneider, R. B., & Bridges, M. R. (2004). Rorschach oral dependency in psychopaths, sexual homicide perpetrators, and nonviolent pedophiles. *Behavioral Sciences and the Law*, 22, 345–356.

Hwang, S., & Akers, R. L. (2003). Substance use by Korean adolescents: A cross-cultural test of social learning, social bonding, and self-control theories. In R. L. Akers & G. F. Jensen (eds), *Social learning theory and the explanation of crime* (pp. 39–64). New Brunswick, NJ: Transaction Publishers.

Jackson, H. J., Lee, J. K. P., Pattison, P., & Ward, T. (2002). Developmental risk factors for sexual offending. *Child Abuse and Neglect: The International Journal*, 26, 73–92.

James, J., & Proulx, J. (2014). A psychological and developmental profile of sexual murderers: A systematic review. *Aggression and Violent Behavior*, 19, 592–607.

Jason, J., Flock, M., & Tyler, C. W. Jr. (1983). Epidemiologic characteristics of primary homicides in the United States. *American Journal of Epidemiology*, 117(4), 419–428.

Jason, J., Strauss, L. T., & Tyler, C. W. Jr. (1983). A comparison of primary and secondary homicides in the United States. *American Journal of Epidemiology*, 117(3), 309–319.

Jennings, W. G., Park, M., Tomsich, E. A., Gover, A. R., & Akers, R. L. (2011). Assessing the overlap in dating violence perpetration and victimization among South Korean college students: The influence of social learning and self-control. *American Journal of Criminal Justice*, 36, 188–206.

Jensen, G. F., & Brownfield, D. (1986). Gender, lifestyles, and victimization: Beyond routine activity. *Violence and Victims*, 1, 85–99.

Johnson, R. E., Marcos, A. C., & Bahr, S. J. (1987). The role of peers in the complex etiology of adolescent drug use. *Criminology*, 25(2), 324–339.

Jones, S., Chan, H. C. O., Myers, W. C., & Heide, K. M. (2013). A proposed sexual homicide category: The psychopathic-sexually sadistic offender. In J. B. Helfgott (ed.), *Criminal Psychology, Volume 2, Typologies, Mental Disorders, and Profiles* (pp. 403–422). Westport, CT: Praeger Publishers.

Kaplan, H. B., Martin, S. S., & Robbins, C. (1984). Pathways to adolescent drug use: Self-derogation, peer influence, weakening of social controls, and early substance use. *Journal of Health and Social Behavior*, 25, 270–289.

Kennedy, L. W. & Forde, D. R. (1990). Routine activities and crime: An analysis of victimization in Canada. *Criminology*, 28(1), 137–152.

Keppel, R. D., & Walter, R. (1999). Profiling killers: A revised classification model for understanding sexual murder. *International Journal of Offender Therapy and Comparative Criminology*, 43(4), 417–437.

Kerr, K. J., Beech, A. R., & Murphy, D. (2013). Sexual homicide: Definition, motivation, and comparison with other forms of sexual offending. *Aggression and Violent Behavior*, 18(1), 1–10.

Khachatryan, N., Heide, K. M., Hummel, E. V., & Chan, H. C. O. (2014). Juvenile sexual homicide offenders: Thirty-year follow-up investigation. *International Journal of Offender Therapy and Comparative Criminology*. Advance online publication. doi: 10.1177/0306624X14552062.

Kienlen, K. K., Birmingham, D. L., Solberg, K. B., O'Regan, J. T., Meloy, J. R. (1997). A comparative study of psychotic and nonpsychotic stalking. *Journal of the American Academy of Psychiatry and Law*, 25, 317–334.

Kinsey, A. C., Pomeroy, W. B., Martin, C. C., & Gebhard, P. (1953). *Sexual behavior in the human female*. Philadelphia: W.B. Saunders.

Kleinbaum, D. G., & Klein, M. (2010). *Logistic regression: A self-learning text* (3rd edition). New York: Springer.

Kline, R. B. (2005). *Principles and practices of structural equation modeling* (2nd edition). New York: Guilford Press.

Koch, J., Berner, W., Hill, A., & Briken, P. (2011). Sociodemographic and diagnostic characteristics of homicidal and nonhomicidal sexual offenders. *Journal of Forensic Sciences,* 56(6), 1626–1631.

Kocsis, R. N. (1999). Criminal profiling of crime scene behaviors in Australian sexual murders. *Australian Police Journal,* 53, 99–102.

Kocsis, R. N., & Irwin, H. J. (1998). The psychological profile of serial offenders and a redefinition of the misnomer of serial crime. *Psychiatry, Psychology, and Law,* 5(2), 197–213.

Kocsis, R. N., Cooksey, R. W., & Irwin, H. J. (2002). Psychological profiling of sexual murders: An empirical model. *International Journal of Offender Therapy and Comparative Criminology,* 46(5), 532–554.

Krohn, M. D. (1986). The web of conformity: A network approach to the explanation of delinquent behavior. *Social Problems,* 33(6), 81–93.

Krohn, M. D., Skinner, W. F., Massey, J. L., Akers, R. L. (1985). Social learning theory and adolescent cigarette smoking: A longitudinal study. *Social Problems,* 32(5), 455–473.

Lalumière, M. L., Harris, G. T., Quinsey, V. L., & Rice, M. E. (2005). *The causes of rape:Understanding individual differences in the male propensity for sexual aggression.* Washington, DC: American Psychological Association.

Langevin, R. (2003). A study of the psychosexual characteristics of sex killers: Can we identify them before it is too late? *International Journal of Offender Therapy and Comparative Criminology,* 47, 366–382.

Langevin, R., Lang, R. A., & Curnoe, S. (1998). The prevalence of sexual offenders with deviant fantasies. *Journal of Interpersonal Violence,* 13, 315–327.

Langevin, R., Ben-Aron, M. H., Wright, P., Marchese, V., & Handy, L. (1988). The sex killer. *Annals of Sex Research,* 1(2), 263–302.

Lanza-Kaduce, L., & Klug, M. (1986). Learning to cheat: The interaction of moral-development and social learning theories. *Deviant Behavior,* 7, 243–259.

Lauritsen, J. L., Laub, J. H., & Sampson, R. J. (1992). Conventional and delinquent activities: Implications for the prevention of violent victimization among adolescents. *Violence and Victims,* 7, 91–108.

Laws, D., & Marshall, W. (2003). A brief history of behavioral and cognitive behavioral approaches to sexual offenders: Part I. Early developments. *Sexual Abuse: A Journal of Research and Treatment,* 15, 75–92.

Lewis, C. J., Sims, L. S., & Shannon, B. (1989). Examination of specific nutrition/health behaviors using a social cognitive model. *Journal of the American Dietetic Association,* 89(2), 194–202.

Liebert, J. A. (1985). Contributions of psychiatric consultation in the investigation of serial murder. *International Journal of Offender Therapy and Comparative Criminology,* 29, 187–200.

Lunde, D. T. (1976). *Murder and madness.* San Francisco: San Francisco Book Co.

Lussier, P. Beauregard, E., Proulx, J., & Nicole, A. (2005). Developmental factors related to deviant sexual preferences in child molesters. *Journal of Interpersonal Violence,* 20, 999–1017.

Lynch, J. P. (1987). Routine activity and victimization at work. *Journal of Quantitative Criminology,* 3, 283–300.

MacCulloch, M. J., Snowden, P. R., Wood, P. J. W., & Mills, H. E. (1983). Sadistic fantasy, sadistic behavior, and offending. *British Journal of Psychiatry*, 143, 20–29.

MacKinnon, C. A. (1984). Not a moral issue. *Yale Law and Policy Review*, 2, 321–345.

Maier, H. W. (1912). Katathyme Wahnbidung und Paranoia [on the subject of catathymic delusions and paranoia]. *Zeitschrift fur die Gesamte Neurologie und Psychiatrie*, 13, 555–610.

Main, M. (1996). Introduction to the special section on attachment and psychopathology: Overview of the field of attachment. *Journal of Consulting and Clinical Psychology*, 64(2), 237–243.

Marcos, A. C., Bahr, S. J., & Johnson, R. E. (1986). Test of a bonding/association theory of adolescent drug use. *Social Forces*, 65(1), 135–161.

Marcum, C. D., Ricketts, M. L., & Higgins, G. E. (2010). Assessing sex experiences of online victimization: An examination of adolescent online behaviors using routine activity theory. *Criminal Justice Review*, 35(4), 412–437.

Mariano, T. Y., Chan, H. C. O., & Myers, W. C. (2014). Toward a more holistic understanding of filicide: An analysis of animal models and 32 years of U.S. arrest data. *Forensic Science International*, 236(1), 46–53.

Marriner, B. (1992). *A new century of sex killers*. London: True Crime Library.

Marshall, W. L. (1989). Intimacy, loneliness, and sexual offenders. *Behavioral Research and Therapy*, 27, 491–503.

Marshall, W. L. (1993). The role of attachment, intimacy, and loneliness in the etiology and maintenance of sexual offending. *Sexual and Marital Therapy*, 8, 109–121.

Marshall, W. L., & Barbaree, H. E. (1990). An integrated theory of the etiology of sexual offending. In W. L. Marshall, D. R. Laws, and H. E. Barbaree (eds), *Handbook of sexual assault: Issues, theories, and treatment of the offender* (pp. 257–275). New York: Plenum Press.

Marshall, W. L., & Eccles, A. (1993). Pavlovian conditioning processes in adolescent sex offenders. In H. E. Barbaree, W. L. Marshall, & S. M. Hudson (eds), *The juvenile sex offenders* (pp. 118–142). New York: Guilford.

Marshall, W. L., Hudson, S. M., & Hodkinson, S. (1993). The importance of attachment bonds in the development of juvenile sex offending. In H. E. Barbaree, W. L. Marshall, & S. M. Hudson (eds), *The juvenile sex offenders* (pp. 164–181). New York: Guilford.

Martin, P. Y., & Hummer, R. A. (1993). Fraternities and rape on campus. In P. B. Bart & E. G. Moran (eds), *Violence against women: The bloody footprints* (pp. 114–131). Newsbury Park, CA: Sage.

McCord, J. (1991a). Family relationships, juvenile delinquency, and adult criminality. *Criminology*, 29, 397–417.

McCord, J. (1991b). The cycle of crime and socialization practices. *Journal of Criminal Law and Criminology*, 82, 211–228.

McCormack, T. (1978). Machismo in media research: A critical review of research on violence and pornography. *Social Problems*, 25, 544–555.

McGuire, R. J., Carlisle, J. M., & Young, B. G. (1965). Sexual deviations as conditioned behavior: A hypothesis. *Behavior Research and Therapy*, 2, 185–190.

McNamara, J. J., & Morton, R. J. (2004). Frequency of serial sexual homicide victimization in Virginia for a ten-year period. *Journal of Forensic Sciences*, 49, 1–5.

Meier, R. F., Kennedy, L. W., & Sacco, V. F. (2001). Crime and the criminal events perspective. In R. F. Meier, L. W. Kennedy, & V. F. Sacco (eds), *The process and structure of crime: Criminal events and crime analysis* (pp. 1–28). New Brunswick, NJ: Transaction.

Meithe, T. D., & Meier, R. F. (1990). Opportunity, choice, and criminal victimization: A test of a theoretical model. *Journal of Research in Crime and Delinquency,* 27, 243–266.

Meloy, J. R. (1996). Stalking (obsessional following): A review of some preliminary studies. *Aggression and Violent Behavior,* 1, 147–162.

Meloy, J. R. (1997). The clinical risk management of stalking: "Someone is watching over me…" *American Journal of Psychotherapy,* 51, 174–184.

Meloy, J. R. (2000). The nature and dynamics of sexual homicide: An integrative review. *Aggression and Violent Behavior,* 5, 1–32.

Meloy, J. R., Gacono, C. B., & Kenney, L. (1994). A Rorschach investigation of sexual homicide. *Journal of Personality Assessment,* 62(1), 58–67.

Mertler, C. A., & Vannatta, R. A. (2005). *Advanced and multivariate statistical methods: Practical application and interpretation* (3rd edition). Glendale, CA: Pyrczak Publishing.

Messner, S. F., & Blau, J. R. (1987). Routine leisure activities and rates of crime: A macro-level analysis. *Social Forces,* 65, 1035–1052.

Michaels, J. W., & Miethe, T. D. (1989). Applying theories of deviance to academic cheating. *Social Science Quarterly,* 70(4), 870–885.

Mieczkowski, T., & Beauregard, E. (2010). Lethal outcome in sexual assault events: A conjunctive analysis. *Justice Quarterly,* 27(3), 332–361.

Mihalic, S. W., & Elliott, D. (1997). A social learning theory model of marital violence. *Journal of Family Violence,* 12(1), 21–47..

Miller, J. E. (2005). *The Chicago guide to writing about multivariate analysis.* Chicago, IL: University of Chicago Press.

Milsom, J., Beech, A. R., & Webster, S. D. (2003). Emotional loneliness in sexual murderers: A qualitative analysis. *Sexual Abuse: A Journal of Research and Treatment,* 15, 285–296.

Money, J. (1990). Forensic sexology: Paraphilic sexual rape (biastophilia) and lust murder (erotophonophilia). *American Journal of Psychotherapy,* 64, 26–36.

Money, J., & Werlas, J. (1982). Paraphilic sexuality and child abuse: The parents. *Journal of Sex and Marital Therapy,* 8, 57–64.

Mustaine, E. E., & Tewksbury, R. (1998). Victimization risks at leisure: A gender-specific analysis. *Violence and Victims,* 13(3), 3–21.

Mustaine, E. E., & Tewksbury, R. (1999). A routine activity theory explanation for women's stalking victimizations. *Violence Against Women,* 5, 43–62

Mustaine, E. E., & Tewksbury, R. (2002). Sexual assault of college women: A feminist interpretation of a routine activities analysis. *Criminal Justice Review,* 27(1), 89–123.

Myers, W. C. (2002). *Juvenile sexual homicide.* San Diego, CA: Academic Press, Inc.

Myers, W. C. (2004). Serial murder by children and adolescents. *Behavioral Sciences and the Law,* 22, 357–374.

Myers, W. C., & Chan, H. C. O. (2012). Juvenile homosexual homicide. *Behavioral Sciences and the Law,* 30(2), 90–102.

Myers, W. C., Burgess, A. W., & Nelson, J. A. (1998). Criminal and behavioral aspects of juvenile sexual homicide. *Journal of Forensic Sciences,* 43(2), 340–347.

Myers, W. C., Chan, H. C. O. Mariano, T. Y. (2014). Sexual homicide in the USA committed by juveniles and adults, 1976–2007: Age of arrest and incidence trends over 32 years. *Criminal Behaviour and Mental Health.* Advance online publication. doi: 10.1002/cbm.1947.

Myers, W. C., Chan, H. C. O., Vo, E. J., & Lazarou, E. (2010). Sexual sadism, psychopathy, and recidivism in juvenile sexual murderers. *Journal of Investigative Psychology and Offender Profiling,* 7, 49–58.

Myers, W. C., Eggleston, C. F., & Smoak, P. (2003). A media violence-inspired juvenile sexual homicide offender 13 years later. *Journal of Forensic Sciences,* 48, 1–5.

Myers, W. C., Husted, D. S., Safarik, M. E., O'Toole, M. E. (2006). The motivation behind serial sexual homicide: Is it sex, power, and control, or anger? *Journal of Forensic Sciences,* 51, 900–907.

Nicole, A., & Proulx, J. (2007). Sexual murderers and sexual aggressors: Developmental paths and criminal history. In J. Proulx, E. Beauregard, M. Cusson, & A. Nicole (eds), *Sexual Murderers: A comparative analysis and new perspectives* (pp. 29–50). Chichester, UK: Wiley.

Oliver, C. J., Beech, A. R., Fishers, D., & Beckett, R. (2007). A comparison of rapists and sexual murderers on demographic and selected psychometric measures. *International Journal of Offender Therapy and Comparative Criminology,* 51(3), 298–312.

Ouimet, M., Guay, J. P., and Proulx, J. (2000). Analyse de la Gravité des Agressions Sexuelles de Femmes Adultes et de ses Déterminants [Analysis of the determinants of the seriousness of sexual aggressions against women]. *Revue Internationale de Criminologie et de Police Technique et Scientifique,* 2, 157–172.

Patterson, G. R. (1975). *Families: Applications of social learning to family life.* Champaign, IL: Research Press.

Pearson, F. S., & Weiner, N. A. (1985). Toward an integration of criminological theories. *Journal of Criminal Law and Criminology,* 76(1), 116–150.

Petersilia, J. (2001). Crime victims with developmental disabilities: A review essay. *Criminal Justice and Behavior,* 28, 655–694.

Polascheck, D. L. L., Hudson, S. M., Ward, T., & Siegert, R. J. (2001). Rapists' offense processes: A preliminary descriptive model. *Journal of Interpersonal Violence,* 16, 299–314.

Pratt, T. C., Cullen, F. T., Sellers, C. S., Winfree, T. Jr., Madensen, T. D., Daigle, L. E., et al. (2010). The empirical status of social learning theory: A meta-analysis. *Justice Quarterly,* 27(6), 765–802.

Prentky, R. A., Burgess, A. W., Rokous, F., Lee, A., Hartman, C., Ressler, R., et al. (1989). The presumptive role of fantasy in serial sexual homicide. *American Journal of Psychiatry,* 146, 887–891.

Presley, C. A. (1997). *Alcohol and drugs on American college campuses: Issues of violence and harassment.* Carbondale, IL: Core Institute, Southern Illinois University.

Proulx, J., Beauregard, E., & Nicole, A. (2002, October). *Developmental, personality, and situational factors in rapists and sexual murderers of women.* Paper presented at the conference of Association for the Treatment of Sexual Abusers, Montreal, Canada.

Proulx, J., Cusson, M., & Beauregard, E. (2007). Sexual murder: Definitions, epidemiology, and theories. In J. Proulx, E. Beauregard, M. Cusson, & A. Nicole (eds), *Sexual murderers: A comparative analysis and new perspectives* (pp. 9–28). Chichester: John Wiley and Sons.

Proulx, J., McKibben, A., & Lusignan, R. (1996). Relationship between affective components and sexual behaviors in sexual aggressors. *Sexual Abuse: Journal of Research and Treatment,* 8, 279–289.

Proulx, J., St-Yves, M., & McKibben, A. (1994). *CQSA: Computerized Questionnaire for Sexual Aggressors.* Unpublished manuscript.

Proulx, J., Beauregard, E., Cusson, M., & Nicole, A. (2007). *Sexual Murderers: A Comparative Analysis and New Perspectives.* Hoboken, NJ: Wiley.

Proulx, J., Beauregard, E., Lussier, P., & Leclerc, B. (2014). *Pathways to sexual aggression.* New York: Routledge.

Reckdenwald, A., Mancini, C., & Beauregard, E. (2014). Adolescent self-image as a mediator between childhood maltreatment and adult sexual offending. *Journal of Criminal Justice,* 42, 85–94.

Reiss, A. J., Jr. (1986). Why are communities important in understanding crime? In A. J. Reiss, Jr. & M. Tonry (eds), *Communities and crime.* Chicago, IL: University of Chicago Press.

Ressler, R. K., Burgess, A. W., & Douglas, J. E. (1988). *Sexual homicide: Patterns and motive.* New York: Free Press.

Ressler, R. K., Burgess, A. W., Douglas, J. E., Hartman, C. R., & D'Agostino, R. B. (1986). Sexual killers and their victims: Identifying patterns through crime scene analysis. *Journal of Interpersonal Violence,* 1(3), 288–308.

Ressler, R. K., Burgess, A. W., Hartman, C. R., Douglas, J. E., & McCormack, A. (1986). Murderers who rape and mutilate. *Journal of Interpersonal Violence,* 1(3), 273–287.

Ressler, R. K., Burgess, A. W., Depue, R. L., Douglas, J. E., Hazelwood, R. R., Lanning, K. V., et al. (1985). Violent crimes. *FBI Law Enforcement Bulletin,* 54(8), 1–33.

Revitch, E. (1957). Sex murder and sex aggression. *Journal of the Medical Society of New Jersey,* 54, 519–524.

Revitch, E. (1965). Sex murder and the potential sex murderer. *Diseases of the Nervous System,* 26, 640–648.

Revitch, E. (1980). Gynocide and unprovoked attacks on women. *Journal of Correctional and Social Psychiatry,* 26, 6–11.

Revitch, E., & Schlesinger, L. B. (1978). Murder: Evaluation, classification, and prediction. In I. L. Kutash, S. B. Kutash, & L. B. Schlesinger (eds), *Violence: Perspectives on murder and aggression* (pp. 138–164). San Francisco: Jossey-Bass.

Revitch, E., & Schlesinger, L. B. (1981). *Psychopathology of homicide.* Springfield, IL: Thomas.

Reynald, D. M. (2010). Guardians on guardianship: Factors affecting the willingness to supervise, the ability to detect potential offenders, and the willingness to intervene. *Journal of Research in Crime and Delinquency,* 47(3), 358–390.

Rossmo, D. K. (1999). *Geographic profiling.* New York: CRC Press.

Rossmo, D. K. (2009). *Criminal investigative failures.* Boca Raton, FL: CRC Press.

Sacco, V. F., & Kennedy, L. W. (1996). *The criminal event.* Belmont, CA: Wadsworth.

Sacco, V. F., Johnson, H., & Arnold, R. (1993). Urban-rural residence and criminal victimization. *Canadian Journal of Sociology,* 18, 431–451.

Safarik, M. E., Jarvis, J. P., Nussbaum, K. E. (2002). Sexual homicide of elderly females: Linking offender characteristics to victim and crime scene attributes. *Journal of Interpersonal Violence,* 17, 500–525.

Salfati, C. G. (2000). The nature of expressiveness and instrumentality in homicide: Implications for offender profiling. *Homicide Studies,* 4(3), 265–293.

Salfati, C. G., & Taylor, P. (2006). Differentiating sexual violence: A comparison of sexual homicide and rape. *Psychology, Crime, and Law,* 12, 107–125.

Salfati, C. G., James, A. R., & Ferguson, L. (2008). Prostitute homicides: A descriptive study. *Journal of Interpersonal Violence,* 23(4), 505–543.

Sampson, R. J. (1985). Structural sources of variation in race-age-specific rates of offending across major U.S. cities. *Criminology,* 23(4), 647–673.

Sampson, R. J. (1987). Personal violence by strangers: An extension and test of the opportunity model of predatory victimization. *The Journal of Criminal Law and Criminology,* 78, 327–356.

Sampson, R., & Lauritsen, J. (1990). Deviant lifestyles, proximity to crime, and the offender-victim link in personal violence. *Journal of Research in Crime and Delinquency,* 27, 110–139.

Sampson, R. J., & Wooldredge, J. D. (1987). Linking the micro- and macro-level dimensions of lifestyle-routine activity and opportunity models of predatory victimization. *Journal of Quantitative Criminology,* 3, 371–393.

Sampson, R., Eck, J. E., & Dunham, J. (2010). Super controllers and crime prevention: A routine activity explanation of crime prevention success and failure. *Security Journal,* 23(1), 37–51.

Sasse, S. (2005). "Motivation" and routine activities theory. *Deviant Behavior,* 26, 547–570.

Schlesinger, L. B. (1996a). The catathymic crisis, 1912-present: A clinical study. *Aggression and Violent Behavior,* 1, 307–316.

Schlesinger, L. B. (1996b). The catathymic process: Psychopathology and psychodynamics of extreme aggression. In L. B. Schlesinger (ed.), *Explorations in criminal psychopathology: Clinical syndromes with forensic implications* (pp. 121–141). Springfield, IL:Thomas.

Schlesinger, L. B. (2001a). The contract murderer: Patterns, characteristics, and dynamics. *Journal of Forensic Sciences,* 46, 108–112.

Schlesinger, L. B. (2001b). Is serial homicide really increasing? *Journal of the American Academy of Psychiatry and the Law,* 29, 294–297.

Schlesinger, L. B. (2001c). The potential sex murderer: Ominous signs, risk assessment. *Journal of Threat Assessment,* 1, 47–72.

Schlesinger, L. B. (2004). *Sexual murder: Cathathymic and compulsive homicides.* Boca Raton, FL: CRC Press.

Schlesinger, L. B. (2007). Sexual homicide: Differentiating catathymic and compulsive murders. *Aggression and Violent Behavior,* 12, 242–256.

Schreck, C. J., & Fisher, B. S. (2004). Specifying the influence of family and peers on violent victimization: Extending routine activities and lifestyle theories. *Journal of Interpersonal Violence,* 19, 1021–1041.

Schwartz, M. D., & DeKeseredy, W. S. (1997). *Sexual assault on the college campus: The role of male peer support.* Thousand Oaks, CA: Sage.

Schwartz, M. D., DeKeseredy, W. S., Tait, D., & Alvi, S. (2001). Male peer support and a feminist routine activities theory: Understanding sexual assault on the college campus. *Justice Quarterly,* 18(3), 623–649.

Schwartz, M., & Pitts, V. (1995). Exploring a feminist routine activities approach to explaining sexual assault. *Justice Quarterly,* 12, 9–31.

Schwartz, M. D., DeKeseredy, W. S., Tait, D., & Alvi, S. (2001). Male peer support and a feminist routine actitivies theory: Understanding sexual assault on the college campus. *Justice Quarterly,* 18(3), 623–649.

Sellers, C. S., Cochran, J. K., & Branch, K. A. (2005). Social learning theory and partner violence: A research note. *Deviant Behavior,* 26, 379–395.

Sewall, L. A., Krupp, D. B., & Lalumière, M. L. (2013). A test of two typologies of sexual homicide. *Sexual Abuse: A Journal of Research and Treatment,* 25(1), 82–100.

Sherley, A. J. (2005). Contextualizing the sexual assault event: Images from police files. *Deviant Behavior,* 26(2), 87–108.

Sherman, L. W., Gartin, P. R., & Buerger, M. E. (1989). Hot spots of predatory crime: Routine activities and the criminology of place. *Criminology,* 27(1), 27–55.

Short, J. F., Jr. (1979). On the etiology of delinquent behavior. *Journal of Research in Crime and Delinquency,* 16(1), 28–33.

Short, J. F., Jr. (1985). The level of explanation problem in criminology. In R. F. Meier (ed.), *Theoretical methods in criminology* (pp. 51–72). Beverly Hills, CA: Sage.

Short, J. F., Jr. (1989). Exploring integration of theoretical levels of explanation: Notes on gang delinquency. In S. F. Messner, M. D. Krohn, & A. E. Liska (eds), *Theoretical integration in the study of deviance and crime* (pp. 243–259). Albany, NY: State University of New York Press.

Silverman, R. A., & Mukherjee, S. K. (1987). Intimate homicide: An analysis of violent social relationships. *Behavioral Sciences and the Law,* 5, 37–47.

Simon, R. I. (1996). Bad men do what good men dream: A forensic psychiatrist illuminates the darker side of human behavior. In R. I. Simon (ed.), *Serial sexual killers: Your life for their orgasm* (pp. 279–312). Washington, DC: American Psychiatric Press.

Smallbone, S., Marshall, W. L., & Wortley, R. (2008). *Preventing child sexual abuse: Evidence, policy, and practice.* Devon, UK: Willan.

Smith, S. G., Basile, K. C., & Karch, D. (2011). Sexual homicide and sexual violence-associated homicide: Findings from the National Violent Death Reporting System. *Homicide Studies,* 15(2), 132–153.

Spano, R., & Freilich, J. D. (2009). An assessment of the empirical validity and conceptualization of individual level multivariate studies of lifestyle/routine activities theory published from 1995 to 2005. *Journal of Criminal Justice,* 37, 305–314.

Spano, R., & Nagy, S. (2005). Social guardianship and social isolation: An application and extension of lifestyle/routine activities theory to rural adolescents. *Rural Sociology,* 70, 414–437.

Spitzberg, B. H., & Cupach, W. R. (2003). What mad pursuit? Obsessive relational intrusion and stalking related phenomena. *Aggression and Violent,* 8, 345–375.

Stein, R. E. (2010). The utility of country structure: A cross-national multilevel analysis of property and violent victimization. *International Criminal Justice Review,* 20(1), 35–55.

Stone, M. H. (2001). Serial sexual homicide: Biological, psychological, and sociological aspects. *Journal of Personality Disorders,* 15(1), 1–18.

Straus, M. (1990). Ordinary violence, child abuse, and wife beating: What do they have in common? In M. A. Straus & R. J. Gelles (eds), *Physical violence in*

American families: Risk factors and adaptations to violence in 8,145 families. New Brunswick, NJ: Transaction Publishers.

Straus, M. A., & Kantor, G. K. (2005). Definition and measurement of neglectful behavior: Some principles and guidelines. *Child Abuse and Neglect, 29*, 19–29.

Streiner, D. L., & Norman, D. L. (1989). *Health measurement scales: A practical guide to their development and use.* New York: Oxford University Press.

Sutherland, E. H. (1924). *Criminology.* Philadelphia: J.B. Lippincott Company.

Sutherland, E. H. (1939). *Criminology* (3rd edition). Philadelphia: J.B. Lippincott Company.

Sutherland, E. H. (1947). *Criminology* (4th edition). Philadelphia: J.B. Lippincott Company.

Tanay, E. (1976). *The murderers.* Indianapolis, IN: Bobbs-Merrill.

Testa, M., & Livingston, J. A. (2000). Alcohol and sexual aggression: Reciprocal relationships over time in a sample of high risk women. *Journal of Interpersonal Violence, 15*, 413–427.

Tewksbury, R., & Mustaine, E. (2000). Routine activities and vandalism: A theoretical and empirical study. *Journal of Crime and Justice, 23*, 81–110.

Tewksbury, R., & Mustaine, E. E. (2001). Lifestyle factors association with the sexual assault of men: A routine activity theory analysis. *The Journal of Men's Studies, 9*(2), 153–182.

Tewksbury, R., & Mustaine, E. (2003). College students' lifestyles and self-protective behaviors: Further consideration of the guardianship concept in routine activities theory. *Criminal Justice and Behavior, 30*(3), 302–327.

Tewksbury, R., Mustaine, E. E., & Stengel, K. M. (2008). Examining rates of sexual offenses from a routine activities perspective. *Victims and Offenders, 3*, 75–85.

Thornberry, T. P. (1987). Toward an interactional theory of delinquency. *Criminology, 25*, 863–891.

Thornberry, T. P., Lizotte, A. J., Krohn, M. D., Farnworth, M., & Jang, S. J. (1994). Delinquent peers, beliefs, and delinquent behavior: A longitudinal test of interactional theory. *Criminology, 32*(1), 47–84.

Tillyer, M. S., & Eck, J. E. (2011). Getting a handle on crime: A further extension of routine activities theory. *Security Journal, 24*(2), 179–193.

Tittle, C. R. (1985). The assumption that general theories are not possible. In R.F. Meier (ed.), *Theoretical methods in criminology* (pp. 93–121). Beverly Hills, CA: Sage.

Tittle, C. R. (1989). Prospects for synthetic theory. In S. F. Messner, M. D. Krohn, & A. E. Liska (eds), *Theoretical integration in the study of deviance and crime* (pp. 161–178). Albany, NY: State University of New York Press.

Tittle, C. R. (1995). *Control balance: Toward a general theory of deviance.* Boulder, CO: Westview Press.

Toch, H. (1969). *Violent men: An inquiry into the psychology of violence.* Chicago: Aldine.

Tseloni, A., & Farrell, G. (2002). Burglary victimization across Europe: The roles of prior victimization, micro-, and macro-level routine activities. In P. Nieuwbeerta (ed.), *Crime victimization in comparative perspective* (pp. 141–162). Dan Haag: Boom Juridische uitgevers.

Tyler, K. A., Hoyt, D. R., & Whitbeck, L. B. (1998). Coercive sexual strategies. *Violence and Victims, 13*, 47–61.

Van Patten, I. T., & Delhauer, P. Q. (2007). Sexual homicide: A spatial analysis of 25 years of deaths in Los Angeles. *Journal of Forensic Sciences, 52*, 1192–1141.

van Wilsem, J., de Graff, N. D., & Wittebrood, K. (2003). Cross-national differences in victimization: Disentangling the impact of composition and context. *European Sociological Review,* 19, 125–142.

Verill, S. W. (2005). *Social structure and social learning in delinquency: A test of Akers' social structure-social learning model.* Unpublished dissertation.

Vetter, H. (1990). Dissociation, psychopathy, and the serial murderer. In S. A. Egger (ed.), *Serial murder: An elusive phenomenon* (pp. 73–92). New York: Praeger.

Vogel, R. E., & Himelein, M. J. (1995). Dating and sexual victimization: An analysis of risk factors among precollege women. *Journal of Criminal Justice,* 23, 153–162.

Ward, T., Polascheck, D., & Beech, A. (2006). *Theories of sexual offending.* Chichester, UK: Wiley.

Ward, T., Hudson, S. M., Marshall, W. L., & Siegert, R. (1995). Attachment style and intimacy deficits in sexual offenders: A theoretical framework. *Sexual Abuse: A Journal of Research and Treatment,* 7, 317–335.

Warr, M. (2002). *Companions in crime: The social aspects of criminal conduct.* Cambridge: Cambridge University Press.

Warren, J. I., Hazelwood, R. R., & Dietz, P. E. (1996). The sexually sadistic serial killer. *Journal of Forensic Sciences,* 41, 970, 974.

Weaver, G. S., Clifford Wittekind, J. E., Huff-Corzine, L., Corzine, J., Petee, T. A., & Jarvis, J. P. (2004). Violent encounters: A criminal event analysis of lethal and nonlethal outcomes. *Journal of Contemporary Criminal Justice,* 20, 348–368.

Wertham, F. (1937). The catathymic crisis: A clinical entity. *Archives of Neurology and Psychiatry,* 37, 974–977.

Wertham, F. (1941). *Dark legend: A study in murder.* New York: Duell, Sloan, and Pierce.

Wertham, F. (1949). *Show of violence.* Garden city, NY: Doubleday.

Wertham, F. (1978). The catathymic crisis. In I. L. Kutash, S. B. Kutash, & L. B. Schlesinger (eds), *Violence: Perspectives on murder and aggression* (pp. 138–164). San Francisco: Jossey-Bass.

White, H. R., & LaGrange, R. L. (1987). An assessment of gender effects in self report delinquency. *Sociological Focus,* 20(3), 195–213.

Wilcox, P., Madensen, T. D., & Tillyer, M. S. (2007). Guardianship in context: Implications for burglary victimization, risk, and prevention. *Criminology,* 45(4), 771–803.

Wilson, C., & Seaman, D. (1996). *The serial killers: A study in the psychology of violence.* London: True Crime Library.

Wilson, W., & Nakajo, H. (1965). Preference for photographs as a function of frequency of presentation. *Psychonomic Science,* 3, 577–578.

Wittebrood, K., & Nieuwbeerta, P. (2000). Criminal victimization during one's life course: The effects of previous victimization and patterns of routine activities. *Journal of Research in Crime and Delinquency,* 37(1), 91–122.

Wolfgang, M. E., & Ferracuti, F. (1967). *The subculture of violence.* Great Britain: Tavistock.

Wong, D. S. W., Chan, H. C. O., & Cheng, C. H. K. (2014). Cyberbullying perpetration and victimization among adolescents in Hong Kong. *Children and Youth Services Review,* 36(1), 133–140.

Zhang, L., Welte, J. W., & Wiecxorek, W. F. (2001). Deviant lifestyle and crime victimization. *Journal of Criminal Justice,* 29, 133–143.

Index

Printed and bound by CPI Group (UK) Ltd, Croydon, CR0 4YY